HISTORY OF ANTINATALISM

How Philosophy Has Challenged the Question of Procreation

editor © Mgr. Kateřina Lochmanová
cover picture © Mgr. Martin Cihlář

ISBN 9798645624255
First edition, 2020

CONTENTS

PREFACE

Antinatalists, represented in philosophy by Arthur Schopenhauer, Peter Wessel Zapffe, Emil Cioran, Seana Shiffrin, or David Benatar, claim it is (almost) always morally wrong to bring new sentient beings into existence. According to at least some of them, a licit exception would occur if procreation of a new sentient being was reasonably expected to prevent a sufficient amount of harm to other sentient beings. Even such antinatalists, however, would consider those exceptions extremely rare, if not purely hypothetical. The focus is on new human beings for humans typically suffer or cause more harm than non-human animals, and are more amenable to quality of life assessments. Yet antinatalists intend to broaden their focus on animals as well.

In philosophy, antinatalists try to justify their view in at least seven ways, all revived in the last two decades especially by David Benatar. Firstly and probably most typically, antinatalists would argue that in the lives of (almost) all sentient beings, harms or bad things markedly outweigh benefits or good things. This is the argument about poor quality of sentient life. It seems to be the most common reason for antinatalism. It is also notable for its alleged implications. Some, including Benatar, see as one implication that it is (almost) always wrong not to abort such a life before the unborn acquires the ability of sentience. Others, including Benatar again and sometimes called exctinctionists, infer as well that it would be better for the overall value in the world if sentient beings never existed, and given that they do exist, if they died out as soon and as painlessly and licitly as possible.

Others, excluding Benatar and sometimes called promortalists, infer that it is (almost) always imprudent not to commit suicide as soon as possible. (Again, here and else the word *almost* is inserted as there might be rare or hypothetical exceptions.) At this moment it should be noted, against possible appearances, that consistent antinatalists need not be utilitarians. Even a promortalist may deem it wrong to kill an innocent and non-consenting human person (at least if they have acquired the ability of sentience), although doing so would do somewhat more good than harm. He may even deem it intrinsically wrong, under any conditions whatsoever, whatever the consequences might be.

Secondly, even when the harms eventually do not turn out to swamp the benefits, they still quite possibly could, and it is wrong, as some antinatalists argue, to take the risk. This is a (pre)cautious or tutioristic argument. Thirdly and similarly, some argue it is wrong to expose an innocent human being to a grave risk to which they never consented. This argument calls for a peculiar sort of respect for autonomy. Fourthly, never existing beings are never harmed by bad things. On the other hand, they never miss any benefit or good thing. Some antinatalists see this as sufficient to make never existing preferable over existence. In that case they endorse the argument for a fundamental axiological asymmetry between existence and never existing.

Fifthly, the preferability of never existing over existence is also the best explanation of why it is typically wrong to knowingly bring into existence a human being who will suffer a serious harm (e.g. from blindness or tragic childhood) while it typically is not wrong not to bring into existence a new human being in whose life benefits or good things would markedly reign over harms or bad things. This is the argument from intuitions common in reproductive or population ethics. So far, all the antinatalistic arguments are altruistic or humanistic as their focus is prevention of harm to new sentient beings, especially to humans. The remaining issues can be called, as Benatar does, misanthropic. Not in the sense that they necessarily articulate hate towards humanity but because their focus is prevention of certain harms that new human beings would cause to the world or to other sentient beings, human or non-human.

Therefore, sixthly, some antinatalists remind that (almost) all new human beings do serious harm, both intentionally and unintentionally, to many already existing beings, human or non-human. And seventhly and finally, some antinatalists note that (almost) all new human beings harm the overall aesthetic value in the world by their unintentional production of many and very ugly things, such as the piles of organic or inorganic waste.

Pronatalists (or, *natalists*) try to defeat all such gloomy reasoning. Both in and outside philosophy, they have dominated since time immemorial. We can find their recent and chief philosophical proponents e.g. in Hans Jonas; nowadays in Elizabeth Harman, Christine Overall, David Wasserman, and Rivka Weinberg. Therefore, firstly, most of the natalists argue that under some feasible conditions, such as normal upbringing in the modern affluence of industrialized countries, harms in the lives of human beings are outweighed both commonly enough and markedly enough by benefits. Notably, some natalists among philosophers of religion would contend that such a favourable balance in terms both of chance and value obtains when we consider the possibility of afterlife, given appropriate moral and religious upbringing, as well as certain arguments for the reality of afterlife itself. Other defenders of afterlife might argue that when the balance does not obtain in the afterlife, the originated human being is morally responsible for that, not their originators.

Secondly, most natalists argue some of these reasons also help to explain why the risk need not be grave (and even acceptable to the new human being that is going to be procreated). Or, thirdly, they discuss why it is not wrong to expose someone who is innocent and non-consenting to a grave risk. An additional reply could be made here, that doing something without another's consent is wrong and disrespectful to their autonomy only if they exist already. Fourthly, natalists would mostly claim, when the benefits markedly outweigh harms, the avoidance of all harm and deprivation by way of never existing does not matter or at least does not suffice to make the never existing preferable over existence. Fifthly, some of them contend likewise that a serious harm (e.g. from blindness) expected in a new life does not matter morally if the expected benefits in it reign overall. Or that it in fact may well be wrong not to start a markedly good new life. Or – if neither is the case – the preferability of never existing may well not be the best available explanation.

Sixthly, most of the natalists would probably try to defend that under feasible conditions, such as upbringing by moral yet appealing models, serious harms imposed by a new human being on other beings are commonly enough swamped by serious benefits imposed on some of those beings (say, one's relatives, friends, or needy strangers) or by benefits attained by the new human being themselves (say, their eventually attained knowledge or virtues; some religious thinkers, would again argue for the availability of blessings attained in the afterlife). Seventhly and finally, the reply to the aesthetic charge against producing new human beings would be very similar.

Why bother? The answer is that antinatalism is as consequential a philosophical position as can be. Just recall not only what it proclaims but also what its implications might be. At the same time, antinatalism is not obviously false, like natalism is not obviously true. At least that much is indicated by the weighty pros and cons. (This is not to say that none of us has made their own mind; that all of us have been sitting on a fence so to speak, be it theoretically or practically. This is a collective monography written by natalists and antinatalists; by people who have, by their own way of life, reaffirmed procreation, as well as by people who have rejected it.) Still, notwithstanding the long history of antinatalism, the recent and quite well-known defence by Benatar, and the less-known reaction from his critics, more work needs to be done before we can say that antinatalism has received attention comparable with its importance and demandingness.

Moreover, antinatalism and its cognates have got growing attention not just in philosophy. In the affluent and industrialized countries such as USA and Italy, more than ten percent of adult women resolve to stay childless by decision. About the same percentage of adults in such countries seem to view life on the whole as bad rather than good or neutral. And the numbers seem to be growing.[1] Sociologists, economists, political scientists, and kindred historians are welcome to explain by their own means why that is the case. Philosophers and historians of philosophy, including the authors of this book, must try to be of help to the thoughtful and discerning reader in figuring out not

---

[1] Cf. Basten (2009); Livingston and Cohn (2010) and Singer (2010).

so much what are the societal correlations or causes of such trends, but rather whether they are moral or prudent, both individually and collectively.

Now, what if antinatalism is false yet hardly refutable, and so too dangerous to be discussed any further? Or what if it is true yet easily misunderstood in its implications, and so once again too risky to be thematised more extensively than it has been already? Note that many would dismiss such caution in case of, say, discussing atheism, nihilism, euthanasia, abortion, or infanticide. Of course, philosophically speaking, perhaps they should not. Anyway, some of us who wrote this book find antinatalism discussed already quite widely, but at the same time they find it false and not so hard to refute. On the other hand, others among us think antinatalism is both true and not so hard to be unpacked correctly. Thus, each side has its own reasons to hope that their contribution shall have the upper hand, and that the book will do more good than harm.

That being said, the structure of the book is organized historically, albeit in a circular rather than linear manner. First of all, we start by a critical discussion of Benatar, a contemporary author, and probably the most articulate and comprehensive philosophical antinatalist so far. We highlight several – and so far never or seldom stated – soft spots in his very choice of the analytic method of writing. Although we initially focus merely on his asymmetry argument, the three-fold rest of the book builds on his argument about the poor quality of human life as well.

In the first part, we start to enlarge the deposit of relevant ideas by delving into the intellectual history of antinatalism in antiquity and the Middle Ages in general, with a focus on neglected tenets of the asymmetry and quality arguments in Aristotle's *Eudemus* and in early Christianity. In the second part, we carry on with modern age up to the present, with a focus on the rarely identified precursors of the asymmetry argument, followed by analyses of some antinatalistic elements in Vladimir Solovyov, and of the almost unknown antinatalistic author bearing the pen name Kurnig.

In the last and third part, we come to the full circle as we return to the contemporary antinatalism (though not just Benatar's), this time to its more or less likely, and surprising, implications in sexual ethics and in the ethics of suicide. We leave to the reader how well-established and acceptable these implications are, and so to what extent they either flesh out or raise doubts about the antinatalistic position itself. Throughout the book, we repeatedly bring attention to some underdiscussed issues that are relevant to the debate between antinatalists and pronatalists. Whatever the side each of us takes, it is our shared aim to help that neither remains nor becomes, in the face of its own opposition, an uncritically accepted ideology.

Vlastimil Vohánka

TO BE OR NOT TO BE
IS ANALYTICAL APPROACH SUITABLE?

INTRODUCTION

In his book *Better Never to Have Been*[2] David Benatar formulated his position regarding the problem of existence, which is typically expressed by question *To be or not to be?*. Benatar's main argument concerns the similar question, but it is hard to determine precisely which one of the following it is: *Is it better never to have been than to have been?* or *Is it better never to have been than to be?* In Benatar's argument, temporal relations are important, so maybe we should differentiate between these two questions.

In my opinion, questions concerning whether to be or not to be are fundamental to a being which is subject to significant suffering. Answers to them are not self-evident. There is no universal agreement on them, too. We can see that from the fact that major religions do not agree on them. For example, Theravada Buddhism and Christianity differ on this matter.

I will not defend here my own answers to these questions. I do not have them. I will instead focus on some problems of Benatar's argument. One of the main problems is, in my opinion, a way in which Benatar approaches the problem of existence, by which I will understand here the problem defined by questions mentioned above. This approach – we can also speak of a method – is like glasses we see the world through, or as an instrument we undertake our philosophical investigations with; typically, we are not aware of it. It is taken for granted by many philosophers.

My suggestion is that Benatar's approach is not appropriate to the problem investigated. In what follows I am going to call this approach – for lack of a better name – *analytical approach*. What I mean by it does not correspond precisely to an approach used in analytical philosophy, although there is significant overlap. In my usage, these words apply to a certain kind of thinking and investigation, which cannot be defined precisely and has no sharp boundaries. Moreover, it changes and evolves. My notion of analytical approach thus shows the characteristics that Wittgenstein described in his famous analysis of a notion of *game* in his *Philosophical Investigations*.[3] These characteristics include: family resemblances, uncertain boundaries, tendency to change over time and

---

[2] Benatar (2006).
[3] Wittgenstein (2009, §65–67).

in response to various specific conditions and contexts. This is not necessarily a bad thing. In some cases this is good and in others it is not. The above mentioned features are not in conflict with systematicness, consistency, logical correctness and other qualities of the results of application of analytical approach.

DEFINITION OF ANALYTICAL APPROACH

Not all categories[4] are classical.[5] When specifying non-classical categories, it is very hard and impractical to construct classical definition, even if such definition were possible in principle. *Classical definition* is a definition that states necessary and sufficient conditions for a given entity to be an instance of defined category (in our case the category is *analytical approach*). In the classical definition, conjunction of all necessary conditions forms a sufficient condition, although also the conjunctions of some subsets of all necessary conditions can constitute sufficient conditions in some cases.

Cognitive linguist George Lakoff uses cognitive models[6] for specifying non-classical categories, but this approach is not useful for me here. When specifying non-classical category *analytical approach* I use simplified method of constructing definition which contains typical features of instances of this category. Therefore, not all instances of analytical approach have to exhibit all of these features. Moreover, some of these features can be present only to some extent. It cannot be precisely defined to what extent they have to be present in order for an instance to belong to the category of analytical approach, too. In using such a non-classical definition I am informed by results of study of our cognition and language provided by cognitive science, mainly by cognitive psychology and cognitive linguistics, and by Wittgenstein.

As Lakoff points out, some of our categories are classical.[7] Classical categories are used more in science, while our ordinary language teems with non-classical categories. In my opinion, classical categories are rightly the ideal of science, because they provide precision and exactness. But when we cannot construct scientific theory, we usually cannot provide them, because precision of one concept requires precision of other concepts connected with it; this requirement of precision thus spreads to wide net of concepts, and the only way how to meet it then is to round up all of these concepts in structure called scientific theory.

---

[4] In cognitive linguistics and cognitive psychology, the term *category* is not used in its philosophical sense; it refers to what in philosophy is termed *concept*. I am following this terminology in this paper.
[5] Lakoff (1987).
[6] Ibid. (1987, p. 13).
[7] Ibid. (1987, p. 160).

When I try to describe approach to thinking I call *analytical*, I am not able presently to construct scientific theory, because thinking and investigation (ordinary, philosophical and scientific) are not currently mature for that: these human processes are so complex that at present we cannot construct scientific theory about them. Because of this, I cannot provide classical definition of analytical approach.

By *analytical approach* I will therefore refer to an approach to thinking and investigation that *typically*[8] shows these features to a *significant* degree:

1.   An effort to be logically correct; this effort can be further specified as an effort to conform to a certain logical requirements considered to be requirements of classical logic.

2.   An effort to think and express ideas in a maximally clear way.

3.   An effort to dissect, decompose and analyze thoughts and ideas – especially the core ones – to a very small parts and relations between them. This analysis has a tendency to create structures more similar to logical structures of formulas of classical logic than are the structures of sentences of ordinary languages.

4.   An effort to dissect, decompose and analyze argumentation – especially its core parts – to a relatively small steps, which should be much more evident than steps of ordinary reasoning. This analysis has a tendency to create structures more similar to the structures of logical proofs of classical logic than are argumentation structures of ordinary reasoning.

5.   An effort to base argumentation on the results of sciences.

6.   An effort to base argumentation on shared, and therefore often on ordinary, experiences.

7.   A notion that there should exist one or more mutually consistent arguments similar in structure to the proofs in classical logic for the thesis defended.

8.   Little or no use of metaphors, images, similes and stories; or an effort to reduce them to literal description; or a belief that such a reduction is in principle possible (for a correct description of something), even if it was not provided or found yet.

9.   A belief that there is one correct point of view; or if more points of view are considered to be correct, a belief that they can be reduced to one of them; or if they cannot be thus reduced, a belief that only one of them (or a certain subset of them, members of which are reducible to one member of this subset) is comple-

---

[8] Notions of *typicality* and *signifficancy*, used here, cannot be defined precisely in this case. I am aware of their vagueness.

tely correct and accurate.

10.   An unimportance of the character of the author.

11.   A tendency or effort towards an economy of expression. One of its constituents is a tendency to non-repetition: even if different accounts or expressions are not exactly identical and if they express the problem described or thesis defended differently, which brings possibility to show it from (maybe only slightly) different perspectives, there is a tendency to unite them into one account or expression.

11.   A relative unimportance of the way a message is to be expressed, if the content was delivered fully and adequately. This includes, for example, a relative unimportance of a writing style.

I am aware that some of these features, at least on the surface, can be categorized to the domain of method, while others seem to belong solely to the sphere of character of expression of results of a given method. Nevertheless, from my point of view, these two domains cannot be completely separated from each other; this is my reason for including them together in one list, which forms the (non-classical) definition of analytical approach.

I do not claim that analytical approach, as defined here, is bad, incorrect or not useful. I would like to show, however, that it is not very good, correct and useful for answering the question *To be or not to be?*. This approach is very fruitful in some areas, not so much in others, and it is quite inappropriate in others still. It is fruitful for answering some kinds of questions, but not other ones. And the provenience of philosophy is so broad that some of its questions fall into one, some to the other domain; and some somewhere in between.

More precisely, the problem opened by our question can be differentiated into parts and aspects that yield themselves to analytical approach in different degrees. But overall, this question, and its most important core, requires stepping beyond this approach, for various reasons. Many aspects of this question fall outside the domain of analytical approach.

THE DOMAIN OF ANALYTICAL APPROACH

Analytical approach is appropriate for many problems and questions. Roughly, it is possible to rank academic disciplines regarding how well their subject yields to this approach. As an example, I will rank some of them in this way now.

Analytical approach is very suitable for problems of logic and mathematics; to a lesser, but considerable degree, it is appropriate in physics and chemistry; still less, but also with great profit, it can be applied in many problems of biology and economics. Its suitability is questionable in many areas of psychology, and it is very doubtful that it can be applied in most research problems of sociology or history. Even more problematic it seems to be in the case of history of arts and in ethics, as well as in wide areas of philosophy.

Analytical approach seems to be very successful in two spheres. Both of these spheres are relative to cognitive or research capacities of a given being or beings and to the level of knowledge they reached. The first of these spheres is

(I)   Relatively conscious (for a given being or beings) creation and study of products of such creation (by these being or beings).

This creation and study can concern both thought and material constructs and systems. Among thought constructs and systems we can count logical formal systems, constructs and systems of mathematics and formalized theories of sciences. Material constructs and systems are material products of technology and science. In the case of study of some formal system we know the origin the propositions of such system can be generated from, like are for example axioms and rules of derivation of logical systems and definition of its well-formed expressions in case of logic, or axioms of mathematics (of set theory) together with classical logic in case of mathematics.

In the case of creation, it is possible to create in such a way that this activity and its results will conform to the tenets of analytical approach, and thus the description of this activity and of its results would also fall very well to the domain of analytical approach. Consider in this respect the work – and also its results – of a logician or a mathematician on one hand, and ability of humans to understand products of their technology on the other.

(II)   Study of relatively simple (relative to cognitive and research capacities of a given being or beings and to their level of knowledge) and recurring (relative to a time period of research conducted by these being or beings) phenomena.

It may not be obvious at first sight that phenomena successfully described by physics, chemistry, or biology are of this kind. But they are much more simple and much less unique (much more recurring) than for example phenomena of human psyche, human society, of history and of art. Many interesting aspects of these layers of reality deal with macroobjects and complex processes, which cannot be modelled by scientific theories we currently have with sufficient precision. These entities and processes are very often unique (non-recurring).

For example, it is possible to calculate the trajectory of a falling man using Newtonian laws of motion. In this case, it is possible to ignore complicated structure of his body (including his brain) and his relations to anything except relevant physical forces. Therefore, in such calculation he can be replaced by a material point. But to calculate or explain why he enjoyed just this book and not the other one, it is not at present possible to proceed using such analytical tools. The structure of his nervous system and his embodiment in social and cultural world cannot be ignored in this case. Both of these are greatly complicated and in many respects very unique.

DOES THE QUESTION OF 'TO BE OR NOT TO BE' LIE IN THE DOMAIN OF ANALYTICAL APPROACH?

Many questions of philosophy and ethics pertain more to the sphere in which analytical approach will not be successful, including many aspects of our problem of whether to be or not to be. This problem certainly concerns human beings and their life in such aspects that are too complex and quite unique. Even such occurrences as *simple* states of happiness and suffering are actually extraordinarily complex, including the simplest pleasure imaginable. Such pleasure seems to us a simple thing only because in ordinary reasoning and in folk psychology we deem it to be simple, fundamental entity, like photon or quark in physics. But in reality, it seems to be a process of enormous complexity and its relations to its causes seem to be no less complex. Consider what intricate activity has to exist in the brain for this simple feeling to arise. This is an activity of such complexity that it is out of reach of the contemporary science to describe. The same thing is even truer of the relation of a given state of mind to its causes, which is relevant for assessing how much happiness and suffering there typically is in human lives.

Moreover, for answering the question of whether to be or not to be we should investigate all possible ways of how to live a life. There are rare people who report that there is a possibility of a deeply blissful existence, in spite of outer limits of human life, and despite inevitable pain stemming from the possibility that our body can be damaged and destroyed. An inner life capable of such bliss and peace can be reached with the help of spiritual practices like are for example meditation, surrender of attachments, self-inquiry, affirmations and negations, prayer, chants, yoga, contemplation and others. A state which can be experienced thanks to these methods for transformation can become perpetual; it can persist throughout daily activities and work, whether it is experienced as an utmost bliss and sacredness, or as a distant undercurrent of peace. It is, moreover, capable of endless enlargement.

In our judgment of whether it is better never to have been, or of whether to be or not to be, we should take into account also reports, experience and lives such as these, however rare and exceptional they currently are. And especially here it is hard to imagine how they could be analyzed using analytical approach. Try to imagine how you would reflect on them using thinking of the kind Benatar uses in chapter 2 of his book.[9] I should note that these lives can contain the pain of a single pin-prick, which according to Benatar makes life not worth starting.[10] Yet it seems obvious to me that it is better to have been born to such a life than never to exist. In order to decide whether it is better to be than not to be, we need to have sufficiently clear insight into the inner experience, including the spiritual and mystical experience. We probably should take into account also meaning, which often makes suffering worthwhile. We should be able to somehow compute with all inner phenomena which have value in order to evaluate them.

But life is so complex and varied. Human mind, soul and inner experience is so intricate that we are currently not able to understand what it actually is: and how then we want to think successfully about it so precisely as Benatar tries to do? Taking into account the complexity of its physical basis, which is nervous system and body as a whole, it is quite plausible we will never be able to unlock its mysteries to the extent sufficient for weighing suffering and happiness so that we would be able to answer whether it is indeed better never to have been. Our ordinary understanding is not sufficient to provide answer of such precision which is implicitly presupposed if we use analytical approach: if we reason in a way Benatar does. I am afraid that Benatar's understanding of our problem area is not sufficiently complex and that we would probably need tools of thought and reasoning of such complexity that are currently not in our reach, if we want to reason about this problem area using analytical approach.

ANALYSIS

I cannot offer here complete analysis of our problem. I will provide only partial analysis, which will deal only with the premises of Benatar's main argument and with some of its implications.

In order to explain methods of assessing truth value of propositions I need to define some terms I will use.

In what follows, I will sometimes call propositions whose truth value cannot be de-

---

[9] Benatar (2006).
[10] Ibid. (2006, p. 48).

termined without experience *empirical propositions* and truth value they have *empirical truth value* (*empirical truth* if they are true, *empirical falsity* if they are false). I will also say they are *empirically true* if they are true and that they are *empirically false* if they are false. I understand experience to include not only personal experience but also scientific observation and experiment.

I will call formal system whose terms are interpreted as referring to something in experience *interpreted formal system* or *empirical formal system*. It contains empirical propositions which have empirical truth value.

I will call formal system whose terms are not interpreted as referring to something in experience *uninterpreted formal system*.

I will call propositions of uninterpreted formal system *formal propositions* and truth value they have *formal truth value* (*formal truth* if they are true, *formal falsity* if they are false);

I will also say they are *formally true* if they are true and that they are *formally false* if they are false.

We can prove some propositions or propositional formulas of a given formal system. If the terms of this formal system are not interpreted as referring to something in experience, the term *truth* used to refer to their truth value if they are true means something else than what it means in the case of propositions like

P1   This apple is green.
P2   Nothing moves faster through space than light.
P3   General theory of relativity is right.
P4   Higgs boson has a spin of 0.

These are empirical propositions with empirical truth value.

In the case of uninterpreted formal system, *truth* is a technical property of propositions defined in the semantics of this system. It is *formal truth*. Examples of formal propositions of propositional logic, predicate logic and mathematics, respectively, are:

P5 $[(p \rightarrow q) \wedge (q \rightarrow r)] \rightarrow (p \rightarrow r)$
P6 $(\forall x)\neg F(x) \leftrightarrow \neg(\exists x)F(x)$
P7   If $x^2 - 4 = 0$, then $x = 2$ or $x = -2$

Such formal system can be constructed in such a way that by its derivation rules we can derive from its axioms only those propositions of this system which have the technical property we call *formal truth*. Such derivation of a given proposition is a *proof* of this proposition. By proof we showed this proposition to be true. But this does not mean that this proposition is true in the sense P1–P4 are true. They are empirically true, but the proved proposition of uninterpreted formal system is not empirically true (like

P5–P7). To say that a proposition of such system is true means just that it has a technical property defined in the semantics of this system we call *truth*. But, if we interpret this formal system, its propositions can be both formally true and empirically true. This is the case of formalized empirical scientific theories: their propositions can be proved by deriving them from axioms or other propositions by system's derivation rules to have the technical property formal truth defined in semantics of a given system, but they can be empirically true as well. To prove that they are empirically true, experience must be utilized in some way. If we introduce derivation rules and axioms and if we interpret suitable terms in such a way that every proposition will be empirically true if and only if it is formally true, then if the premises of a given argument will be formally true, they will also be empirically true, and if this argument is sound, its conclusion will be both formally true and empirically true. In such design, formal truth overlaps with empirical truth, and we achieved precision and exactness, which is the aim of formalizing of a description of some experiential domain.

Examples of such uninterpreted formal systems are various logical systems (propositional calculus, predicate logic, modal logics) and mathematics. We have to be cautious, though, because these uninterpreted formal systems or their parts can be interpreted. By this process of interpretation, new theoretical entity is created, which we should distinguish from its uninterpreted origin.

As an example we can mention Euclidean geometry. This formal theory is uninterpreted only if it is not considered to model physical space. As soon as we interpret its terms so that the space of Euclidean geometry refers to physical space, it is no longer uninterpreted. In such case it is in fact a theory of physics, which can be either empirically true or empirically false. According to General theory of relativity it is empirically false. But uninterpreted Euclidean geometry, which is part of pure mathematics, is neither empirically true nor empirically false. It is not true or false in the ordinary sense of the words *true* and *false*; it is not true or false in the sense P1–P4 can be true or false.

Examples of interpreted formal systems are theories of physics, like special and general theory of relativity, quantum physics and so on. In these cases, classical logic and mathematics are actually parts of these theories, which thus form formal systems.

Part 1

Let us now turn to Benatar's main argument. Benatar bases his argument on these premises:

"1.   *The presence of pain is bad.*
2.   *The presence of pleasure is good.*
3.   *The absence of pain is good, even if that good is not enjoyed by anyone.*
4.   *The absence of pleasure is not bad unless there is somebody for whom this absence*

is a deprivation."[11]

How would we prove or show that these premises are true? Or how would we assess their truth or falsity, or at least their likelihood?

We can go through successful ways of how to show that some propositions are true. Let us call the following methods M.

Method 1:

We can prove some propositions or propositional formulas of a given uninterpreted formal system by deriving them from its axioms by its derivation rules. As we already mentioned, examples of propositions of uninterpreted formal system are P5–P7.

The premises (1)–(4) are not propositions of some uninterpreted formal system, so they cannot be proved to be true by this method. If we constructed some uninterpreted formal system, created the replacements of (1)–(4) in the language of this system and proved them in it by this method, they would be true only in a technical sense of formal truth. This would not be sufficient for Benatar since he certainly claims something more than what we call formal truth for his premises and conclusions.

Method 2:

We can prove some propositions of a given empirical formalized theory, which we call interpreted formal system here. In this case we have a formal system of a kind mentioned in Method 1, but now the terms of this system are interpreted to refer to something in experience. In this case also we can prove some propositions of this theory, based on derivation rules, axioms and other premises, because empirical formalized theories presuppose classical logic (and its derivation rules), which should be counted to be part of the system in question. If formal truth overlaps with empirical truth, if all premises of argument are empirically true and if by derivation we can derive only at those propositions whose formal truth is secured by the formal truth of premises from which we derive conclusion, then what we thus proved will also be empirically true.

Examples of propositions of interpreted formal system are:

P8 $s = v*t$
P9 $m_3 = 2{,}35$ kg

Premises (1)–(4) are not parts of empirical scientific theory of this kind, though, so they cannot be proved to be true by Method 2.

---

[11] Benatar (2006, p. 30).

Method 3:

We can find out whether some empirical propositions of ordinary language or some empirical scientific propositions are true using our senses or measuring instruments. Examples of empirical propositions of ordinary language are:

P10   This computer is turned on
P11   Now it is five o'clock

Examples of empirical scientific propositions are:

P9 m_3 = 2,35 kg
P12 t_2 = 25 s and s_2 = 5 m

How would we assess whether the proposition *This computer is turned on* is true or not?
A person who has a good sight and is in the appropriate distance and position, can see whether the screen is on, or whether the light indicating that this computer is turned on is on; a person who is not deaf can under suitable circumstances find out whether the computer is emitting a sound of a certain kind.
How would we assess whether the proposition *Now it is five o'clock* is true or not?
Knowing that operating system in my computer works reliably, and that it is synchronized with worldwide web, I can look at the right low corner, or wherever an actual time is displayed. Or knowing a given clock works reliably and were properly set, I can look at it.
How would we assess whether the proposition *m_3 = 2,35 kg* is true or not? For example, we could use some reliable and functional measurement device with sufficient precision to determine the weight termed m_3, which belongs to a given physical object.
These descriptions are not complete, but it seems to me they cannot be; if not for other reason than because they cannot at present be formulated in some scientific theory. This is true also about scientific empirical propositions: Method 3 of determining whether they are empirically true (but also other methods M) cannot be at present itself described fully by some empirical formalized theory, even if it is used in creating such theory.
Again, Benatar's premises do not fall into this category, so they cannot be shown to be true in this way.

Method 4:

We can scientifically prove some empirical general propositions, hypotheses, and theories. This category of propositions contains general propositions which can emerge as proved in scientific process. This method does not use proofs which are used in Methods 1 and 2, nor does it use senses or measuring instruments as directly as Method 3. Measurements (observation and experiment) are crucial, but many of them have to be performed in order to arrive at conclusion that these general propositions, hypotheses or theories are right. Scientific process generating them probably uses something like Popper's falsification, and other ways of discovery.

Many such propositions emerged in physics, chemistry, biology and other sciences. They need not be parts of some empirical formalized theory. Examples of them are:

P13 $E = mc^2$

P14 $s(t) = \int v(t)dt$

But premises (1)–(4) are not results of empirical scientific research, so they cannot be proved to be true by this method.

If there are other successful methods for showing that something is true, we should ask whether Benatar's premises can be showed to be true by these methods. But what are other such methods?

It is very questionable that some reasonable method for assessing truth value can be offered in the case of (1)–(4).

We can even ask whether (1)–(4) really are propositions and not, for example, commands or other different speech acts, which have not a function of informing about something. On the surface, on the syntactical level, they seem like sentences that describe something (and the acts of uttering them therefore seem like acts of informing about something), but a deeper analysis could show otherwise. Maybe the proposition *The presence of pain is bad* is actually a command *Avoid pain!;* this command could have been *given to us* by nature. Maybe its expression in the form *The presence of pain is bad* is deceptive: this proposition seems as informing us about some objective relation – about an objective fact that some state of the world (*presence of pain*) has some property (*being bad*). But it need not be so.

If propositions (1)–(4) indeed are informative, we can ask whether they inform us about something more than about our subjective values – or values of our society (or values prevalent in our society). This is a reasonable possibility, too.

Benatar says that (1) and (2) are uncontroversial.[12] But is there a good reason for them to be uncontroversial? If not, then their being uncontroversial is irrelevant for our inquiry seeking to unravel the truth. In other words: is there a good reason for us to accept them? Many propositions were uncontroversial in the past and now we know that they are false.

We can, of course, use the concept of intuition. This could be a move towards greater

---

[12] Benatar (2006, p. 30).

clarity, as to the status of (1)–(4), and as such it could shed some light on our problem. If we said that (1)–(4) are intuitive for us in the sense that we have a strong feeling that they are true, or that they are intuitive for us in the sense that we have a strong tendency to accept them, we could make a step forward in illuminating their truth status. This would indicate that we do not have any methods similar to M for assessing their truth value.

If we tried to use more philosophical notions of intuition we would stray into more significant problems connected with them. Understandings of intuition just mentioned have a virtue of not going too far from what is certain. Therefore, it would be good to stick to them in our descriptions of why we accept some or all of premises (1)–(4). Personally, I could label as *intuitive* only (1) and (2). But this does not mean that they are true or even likely, only that I have a feeling that they are true or likely or that I have a tendency to accept them.

Part 2

One of Benatar's main theses can be formulated thus:

T1   Future life containing any pain is worse than no life.

Does T1 follow from Benatar's premises (1)–(4)? It does not. In order to deduce it we need more premises: we need to state how to calculate with pleasures and pains and which sets of them are relevant for comparing given lives, or for comparing a given life with no life. These can be considered to be hidden premises of Benatar's main argument, or at least premises he is not aware are needed for deducing T1, although he expressed them and considers them to be true. In fact, that what we need to add to (1)–(4) in order to deduce T1 is partly hidden for Benatar (according to his book)[13] and partly he expressed it but did not say it is part of his premises. Because of that, we need to both construct and reconstruct, in order to develop full and precise argument for deducing T1: we need to construct that part of premises he did not expressed and reconstruct that part which he did, but not in a clear way; this second component is scattered among his other statements.

We will start with Benatar's premises (3) and (4) and skip (1) and (2), because, as we will see, (2) is not needed for deducing T1 and what (1) wants to say will be incorporated into our version of (3).

Benatar's premise (3) states:

(3)   The absence of pain is good, even if that good is not enjoyed by anyone.

---

[13] Benatar (2006).

a

Since this would imply that a universe with no life is not neutral, but good, it would be better to restate this premise to:

> The absence of pain is better than its presence, even if this absence or presence of pain is not enjoyed by anyone.

If we admit the possibility of comparing no life with specific life, we need not explicitly state that absence of pain is better than its presence even if there is no one in whom a given possible pain would be absent:

> The absence of pain is better than its presence.

We will see that Benatar's argument presupposes that when we decide about the existence of future life – a life that has not yet started – we should collect pains and pleasures to a certain sets and not to others. How we make evaluations of pains and pleasures of past and actual beings can be left open for our purposes, but in the case of future beings we have to introduce calculation mechanism of pains and pleasures, which presupposes pains, pleasures, their values and sets of pains and pleasures and their values. The reason is that Benatar presupposes that unit which is relevant when we decide about the existence of the future life is the set of all pains and pleasures only in that one life.

According to him, this unit cannot contain only some of the pains and pleasures of a given future being: we have to include in it all pains and pleasures felt be this being in its life. We also cannot extend this unit to pains and pleasures of other beings: if we are deciding whether to create a life, we should take into consideration only pains and pleasures felt by a being which has this life, but not pains and pleasures he or she may cause in other lives. This premise will be expressed in one of our additions to Benatar's premises, but we need now to introduce concepts used in the mechanism for calculating with pains and pleasures, because premise (3) needs to be rephrased in them.

We need to introduce not only pains, pleasures and their values, but also sets of pains and pleasures and values of these sets, because when Benatar evaluates future lives, he takes into account all pains and pleasures in a given life, and thus he uses sets of pains and pleasures for this evaluation. To compare values of pains and pleasures is not the same as to compare values of sets of pains and pleasures, if we do not consider sets of pains and pleasures to be the only units we use in evaluation and if we do not understand individual pains and pleasures to be a sets with one element; in such case our mechanism can cover both the sets with more elements and those with only one element.

Let us make a distinction between values of pains and pleasures and values of sets of them:

We will call V(p) the value of pain or pleasure p.

We will call SV(S) the set value of set of pains and pleasures S.

If we want to rephrase now our version of (3) in terms of our mechanism for calculating with pains and pleasures, we need not to assign values to absence of pain or pleasure, because we can construct our formula for calculating set value of a given set of pains and pleasures so as to guarantee that absence of pain or pleasure will have a desired effect on the set value of a given set of pains and pleasures. Our desired effect is that it should have no effect on this set value. Thus we can restrict our version of (3) only to setting values for pains:

PA   The value of any pain is < 0.

Let us move to Benatar's premise (4), which states:

(4)   The absence of pleasure is not bad unless there is somebody for whom this absence is a deprivation.

Let us proceed in steps similar to our transformation of (3). First, we do not want the following proposition to be derivable from our replacement of (4):

The absence of pleasure is bad if there is somebody for whom this absence is a deprivation.

In such case the life of a being which does not contain any pleasures or pains would contain something bad, which we do not want; such life should be neutral. Again, it will be better to express comparison:

The absence of pleasure is worse than its presence only if this absence or presence of pleasure concerns actual being.

Since we want to reason about future beings, we will formulate our premise thus:

The presence of pleasure is not better than its absence if this presence or absence of pleasure concerns future being.

Anyway, we do not have enough information from Benatar's book concerning evaluation of lives of past beings in this way.

We probably want to value the state without pleasure and pain (or without any positive or negative feelings generally) neither positively nor negatively. Premise (4) wants to say that presence of pleasure is not better than this state in the case of future beings. But presence of pleasure should not be worse than its absence, even for future beings.

Therefore it seems best to set the value of presence of pleasure in a future life to 0. Our version of premise (4) thus gains the form:

PL   The value of any pleasure in a future life is 0.

We want to make evaluation of future lives. Our mechanism for calculating with pleasures and pains of future beings should therefore contain the formula for this evaluation. If we want to be faithful to what Benatar says in his book, the formula for calculating set value of the set S of pains and pleasures has to be of the form:

$$SV(S) = \sum M(p)V(p)$$

where p is an element of S, the sum $\sum$ is considered to run through all the members of S and M: P $\rightarrow$ R$^+$ is a function which assigns positive real number to an element of a set of all possible concrete pains and pleasures in the future P. Positive real number M(p) is a multiplier of a real number V(p) which represents the value of pain or pleasure p.

It seems to me that this formula is most general we can use if we want to be faithful to Benatar's exposition. If M(p) could be 0 for some p, then some pleasures or pains could have no effect on our evaluation of future life. If it could be negative, some pleasure could have negative effect on our evaluation and some pains could have positive effect on it. None of these things seems to be consistent with Benatar's argument.

We also cannot add to or subtract from V(p) for the same reason. If we did, either some pleasures could have negative or no effect on our evaluation or some pains could have positive or no effect on it.

More generally, it seems to me that any function F[V(p)] in our formula for SV of the form SV(S) = $\sum$F should be equivalent to a function of a form M(p)V(p), where M: P $\rightarrow$ R$^+$, for the same reason.

But we could be more specific and set M(p) = 1 for all p. In the case of such constant multiplier we would get

$$SV(S) = \sum V(p)$$

Maybe, we also can interpret M as representing a probability of a presence of given element of P (of a given concrete pain or pleasure in the future) and limit the values of M to the interval $\langle 0, 1 \rangle$.

In our mechanism for calculating with pains and pleasures we used calculation mechanisms already present in mathematics, which included the order of real numbers, operations of adding and multiplying, sets and functions. We need not to use mathematics but then we need to invent another calculus for calculating with pleasures and pains.

To see this note that future life may contain more than one occurrence of pleasure or pain. In such case we need to evaluate some collection or set of pleasures and pains. We need to specify what the value of the whole collection or set will be, because it cannot always be equated with the value of its member (since there can be more than one such member). It is also not *a priori* true that we should add the values of all the members; in general, we need to consult experience in order to know which formula models the value of set of pleasures and pains best. Since we try to model Benatar's conceptualization of this evaluation, we need not to consult experience at his stage of our analysis, but we need at least to explicitly state what formula we will choose for evaluation, because it is not the only possible one. Since this formula is a premise of Benatar's argument, it will thus become explicit, too.

For example, if a future life contains one occurrence of pleasure and one occurrence of pain, it is not a priori true that its value is negative. But this is exactly what Benatar says, if we want to make his position more explicit. We need to do it more explicit in order to be faithful to the way he argues, especially in the chapter 2: his way of thinking and investigation can be included under analytical approach. But if we do not want to make it more explicit by utilizing mathematics, we need to invent some system similar to it in many respects, since Benatar admits that pleasures and pains can have different intensity and duration (and thus different value), and that they can be compared. The set of real numbers already contains all the machinery we need to model this, so it is wise to utilize it. Set theory, arithmetic and the notion of function provide tools for calculating the values of sets of pains and pleasures.

If we wanted to try to avoid the use of some calculus and say that our premise is that if there will be any pain in the future life the value of this life will be negative regardless of anything else we would have declared our conclusion to be the premise. And it would not be entirely appropriate to say that we avoided the use of some calculus. It seems it would be equally appropriate to say that we used very simple calculation mechanism which assigns some value – let us call it *Negative* – to all future lives which contain at least one occurrence of pain and some other value – let us call it *Indifferent* – to all future lives which do not contain any pain.

We will use mathematics, and since it presupposes classical logic – predicate logic of higher order with identity – we need not to declare this logic to be basis of our reasonning independent of mathematics. But it is not customary to state that mathematics or logical system are premises of an argument, even if they are used in it and thus form its basis too. Because of that, we will explicitly declare as premise only our formula for evaluation of sets of pains and pleasures:

PE   Set value SV of set of pains and pleasures S is $SV(S) = \sum M(p)V(p)$, where p is an element of S, the sum $\sum$ runs through all the members of S, M is a function

$P \rightarrow R^+$, where P is a set of all possible occurrences of pains and pleasures in the future, and V(p) is a value of p.

Finally, we need to state what sets of pains and pleasures are relevant for evaluation of a future lives L_x and L_y and how we will evaluate them:

PR   If L_x and L_y are future lives or no life (L_0), and S_x is a set of all pains and pleasures that will be felt in L_x if L_x is future life or an empty set if it is L_0, and S_y a set of all pains and pleasures that will be felt in L_y if L_y is future life or an empty set if it is L_0, then:

L_x is worse than L_y if and only if $SV(S_x) < SV(S_y)$,
L_x is better than L_y if and only if $SV(S_x) > SV(S_y)$,
L_x is neither worse nor better than L_y if and only if $SV(S_x) = SV(S_y)$.

Because it is not a priori true that relevant set for evaluation of a given life is a set of all pains and pleasures felt in just that one life, we declared PR to be a premise.
Now we constructed or reconstructed all the premises and definitions needed for proving T1: from the conjunction PA $\land$ PL $\land$ PE $\land$ PR we can prove T1.

Proof:

We want to compare future life L with at least one occurrence of pain with no life L_0. By PR, empty set $\varnothing$ corresponds to no life L_0. By PE, set value of $\varnothing$ is $SV(\varnothing) = \sum M(p)V(p)$. Since empty set has no elements, sum of values of its elements multiplied by positive real numbers is 0. Set value of $\varnothing$ is thus $SV(\varnothing) = 0$. By PR, set S of all pains and pleasures that will be felt in L corresponds to L. By PE, set value of S is $SV(S) = \sum M(p)V(p)$. S can contain many occurrences of pleasure, but by PL, all of them have value 0, since L is a future life. By PA, value of any pain, whether in past life, actual life, or future life, is negative. By PE, set value of S will be the sum of all values of pleasures and pains in S multiplied by positive real number. Since multiplier M is always positive, all contributions of all occurrences of pleasure will be 0, and all contributions of all pains will be negative. Since there is at least one occurrence of pain in S, the sum in formula for set value of S will be negative: $SV(S) < 0$. By PR, we can conclude that the future life L with at least one occurrence of pain is worse than no life L_0, because $SV(S) < SV(\varnothing)$.
I am aware that the proof is trivial. My aim here was to uncover hidden premises and explain some problems I see with Benatar's argument. I formalized it in order to show these problems in a maximally clear way. I will now discuss them.
The fact that we can prove T1 from PA $\land$ PL $\land$ PE $\land$ PR means that the following argument is valid:

$$PA \wedge PL \wedge PE \wedge PR$$
T1

But the validity of an argument does not imply that its conclusion is true. It only implies that if all the premises of this argument were true, conclusion would have to be true as well. But are PA, PL, PE and PR all true? If not, T1 may be false.

Is PL true? Is it really true that any pleasure in a life of a future being is of no worth? I personally do not think so. Even if it is not obligatory to create a life full of happiness with no suffering which would be too great, it does not follow that such a life has no worth, as I will try to explain below.

In our analysis, we uncovered that to deduce something like T1 we need some mechanism for calculating with pains and pleasures. But is our candidate for such a mechanism appropriate? This is quite questionable.

It is possible that our formula for evaluation of future lives should contain some thresholds, for example a threshold modeling that suffering which will exceed some intensity for some duration of time will outweigh any happiness. It is also possible that we should count with some marginality effect similar to that described in economics; it is possible that every pleasure or pain added to previous pains or pleasures will contribute less or more than is its value to the set value of the set of pains and pleasures which will be created by its addition. Thus PE is problematic.

Why only pains and pleasures felt in the future lives are relevant for their comparison? A future being will influence other beings and although it suffers it may bring great good to others. What if this suffering will be a suffering of a great scientist whose discoveries will help many others? A future being may be a saint who will help many people, or a mystic or spiritual teacher who will help others through his or her teaching. Maybe it will be a great artist whose work will bring pleasure to many.

Even if it were true that the majority of people will not be responsible for great amount of good in the lives of others, we still have to change PR in order to extend relevant sets of pains and pleasures beyond those felt by a being whose life we evaluate. It is important to note that Benatar really presupposes, at least implicitly, that the pains and pleasures relevant for comparing future life with no life are limited to an individual being whose life we are comparing with no life. We can see that from T1, which states that any life with any pain is worse than no life, regardless of anything else; it is therefore worse than no life regardless of whether this life belongs to someone who will bring much happiness or alleviate much suffering in a life of someone else. I personally think that if we wanted to approach matter analytically we would need to change PR in this respect; and whether we want to approach matter analytically or not we should take into account also influence of a given future being on others. In the case when we do not know what influence a future being will have on others we should still take into account the general truth that this influence will very probably exist, because this being will probably not live in total isolation from others.

Another problem stems from the fact that we imagined that inward states with some value can all be classified either as pains or pleasures. Benatar says that we should imagine pains and pleasures only as exemplars of harms and benefits,[14] so he is aware that we perhaps should generalize our argument towards the latter. Our model nonetheless presupposes just pains and pleasures, although replacement of pains with harms and pleasures with benefits is easy. But if positive and negative states have more complicated structure than that captured by two categories with opposite values of its members, generalization may be more difficult. Our model also presumes that values of members of these categories are one-dimensional. We could find also other problematic features, I believe. The last one I will mention here is whether pleasures have positive value. This only strengthens Benatar's argument, but our model should be changed if they indeed do not; the change would be trivial, if pleasures are all plainly negative, but it may be difficult if their structure relevant for their evaluation is more complex.

My experience suggests that we maybe should distinguish different kinds of inward states which are felt as positive in a moment of their presence. It is possible that we should introduce two quite different categories of such states; I will refer to them by the terms *pleasure* and *happiness*. So called pleasures seem to tend to strengthen and feed a certain mechanism which we can call the mode of seeking pleasures. In this mode, although it may seem that pleasures fill feed us, they in fact do not. They only appear to satisfy us for a little while, while in the long run they only magnify the hunger for more of them. If pleasures themselves have this character, then it should be considered to be essential for them and we should maybe regard them as negative. On the other hand, there seems to be something different which does not have this effect, which I call happiness. Moreover, pleasures seem to close us to the world and make us more selfish, while happiness seem to opens us to others and make us responsive to their needs in a better way. I am not saying this account is accurate; maybe the problem lies only in the mode of seeking pleasures and not in the pleasures themselves, or maybe I am wrong here in something else. I only want to point out another possible problem with the model I presented above.

In summary, I personally am inclined to agree only to PA; other premises seem to me to be quite problematic.

Part 3

Let us return to PL, because there is another way of how to reveal it is problematic. Benatar admits that the following proposition is one of the consequences of his premises:

---

[14] Benatar (2006, 30).

C   *"A life filled with good and containing only the most minute quantity of bad –
        a life of utter bliss adulterated only by the pain of a single pin-prick – is worse
        than no life at all."*[15]

If we want to stick with talking about pains and pleasures, because only they were mentioned in the original premises (1)–(4), and if we want to formulate this proposition in
the terms of our model, we should reformulate it, for example in this way:

T2   A future life containing great amount of pleasure and almost no pain is worse
        than no life.

We of course had to add also explicit reference to the future. As we already pointed
out, in Benatar's argument, temporal relations are important. Both T1 and T2 concern
future lives. Benatar does not say that we should prefer no life over *actual* life with any
suffering, but that we should prefer no life over *future* life with any suffering.
T2 also follows from premises PA, PL, PE and PR. The proof is again trivial. Even great
amount of pleasure cannot overweight the smallest pain, because the values of all pleasures in future life are 0, but the value of even the smallest pain is negative.
Let us call the conjunction of PA, PL, PE and PR our hypothesis, H:

$H =_{def} (PA \wedge PL \wedge PE \wedge PR).$

We can then express the fact that T2 follows from our premises simply as:

$H \rightarrow T2.$

If our hypothesis is true, T2 has to be true as well, since it follows from it. This can be
expressed in the form of modus ponens, by which we will get the following argument:

$$\text{MP} \quad \frac{\begin{array}{l} H \rightarrow T2 \\ H \end{array}}{T2}$$

But we do not know whether H is true. We saw that at least three of its premises are
problematic. So we cannot say T2 is true, even though it follows from H.
But why not try to assess the truth value of T2 in another way? T2 cannot be assessed
with the help of methods M, but if we have to somehow estimate its truth value, would
this estimate be more likely true than estimate of the truth value of H? If so, then if we
want to accept the estimate of the truth value of H, we should accept the estimate of
truth value of T2 even more willingly. I personally think that it is more likely that T2 is

---

[15] Benatar (2006, p. 48).

false than that H is true: I personally think that it is more likely that *it is not true that life of utter bliss adulterated only by the pain of a single pin-prick is worse than no life at all* than that *premises H of our previous argument are true*. In other words, I think that the negation of T2 is more likely to be true than H.

If negation of T2 is true then we can use another valid rule of propositional logic to arrive at a different conclusion. We can use modus tollens to construct an argument:

AMT $H \rightarrow T2$
$\underline{\neg T2}$
$\neg H$

If ¬T2 is more likely to be true than H, premises of AMT (H → T2, ¬T2) are more likely to be true than premises of AMP (H → T2, H). Therefore, the use of AMT is more or at least equally reasonable as the use of AMP for deriving any conclusions. Because of that, to accept the conclusion of AMT (¬H) is more or at least equally reasonable than to accept the conclusion of AMP (T2). Thus it is more or at least equally reasonable to conclude that at least one of the propositions constituting hypothesis H is false than to accept T2.

I personally think that ¬T2 is more likely to be true than H, therefore I would rather use AMT than AMP. Because of that I think it is more likely that at least one of the propositions constituting hypothesis H is false than that T2 is true.

If we can use terminology of Karl Popper even if we are not talking about scientific hypothesis (because I do not claim that H is scientific hypothesis), we can say that I think it is more likely that ¬T2 falsifies hypothesis H than that hypothesis H proves T2.

Part 4

I will continue by offering a different view on one of the problems Benatar claims his premises solve.

Benatar's premise (4) is particularly problematic. It seems to me that there indeed is asymmetry between a good and a bad life, concerning bringing new beings into existence. But I have a tendency to explain this asymmetry differently from Benatar. I would firstly introduce a distinction between two meanings of good and bad:

D1   A possibility is *ethically good* if we should choose it; I will also say that we have an *ethical obligation to choose it.*

D2   A possibility is *ethically bad* if we should not choose it; I will also say that we have an *ethical obligation not to choose it.*

D3   A possibility is *good as a gain* if it is in some sense a gain to choose it, relative to not choosing it; I will also say it is a *gain.*

D4 A possibility is *bad as a loss* if it is in some sense a loss to choose it, relative to not choosing it; I will also say it is a *loss*.

Please excuse my inability to produce better definienda than *good as a gain* or *gain* and *bad as a loss* or *loss*.

I introduced these distinctions because I feel that there are some possibilities which are in some sense gains, but which we have no ethical obligation to choose. For example, it is a gain for me to choose happiness for myself, if I do not lose anything good by this choice, but I do not have ethical obligation to choose in this way; nor I have an ethical obligation not to make this choice, if I do not influence others in a bad way by it.

I would like to note that I am not sure whether these definitions are appropriate, mainly because I think that most of the ethical domain does not currently belong to the domain of analytical approach for human beings.

Using these meanings of good and bad I can now state:

S1 We have an ethical obligation not to bring into existence a being whose life will be full of extreme suffering without sufficient meaning to this suffering.

S2 We have not an ethical obligation to bring into existence a being whose life will be full of happiness and which will not contain too much suffering.

S3 It is a gain to bring into existence a being whose life will be full of happiness and which will not contain too much suffering, in comparison to not bringing it into existence.

S4 It is a loss not to bring into existence a being whose life will be full of happiness and which will not contain too much suffering, in comparison to bringing it into existence.

I would like to note that I am not sure whether these statements are true or precise, again mainly because I think that most of the ethical domain does not currently belong to the domain of analytical approach for human beings.

Last two of these statements express my feeling that it would be some kind of gain (*a gain for the world/for the universe/for the All*) if there was a being whose life would be full of happiness and without too much suffering, in comparison to the state of the world in which this being would not come into existence; and that it would be some kind of loss, if there was not such a being, in comparison to the state in which this being would come into existence.

It seems to me that there is a more general asymmetry between positive internal states and negative internal states. In a first approximation, it seems to me that something like this may be true: we do not have an ethical obligation to create positive internal states in others, but we have an ethical obligation not to create negative internal states in others. For example, it seems to me that I have no ethical obligation to make others happy, but that I have an ethical obligation not to make others suffer, if there is no sufficient justification for it. But it is good to make others happy. In the terminology introduced in D1–D4 we can express it in this way: it is not ethically good to make others happy, but it is a good as a gain to make them happy. If we would like to start building some theory using analytical approach, we could introduce more general premises. For example, we could start with something like the following and then try to refine them further:

G1   We have an ethical obligation not to create negative mental states in others.
G2   We have not an ethical obligation to create positive mental states in others.
G3   It is a gain to create positive mental states.
G4   It is a loss not to create positive mental states.
G5   It is a gain not to create negative mental states.
G6   It is a loss to create negative mental states.

I am neither satisfied with these premises nor do I think that I can refine them to be a solid basis for precise ethical decision making. The reason is, again, that I think we cannot at present build exact theory of ethical domain or some significant part of it, because this domain does not currently belong to the domain of analytical approach for us.

I expressed these statements because I wanted to present some outline of how more general premises from which we could derive premises about starting future lives could look. Statements S1–S4 are consistent with the existence of the asymmetry Benatar talks about. It is questionable whether they explain it, but only because they just state it and are not general enough to be the basis for deriving it. The more general premises G1–G6 expressed now provide an outline of this more general basis from which the existence of the asymmetry could be derived.

I admit that neither S1–S4, nor G1–G6 can be justified by methods M, just like Benatar's premises. Both my and Benatar's premises are structures from which we can deduce some propositions we believe in. It is fairly possible that they may seem to be true to somebody only because they provide propositional material from which he can deduce what he already tends to accept. What if we have a tendency to build structures like these, because equipped with them we have a feeling that with the help of them we based some of our beliefs on a firmer ground or explained them? And what if, in fact, they are not better basis or explanation of our beliefs in virtue of implying them?

CONCLUSION

To somehow cope with such question as is the question of *To be or not to be*, we have to – due to enormous complexity, depth and width of the problem domain opened by it – use less precise, less exact, less detailed, and maybe even less consistent thinking, because analytical approach cannot provide us with a good enough answer. In a real life, which requires ethical deliberation and some, at least implicit, stance on whether we want to live or have children, we do not and cannot use precise and exact theories and sometimes we even have to make friends with paradox or contradiction.

The reason is that most problems of real life do not fall into the sphere delineated in (I) and (II). Therefore, it is wise, I think, that we are almost always imprecise and inexact and that we sometimes make use even of paradox or contradiction; sometimes we do this with great and true benefit. Is it not so, that sometimes, only paradox or contradiction enabled us to solve some problem of our existence or brought us peace or understanding? This is no coincidence, in my opinion, nor stupidity or folly, but wisdom of our ordinary existence, which we maybe do not appreciate. We have to move almost constantly outside the analytical approach in our real life because most of its problems do not fall into the domains described in (I) and (II).

Similar thing holds also for the home domain of our questions of *To be or not to be* and *Is it better never to have been than to be*, which belong to many spheres simultaneously; we can speak loosely of spheres of *ethics*, of *meaning*, of *inner experience*, of *spirituality*, and maybe others. The reason I speak about less precise, less detailed or less consistent or paradoxical thinking is that some people may solve these questions for themselves by it, and – I think such solution may be right or wise in many cases.

But the stance we have to have, at least in implicit form, to the question of *To be or not to be* need not be affirmative or negative. The stance of not knowing is also a possibility, and it has implications for real life decisions. If I do not know whether to be or not to be I can continue on and see what will happen and what will I come to know in the future; maybe I will find an answer to this deep question and maybe I will not. Similarly with the question of having children I can at present use my best estimate based on conscience, feelings, my beliefs and facts, even if I am not sure, because I am not able to answer this question using analytical approach: no theory, whether scientific, ethical or philosophical, provides good enough reasons for affirmative or negative answer.

I do not claim that it is better to exist than never to exist, I only suggest that the way Benatar approaches this question is not currently appropriate for it. The questions of *To be or not to be* and *Is it better never to have been than to be* are not at present answerable well enough using analytical approach as defined here, because we do not have sufficient knowledge, or cognitive or research capacities for that. I think that precise truths about happiness and suffering, which we would need for deducing answers to these questions, are not as simple as Benatar's premises (1)–(4), if we want to reason with the precision he implicitly presupposes in the way he argues. His pursuit of precision, logical consistency and truth is the pursuit of scientific theory, whether he is aware of it or no. Such pursuit cannot stay halfway between ordinary reasoning and scientific theory, if it wants to be consistent. But scientific theory concerning these matters is, I think, impossible for us at present.

Michal Kutáš

PROTOHISTORY OF ANTINATALISM

AUTHORS:

Kateřina Lochmanová
PROTOHISTORY OF ANTINATALISM:
Antiquity and the Middle Ages
(pp. 37–52)

Filip Svoboda
ARISTOTLE AND HIS EUDEMUS
(pp. 53–67)

Théophile de Giraud
ANTINATALISM IN EARLY CHRISTIANITY
(pp. 69–88)

PROTOHISTORY OF ANTINATALISM
ANTIQUITY AND THE MIDDLE AGES

INTRODUCTION

Of course there is nothing new about antinatalistic spirit at all: the preference of non-existence over existence has its roots in antiquity, when explicit references to the asymmetry of good and evil applied to the question of existence first appeared, along with nineteenth century thinkers. It seems that Benatar, however, does not turn his attention to such a tradition in any sufficient manner and thus, despite the uniqueness of his argumentation owing to its philosophical strife according to Coates,[16] he is somewhat lacking in this historical context. But if the stream of analytical philosophy, or rather analytical existentialism that Benatar has professed, should be considered as just an episode in a long-running series called *philosophy*, then Benatar's argumentation needs to be broadened by this tradition a bit more, as Michal Kutáš points out in his chapter. And that is precisely the task which we have set to ourselves: to describe the history of antinatalism.

However, the history of antinatalism has not been monolithic by any means and even at first glance it's obvious that at least three quite different periods could be outlined. The first one belongs to the era of antiquity, which overlaps with the Middle ages, when antinatalistic discourse was significantly weakened because of the spread of Christianity. The second one begins soon after in the modern era, and afterwards got rejuvenated as late as in the nineteenth century, and we see a third rejuvenation within the third period, in the twentieth and the twenty-first century, whose influence has persisted until the present.

---

[16] Apart from its philosophical impact, according to Coates, Benatar's originality lies also in his narrow focus on procreation ["*in his focus on procreation and in his strong advocacy of anti-natalism on philosophical grounds*" (Coates 2014, p. 264)].

The first of the three periods, the period of Antiquity and the Middle ages, is elaborated within the first section of this book. Starting with this chapter, we are trying to document the protohistory of particular antinatalistic suppositions and then map how the reception of said suppositions changed with the advent of Christianity. The first section is thus going to be commenced by an era, when some reasons for antinatalism were already concerned, but this was not the case of Benatar's asymmetry argument, nor any of its earlier variations. Within the second section of the book, we then focus on the period when the topic of antinatalism has gradually been enriched by a new type of arguments; since this was the time when Benatar's so-called asymmetry argument begun to be formed, besides the on-going argumentation concerning the low quality of life. The third section of the book is devoted to contemporary antinatalism, introduced finally as an established and seriously intended alternative to traditional catholic ethics.

Ken Coates has already set a similar goal as well, resulting in a monography entitled *Anti-Natalism: Rejectionist Philosophy from Buddhism to Benatar*,[17] providing a collection of antinatalistically relevant views by selected spiritually, philosophically or literary-oriented thinkers across the history of mankind. Within this monography, we aim to supplement Coates' book with other names, yet somewhat inversely. While Coates dealt with religious antinatalism concerning some typically Eastern types of Buddhism and Hinduism, we are trying to find reflections of antinatalistic spirit within Greek mythology and Western Christianity. While Coates focused on the 19th century German philosophers Arthur Schopenhauer and Eduard von Hartmann, we are particularly interested in a Russian philosopher called Vladimir Solovyov and an unknown author going by the pen name Kurnig. We devoted much more space to the Jewish philosopher Hans Jonas, instead of the typically atheistic writers of the 20th century like Samuel Beckett and Jean-Paul Sartre, but we mention many other thinkers as well, ranging from antiquity to the 21st century. Among the authors which both of these books are dealing with, it is especially David Benatar who need not be absent, since he is the one who disfavours the historical part of antinatalism over the contemporary part, as an explicitly defined direction. That is the reason why we opened the whole book preciously by the analysis of his approach.

As the subtitle of this book indicates, we attempt to capture the development of antinatalistic philosophy precisely in the context of the changing social situations in Europe, so that we focus on the question of whether and to what extent antinatalistic ideas have broke through in competing with alternative approaches, and to what extent antinatalistic ideas have spontaneously sneaked even into these alternative approaches.

---

[17] Coates (2014).

Although such a collection could hardly be called exhaustive, that should still be considered as better than nothing; as long as Leibniz's thesis that something is better than nothing still holds (being a bit shakened by Benatar, truth be told).[18]

ANTIQUITY

According to Patočka, philosophy from its very beginning, *"has been forced to radicalize itself again and again by revelation of the reality of human misery and suffering; it had to result not only into a calm and dismantling resignation, but also into a radicalization of human demands on the world and destiny."*[19] Philosophers, indeed, could find their inspiration from their own experiences, since, as stories of philosophical martyrs such as Zeno of Elea, Anaxagoras, Socrates or Boëthius show, the history of philosophy is also parallel to the history of philosophers' suffering.[20] Even if this holds true not only specifically for philosophy[21] or merely for Western thinking in general – myths and religions had attempted to cope mainly with the crushing psychological effects of death, a notion supported by the first preserved literary piece ever, the *Epic of Gilgamesh*[22] – the confirmation of such a perspective comes soon: death has been regarded as natural and comprehensible, while life has always been regarded as problematic.[23]

In spite of this, the topic of antinatalism had been perhaps most extensively developed within myth, which was nevertheless subsequently rewritten by a philosopher, namely Aristotle in his *Eudemus*.[24] Aristotle reports that when Midas asked his captive Silen

---

[18] Let us now leave the very question why *"(...) books should have existed at all times; why there should be books at all, and why they should be written in this way"* (GP, VII, 302–308) for Leibniz any more.

[19] Patočka (1996, p. 68).

[20] Olišk (2009, p. 91).

[21] The proverbial pessimism of Greeks has been noticeable in various cultural areas. Melancholy and skepticism, far from being manifested solely by means of dialectic and poetic, has been deeply experienced by the Greeks, leaking their entire being. The pessimistic spirit, however, had found its counterpart in a typically Greek playfulness and joyfulness that contrasts with an otherwise more pragmatic orientation of ancient societies. Such a marvelous ambivalence of Greek temperament is thus a repercussion of their enschrining in a real, equally ambivalent world: their pessimism had been supported empirically, while optimism had been a reflection of the artistic aspect of the greek soul. Contrary to the roman *vale*, i.e. *be strong* or *salve*, i.e. *be well*, the Greeks used to greet each other saying χαίρε, i.e. *rejoice*; contrary to the Indian pessimism the Greek one lacked the metaphysical power, which captures even deepest parts of a soul (Friedell, 2009, p. 559).

[22] Chalupecký (2005, pp. 92n.).

[23] Jonas (1997, p. 28).

[24] In isolation from reflections contained in *Eudemus*, there is even some kind of germinal formulation of the asymmetry between good and evil by Aristotle, for Aristotle was convinced that painful memories are kept in mind with much higher intensity than joyful ones. It is difficult to say, however, whether Benatar would agree with such a statement, since Pollyanna Principle sides, at least in the moment of balan-

what mankind desired the most for itself, Silen stayed silent for a long time at first, till he finally, even if reluctantly, as a result of Midas' insistence, nearly erupted: *"Ephemeral offspring of a travailing genius and of harsh fortune, why do you force me to speak what it were better for you men not to know? For a life spent in ignorance of one's own woes is most free from grief. But for men it is utterly impossible that they should obtain the best thing of all, or even have any share in its nature (for the best thing for all men and women is not to be born); however, the next best thing to this, and the first of those to which man can attain, but nevertheless only the second best, is, after being born, to die as quickly as possible."*[25]

In the next chapter, the myth of Eudemus, the oldest pessimistic source according to Aristotle, is discussed in detail. However, now I would like to point out a theory emerging there, which is now known as the Pollyanna Principle, i.e. a tendency to not focus unpleasant experiences in favor of pleasant ones (*"For he lives with the least worry who knows not his misfortune."*) and partly the similarity between this passage from Eudemus and another non-philosophical source, namely a tragedy by Sophocles: *"Not to be born is, beyond all estimation, best; but when a man has seen the light of day, this is next best by far, that with utmost speed he should go back from where he came."*[26]

The observation that the greatest wisdom is to not be born at all appeared in a number of variations and also the notion ὁ ἀποκαρτερῶν, i.e. *who can no longer bear life and therefore be kills himself by hunger*, which Hegesias used for entitling his book on suicide, was usual at that time.[27] One tragedy by Euripides doesn't sound any different: *"Where a man is born we should assemble only to bewail. His lot in coming in so much evil. But when one dies and comes to the end of trouble then we should rejoice and praise his happy departure."*[28]

Seneca also wrote that nobody is born without suffering some harm,[29] while Marcion traced similar claims even by presocratics, namely Heraclitus and Pythagoras, but also by Socrates, based on the fragment retained thanks to it by Clement: *"Does not Heraclitus call birth death, just as Pythagoras and Socrates in the Gorgias,*[30] *when he says: 'Death is what we see when we are awake; and what we see in our sleep is a dream.'?"*[31]

In the case of Heraclitus, another fragment could be taken into consideration too:

---

cing, with the joyful memories. Moreover, Aristotle did not reevaluate his own views on procreation on the grounds of it: he was contented with a suggestion that *"rather the procreation of children should be limited than possession, so that over a certain number of children being yet more fruitful would not be permitted"* (Pol. 1265b). But this is discussed in more detail within next chapter.

[25] EU (115b–e; section 27, p. 179).
[26] Sophocles (1889, verses 1225–1229).
[27] Friedell (2009, p. 559).
[28] Strom. (III, 15).
[29] MD (VI, XV, p. 182).
[30] Gorg. (492e).
[31] DK (B 21).

"When men are born they are fain to live and suffer death, or rather go to their rest, and they leave children who also suffer death."[32] Herodotus attributes to Solon a statement: *"O Croesus, every man is a misfortune,"* while his rendering of the myth about Cleobius and Biton depreciates life in favor of death.[33] Also Empedocles complains: *"When I saw the place, so strange it was, I wept and wailed"*[34] and continues lamenting: *"Woe, unhappy race of mortals, wretched men!"*[35]

Clement, however, does not interpret the passages cited above as being antinatalistic,[36] which he justifies through an example of the Pythagorean ban on bean consumption. Beans were, indeed, according to him, forbidden by the Pythagoreans for they were believed to have contraceptive effects.[37] Even I am to take Clement's point, not only because Pythagoras, like Anaxagoras, saw a reason to be born even in the very possibility of seeing the sky and the order all around the world.[38] In fact, the Pythagorean symbol is a pentagram, also called γάμος, a breeding archetype, the number of the goddess of a fruitful intercourse, Aphrodite. Pentagram is a result of a sum of an even number, multiplying by division (maternal dyad) and an odd one (male triad). Even though the dyad was considered to be bad and unpredictable, the triad was not. The number five is thus a combination of order and disorder, happiness and misfortune, life and death. On the one hand, it was a terrible image of the evil principle, but on the other it has also been a symbol of wedding and the goddess Juno connected with wedding, of a life essence, a reviving spirit, universal quintessence.[39]

Nevertheless, even Clement admitted that *"(...) from a dislike of its inconveniences the Greeks have made many adverse observations about the birth of children."*[40] It is, however, clear from passages mentioned above that the ancient antinatalianistic way of thinking did not yet even touch the way of argumentation in the manner of Benatar's asymmetry argument. Although coming into the world was regarded as extremely undesirable for the given individual, such a fact was justified by the very claim about the

---

[32] DK (B 20).

[33] Strom. (III, 16).

[34] DK (B 118).

[35] Strom. (III, 14).

[36] Strom. (III, 21, 1).

[37] Strom. (III, 24). By the way, from the 7th century b.c., the Greeks kept using various plants with contraceptive properties, which is well documented by numerous ancient writers on gynaecology, for instance Hippocrates (Smith, 2013, p. 7).

[38] Aristotle (PEP, B 18; EE, 1216a 11). Svoboda comments on it: *"It may seem strange that Anaxagoras should be attracted by observation of hot pieces of metal so much that he would desire to be born due to it"* (Svoboda, 2015, p. 106), but for the Greeks observation, discovering and creativity, in which they were real masters, represented the deepest possible consolation whatsoever (Friedell, 2009, pp. 559n.). For instance, a fragment of Democritus is peculiar in this regard: *"Democritus said that he would rather like to find a single one causal explanation than to obtain the kingdom of the Persians"* (DK, B 118).

[39] Ghyka (2016, p. 28); Ragon (1938, p. 4).

[40] Strom. (III, 22).

poverty of human conditions. Apart from some rare exceptions,[41] the ancient antinatalistic reflections should be marked as rather passive, since neither of those lamentations result in a proposal for a concrete solution. Natality, as well as death, was considered to be a natural fact of life (greek φύσις, i.e. *nature*, is derived from φύομαι, i.e. *I am being born*).[42] Therefore, according to Jonas, *"none of former ethical principles that had taken human constants for granted had grown mature to encounter them polemicaly."*[43] People, rather, tried to imitate the natural cycle of rebirth through various sorts of feasts.[44]

Considering that in the Middle ages antinatalistic spirit began to be marginalized even more than within antiquity, it is significant that especially Epicurus, living within a period immediately preceding the Middle ages, viz. within Hellenism, commenting on one of those above mentioned antinatalistic sources, namely the passage from the tragedy of Sophocles, outrightly overlooks its antinatalistic aspect: *"Yet much worse still is the man who says it is good not to be born but once born make haste to pass the gates of Death at once. For if he says this from conviction why does he not pass away out of life?"*[45] Moreover, contrary to some more recent antinatalistic presuppositions, Epicurus did not accept the assumption that the evil should be considered as a far more serious issue than the good, by contrast, he attributed a higher value to the good. According to him, it is rooted in the fact that while the highest good is very easy to achieve, the highest evil is either transient or causing only minor suffering.[46] The good, outright the

---

[41] To the very first of the Miletus philosophers, Thales, is attributed a statement that he has no children owing for his love for children (DL, 1 26). According to Herodotus, also Chilon gave an advise to Hippocrates that he should not get married to a fertile woman, otherwise he should forsake her (DL, 1 68, fn. 155).

[42] Kratochvíl (2016, p. 11). Greek philosophy thus accurately imitates mythical reflections in this respect, despite that its classification as a separate way of thinking free from mythical explanation is paradoxically usually being based just on the concept φύσις (Šíma, 2013, pp. 164n.). Eleatics are an exception in this respect, for although Parmenides also used myth in order to explain his doctrine, unlike the Ionian philosophy that emerged in a close connection with observations of variable nature, Eleatics denied the possibility of any change. Such a deflection from practical life was, however, considered as undesirable in that time, and so they remained largely misunderstood (Farrington, 1953, p. 57). Not only Plato, but also Aristotle, partly followed them up afterthought, but even by Aristotle there is, beside some Eleatic motifs, also easy to identify a Platonic one of μίμησις, when the cycle of births and deaths becomes an image of periodically repeated movements of a supralunar sphere, which itself imitate the perfect ενεργεια of the first mover whatsoever (Wagner, 1956, pp. 287n.).

[43] Jonas (1992, p. 50). Maybe a statement by Democritus could be considered as an exception: *"For people having children seems to be one of the necessary things from nature as well as from some ancient establishment. Certainly it seems to other animals this way too, since they all have got offsprings in conformity with nature and not for their profit. By contrast, when babies are born, everyone is straining, nourishing them as much as possible, looking after them when they are small, and grieving when something happens to them. Such is the nature of all creatures that have a soul, and for man it becomes even a common vision that they have got some benefit from the descendant"* (DK, B 278).

[44] Keller (2008b, p. 73).

[45] Men. (126n.).

[46] Men. (133).

highest possible one, has been accompanying us since our birth: *"The origin of the ulti-mate good ought to be seeked, I guess, by the birth of living beings. As soon as a person is born, she feels joy, she is thus of delight, and longs for it as for something good, despi-sing pain as evil."*[47]

THE MIDDLE AGES

In the Middle ages the social situation began to develop disadvantageously for anti-natalism even more significantly than in antiquity, for under the influence of the Old Testament life became utterly sacred, which had not quite happened in antiquity.[48] The widespread contempt for labour, eking and giving birth, along with the postponing of giving birth, together with conditioning the value of life by associating it with good health, all this, according to Arendt, ended as a result of the development of Christia-nity.[49] Immediately on the threshold of the Middle ages, procreation was finally per-mitted by Saint Augustine himself: *"(...) Necessary sexual intercourse for begetting is free from blame, and itself is alone worthy of marriage."*[50] Apart from rejecting the antinata-listic solution regarding the non-existence issue,[51] he thus regarded procreation to be praiseworthy [of course, only if performed for the sake of God, not for the potential individual's sake: *"Even they who wish to contract marriage only for the sake of children, are to be admonished (...)*].*"[52]

Owing to Augustine's authority, his opinion could not vanish as just a subtle sigh, as just one among countless of others in the course of history. Rather he marked out the beginning of a systematic suppression of antinatalism, in spite of a good many of ex-plicitly antinatalistic passages even by Augustine and in the *Bible* itself,[53] despite that the early Christianity, inspired by Augustine, kept refusing all the popular mysteries of the past (the cult of Mithra or Dionysius), among others *"since many of their practices were associated with celebration of immortality of the deity of fruitfulness and for their lascivious character,"*[54] as well as their affairs attributed to the Greek, Egyptian or Hindu

---

[47] Cicero (DFBM, II 10, 31).
[48] Arendt (1998, p. 107).
[49] Ibid. (pp. 107, 315).
[50] Augustine (1887, p. 404, §11).
[51] Augustine considered the preference of non-existence to the unfortunate existence as absurd, for the choice of non-existence, i.e. of nothing, is not able be a choice, i.e. to be something (Sully, 1877, p. 49).
[52] Augustine (1887, p. 403, §9).
[53] For example Jr (20:14–18); Jb (3:2–4, 6, 10n., 13, 16); Iz (54:1).
[54] Svoboda (1973, p. 402).

deity has been alien to Christianity.[55] But this is discussed in better detail in one of the following chapters.

This institutionalized form of Christian religion was actually formed in the context of much more tranquil conditions than these, which shaped the mentality of the first Christian thinkers, including Augustine.[56] A poem by Bernard Silvester titled *De universitate mundi*, describes how the universe was created by a feminine emanation of a transcendental God, and nature is described as a tireless breeding womb (*generationis uterus indefesius*), culminating with man, and – considering the amount of extant copies – became one of the most widely read texts of the Middle ages. According to Curtius, all of Silvester's philosophy is interweaven with a cult of fertility, with a mixture of religion and sexuality, and it was not any different in the case of the philosophy of Bernard's contemporary Guillaume de Conches.[57] Also Juliane de Norwich or Hildegard von Bingen emphasized the unity of father – and mother – like qualities of God.[58]

Especially during the 11th and the 13th century, western Christianity was somewhat ambivalent, oscillating between fidelity to the the New Testament and some pagan Hellenistic traditions as well as barbarian ones, between a condemnation of the world and a love of it.[59] Only gradually, in the context of production/mechanization, God began to be understood as a producer and creator, rather than a procreator, for his creative act got by even without copulation, also Maria's conception was immaculate (*genitum, non factum*).[60] From there, only a short step is left to realize that the Christian marking of a yet initiated life as a sacred one, is in itself far from exhausting not only the question of how and what intentions with to begin such a life properly, but also the question of whether to begin it at all.

Some, like Benjamin, deny Christianity even the patent on the very dogma of the sacredness of life, which is, in their view, likely to be a much younger product of the secularization of the Western society. Religious bans on murder had allegedly originated elsewhere.[61] Keller, however, tends to reproach modern society for the opposite tendency, since it does not esteem life as an autonomous value apart from prosperity; life is being esteemed as valuable only as long as it serves to prosperity. According to him,

---

[55] Sloterdijk (2001, pp. 26n.).

[56] Whitehead (1967, pp. 15n.).

[57] Chalupecký (2005, p. 184).

[58] Farkašová (2006, p. 22).

[59] Chalupecký (2005, p. 185).

[60] Sloterdijk (2001, p. 27). The heavens and the earth, including its inhabitants, have become merely a God's handwork, not an image, reducing thereby all nature into a single ontological category of *creation*, i.e. equal for God (Jonas, 2001, p. 71).

[61] Benjamin (1991, p. 202).

it has been caused by the devaluation of death and the sacredness of life during experiments with animals, in action movies, by development of transportation and propagation of addictive substances.[62]

Also Rádl, according to whom it was very difficult in the Renaissance era to get a corpse for a public dissection for "(...) *since prehistory until then people believed in the sanctity of the human body*"[63] or Jonas developed a similar interpretation that modern science has neutralized the value of life so much that we now "(...) *shiver in the nakedness of a nihilism in which near-omnipotence is paired with near-emptiness.*"[64] In short, he also insists that the category of *the sacred* has been most thoroughly destroyed by the scientific enlightenment.[65] The myth that "*medieval people (...) all thought that the Earth was flat while the Church allegedly banned human dissection and burnt scientists at the stake*" indeed refuses to die, as Hannam points out.[66]

If, however, we were to draw on Keller's reflection that the conditionality of the value of life is, among others, related to its desacralization during animal experiments, we would eventually have to agree with Benjamin, since the origins of such an approach could be traced back to antiquity and its theoretical justification – and thus not a rejection – followed in the Middle ages. I try to support it below, to confirm simultaneously Benatar's statement too, that "(...) *my arguments are not as incompatible with religious thinking as many people might think*"[67] and, on the contrary, to question the initial interpretation of Arendt, Magee and Coates, according to which it is certainly not just a coincidence that the first properly antinatalistic philosopher, i.e. Schopenhauer, was also the first properly atheistic philosopher.[68]

Regarding animal experiments, they were already routinely practiced in antiquity. It is thus not true that, as Šiler writes, despite the considerably degrading attitude to animals during ancient cultures, that vivisection would be simply unthinkable then, just because it was not yet justified metaphysically, as later by Descartes.[69] Not only dissections, but also vivisections were carried out (in spite of Pythagoras' sympathies to-

[62] Keller (2008a, pp. 181n.).
[63] Rádl (2000, pp. 93n.).
[64] Wiese (2007, p. 110).
[65] Ibid. (p. 111).
[66] Hannam, 2010, s. 5.
[67] Benatar (2006, p. 16).
[68] Magee (1978, p. 213); Coates (2014, p. 125).
[69] Šiler (2005, p. 28).

wards a dog being beaten)[70] both by the Pythagoreans[71] and Peripatetics.[72] Moreover, antiquity includes not just ancient Greece, but ancient Rome as well, while, as Šiler admits, a status of mere things appertained to animals within the Roman law. *"Considering soul, suffering, life was absolutely pointless. Animals therefore, used to be killed, eaten or used in circuses for fun without any moral scruples. Roman law-thinking has considerably influenced the further degradation of animals in the European cultural tradition till the level of a machine."*[73]

Šiler, however, is right in claiming that in Greece, besides such inhumane practices, the originally mythic conception still reverberated, according to which the imperfect and mortal man was created as a God's image and nature itself was by no means the mere object of his will.[74] For example, God from Plato's *Timaeus* created the world as a *perfect animal* or a *visible God,* as soulful and intelligent. Everything changeable was intended to be similar to him. Passive matter itself would not be able to remain in the process of passing of forms and proportions imprinted on it, and the lesser would it be able to provide a drive for such transformations themselves, based on which each proper copy must forever imitate its pattern. In order to provide a spontaneous cause of motion, the existence of the soul was required, just as it was also needed to provide intelligence as the cause of rational motion. It is just this dualistic aspect of the soul that Plato considered to be the cause of motion and order. Based on those requirements, Plato made the soul a universal physical principle,[75] while just this religious respectability of cosmos

---

[70] *"Walking once around a maltreated puppy, he felt regretful about it and made such a statement: Give it up and do not beat it any more, for it is the soul of a man, a friend after all, that, hearing its sound, I have recognized"* (DK, B 7). Even Šiler works on the assumption that *"the Pythagoreans had tended to some kind of pantheistic mysticism. They had believed in reincarnation of souls, and therefore had refused to kill and eat animals"* (2005, p. 27; cf. Shea, 2007, p. 12).

[71] Namely Alcmaeon of Croton, who has been assigned among Pythagoreans (Farrington, 1953, pp. 53n.).

[72] Aristotle's enthusiasm for vivisection, out of which he finally exploited works such as *The Origin of Animals* or *Parts of Animals,* appears to be somewhat excessive even at present, when the same process became to be a part of a prevalent scientific routine. Aristotle, however, had gained countless of remarkable insights due to it, for example on how long an animal with revoked guts is able to survive (Leroi, 2012b, 4:16, 6:20, 9:06, 12:47). Selected passages of *Corpus aristotelicum* despite it suggest that he had been willing to attribute to animals (besides the vegetative and animal parts of the soul) even νοῦς, i.e. the human part of the soul, as Filip Svoboda supports in next chapter. Besides it, Aristotle had attributed a specific kind of soul to every single organ of even the most primitive animal whatsoever, and he had seen a reflection of something divine in each of them, but nothing of that prevented him from performing vivisection (Leroi, 2012c, 0:42; 2012a, 10:04). For becoming familiar with Aristotle's biology the author owes to Filip Svoboda.

[73] Šiler (2005, pp. 27n.).

[74] Wiese (2007, p. 116), Svoboda (1980, p. 8). *"The Epicureans also refused to kill animals, albeit rather from aesthetic-ethical reasons, Socrates was a vegetarian and Plato promoted active protection of animals"* (Šiler, 2005, p. 27).

[75] Jonas (2001, p. 70).

as a whole – not for its size, but for the consistency of its intelligibility with its intelligence – subsequently underlines its visual beauty as well.[76]

On the other hand, even Plato, and in his footsteps later Aristotle too, still considered motion in nature to be somehow derived, so that its self-motion capacity seemed to them to be rather illusive. In particular, Plato in *Timaeus* argues that all motion, including the motion of the primary matter, is a result of the motion of the world's soul. The world's soul was created by Demiurgos and is also dependent on him,[77] the motion of the soul itself is thus secondary.[78] Although Aristotle, in the second book of *Physics*, defines φύσις as the principle of self-motion,[79] even from him we find out that this motion itself is also merely a response to an external stimulus,[80] which applies not only to particular living beings, but also to nature in general, whose motion is derived from a pure act, the first mover whatsoever.[81] Neither Plato nor Aristotle, but rather the Milesian hylozoists or Stoics therefore had rendered the motion in nature to be immanent.[82]

For the emerging Christianity, however, the hylozoistic-pantheistic approach already posed a downright threat, which the western Christian thinkers took the charge to respond with a strict dualism. It is easy to understand that the Catholic Church establishing its official doctrine, consequently looked after the already existing partly dualistic philosophy of Aristotle, adjusted through Thomas Aquinas, for the needs of Christianity of course. The Christian dualism of God and the church versus the world, philosophy versus theology and man versus nature later exalted in the form of protestantism, especially the Calvinistic one. While the Renaissance philosophy of nature and Lutheran Pietism, likewise Catholic mysticism with its pantheistic love for nature as well as Arabic philosophy attempted to overcome such a dualism, immediately after the reformation dualism, formulated this time by Descartes, broke through once again (from various, not exclusively religious, motives).[83]

The objection offers itself, that after the modern age emancipation of science from the aegis of theology there has been nothing to prevent the emerging science from re-establishing the hylozoism abandoned by the Middle ages, all the more so since science discovered the glamour of motion meanwhile. In fact, the opposite is true: hylozoism did not correspond even with the needs of science and with the new mathematical

---

[76] Jonas (2001, p. 71).

[77] Tim. (27d–e).

[78] Leg. (X 889b–e, 891c).

[79] Phys. (II 8, 198b 22nn.).

[80] Phys. (VIII 2; VIII 8, 253a 11–21; 259b 1–16).

[81] Phys. (VIII 5, 257b 31n.).

[82] Mikeš (2008, p. 144).

[83] Šiler (2005, pp. 27n.).

conception of motion, for a spontaneous, teleological motion is unsuitable for calculating.

In the ancient times this was yet not the case, since Greek mathematicians focused exclusively on relations of rigid figures and bodies, till the abstract algebra of analytical geometry and infinitesimal calculus newly allowed to express the geometric form itself as a function of variables or phases in their continuous increase.[84] Motion, not the fixed space proportions any more, thus suddenly became the main object of measurement and such a primary interest in motion had just been the motive that resulted into application of algebraic methods not only in geometry but also in physics.[85] Motion of nature has since no longer been understood as a spontaneous one, instead of it a belief in some kind of strict natural law began to develop.[86]

Perhaps the only major exception to this newly launched trend was represented by Leibniz, who was likewise utterly immune to any categorization whatsoever. Immediately after adopting the new scientific method, he began to look for its interconnection with hylozoism, for if nothing would be self-acting, then nothing could be active at all. What other reason would such an activity have if it did not come from the nature of things?[87] But other modern mechanics, whichever way they got motion into their conception, agreed on the following according to Leibniz: motion is not reducible to the nature or essence of a body, nor has it been caused by it, it is just a kind of fundamental feature of the body instead. Leibniz himself considered this position unacceptable.[88]

We should not be astonished, he writes, by the fact that the Cartesians denied the existence of anything such as a soul in the body, for there had not been any reason for such a denial, nor did the non-existence of anything follow from the lack of any sensory image of it. *"For a long time it has seemed ridiculous to me that the nature of the universe would be so stingy or grudging that the soul would be provided solely to such unimportant masses as human bodies on this earth, if it could be provided to all bodies in harmo-*

---

[84] Jonas (2001, p. 68).

[85] Ibid. (p. 67). Strictly speaking, however, this final adjustment of mathematics for the needs of the new natural science should be credited to Descartes, Newton and Leibniz, for even Galilei was not yet to abandon the traditional conception, as long as he considered such geometric figures as triangles or circles to be the symbols of the mathematical language of nature. For although such figures were still used as auxiliary constructs in dynamic analysis, it would be much more progressive to identify mathematical symbols with constants and variables, functions and equations, in short: with the language of algebra (ibid., p. 69).

[86] Ibid. (p. 72). In this respect, the turn could be identified already by Grosseteste (Ruby, 1986). Although, strictly speaking, already Thales and Anaximander *"(...) taught that the cosmos and the motions of the stars were governed by laws of nature (...),"* by the term *laws* they meant something different than modern scientists do and, in addition, *"this was a new idea, one that would take a while to catch hold (...)"* (Shea, 2007, p. 10).

[87] GP (II, 262–265).

[88] Jolley (1995, p. 74).

ny with other targets."[89] In each body there must therefore be a kind of spiritual principle, which is indeed a somewhat hylozoistic claim. Leibniz's philosophy thus gradually turned into some kind of immanent dynamism, which was yet in his early writings refused precisely for he considered it incompatible with monotheism. However, due to some difficulties associated, among other things, with strictly mechanical collision laws, he had finally no other choice but to adopt such a hylozoistic position.[90]

Unlike Descartes, therefore, Leibniz considered the idea of an animal degraded into the role of mere machine – except that it is a speculation exceeding the phenomenal experience – to be in conflict with the order of things.[91] He hoped, however, in the ability to reconcile the concept of animal as a mere mechanism with its explanation through final causes. *"Both is good, both might be useful (...), only the authors who go through these different paths should not deflame each other,"*[92] especially if the Christian mathematicians, including Descartes, still did not deny the existence of immaterial substances, even though they separated them strictly from a pure matter. Nevertheless, later the mathematicians, following the example of ancient atomists, admitted merely bodies. Not the mathematical, but the metaphysical principles thus should be opposed to the materialistic conceptions. While Pythagoras, Plato or Aristotle still had certain ideas about such principles,[93] starting with the Christian dualism, these ideas have gradually began to fade away.

Not only mind, but also soul, and consequently life as such became in the course of time almost unnecessary for the sake of understanding the world. Motion without a soul assumed power without appetite, for the nature of power became inertial instead (it has been a kind of quantitative constant transmitted from moment to moment in an endless series), while life requires spontaneous and teleological movement. Just such a world without consciousness and without life, *dead matter,* as the Christians exposed it, became scientific standard of all intelligence. Descartes' theory of organism as a mere machine thus could be considered as a direct and inevitable consequence of these originally Christian metaphysics, while maintaining human dignity in an otherwise completely inanimate world is, according to Jonas, to be regarded as mere inconsistency, or perhaps rather a guise, but not an argument capable of defending such a conception of Descartes. La Mettrie's *L'homme machine,* likewise later behaviorism as well, were only the heirs to this Cartesian dualism, this time even robbed of its spiritual part. Modern sciences, with their quantitative measurement, have then passed the baloon further.[94]

---

[89] GM (III, 551–553).
[90] Moreau (1956, p. 66).
[91] GP (IV, 477–487, fn. 2).
[92] Leibniz (GP, IV, 447, §22).
[93] LC (L.2.1).
[94] Jonas (2001, p. 74).

Indeed, the metaphysics, on which modern science grew, took up this opportunity posed by the Jewish-Christian transcendentalism, whose dominance could be undoubtedly contributed to the close connection of official church doctrine with Tomism.[95] Even particular biological or sociological branches have taken over their basic postulates from the previous victory of mechanics, especially the assumption that the explanation requires proceeding from the least, i.e. from elementary units of regularly changing relations, while these clearly defined mechanical postulates somewhat contrast with vagueness of some key concepts which these sciences operate with.[96] Darwinism succeeded in overcoming the last bastion of theism, the mystery of life, since life is explicable entirely naturalistically through Darwinism.[97]

Let us add that, at the same time when sociobiology began to humiliate, besides animals, even human beings as well, voices calling for ethically motivated animal protection have began to sound more and more frequently. However, such a tendency was not the result of sociobiological research itself, but rather of a protest against it.[98] The above stated thus raises a question of whether is it really antinatalists, to whom life does not seem sufficiently sacred. Evidence challenging this relatively widespread view might bee seen not only in the fact that the very first antinatalistic philosopher, namely Schopenhauer, is at the same time regarded as the first atheistic philosopher, but above all the fact that the founder of antinatalism, namely Benatar, is at the same time a defender of animal rights and a vegan.

Regardless of whether Christianity treats life as something sacred or not, however, in the Middle ages its ideological impacts were so far predominantly pronatalistic, despite the fact that the religious conception of marriage, the ban on divorce and the institutional celibacy allegedly led to a population decline according to Montesquieu.[99] However, contrary to Buddhism, celibacy is merely a marginal issue in Christianity,[100] it even disappeared for a certain period of time, so that, starting with the eleventh century, the popes had to begin to push it through again,[101] and, moreover, not the fornication itself, but rather marriage as an institution were an obstacle to progress higher through the hierarchy of church.[102]

Already Héloïse in her letter to Abaelard was taken aback by such a paradox: *"(...) When we took steps to correct what we had done, to cover the illicit with the licit and repair our fornication with the proper rites of marriage, the Lord raised up an angry hand against*

---

[95] Jonas (2001, p. 72).
[96] Burtt (1951, p. 17).
[97] Beiser (2016, p. 6).
[98] Šiler (2005, p. 28).
[99] Montesquieu (1950, p. 231).
[100] Küng (2005, p. 163).
[101] Chalupecký (2005, p. 184).
[102] Tomkins (2006, p. 110).

us and struck our now-chaste bed when he had winked at our unchaste bed for so long before."[103] Héloïse's reaction sounds almost antinatalistic: *"Was it my sorry birthright to become the cause of evil (...)?"* But Héloïse does not regret her own birth because of herself: *"(...) the well-known curse of womankind to lead the greatest men to greatest ruin,"*[104] she does not regret her pregnancy and her sighing is of only a conditional individual validity, so it is antinatalistic only seemingly.

Much more antinatalistic seems to be the interpretation of those historical facts by Otisk, according to whom, Abaelard was castrated on the basis that Héloïse became first his mistress and later the mother of his son. Héloïse allegedly rejected the marriage proposal since, as a matter of fact, she did not believe in a functional possibility of connecting marriage with philosophy.[105] The realization of the marriage, however, documents also Abaelard in *Historia calamitatum mearum*,[106] but Otisk points out that the authenticity of this source is still a subject of some disputes.[107]

CONCLUSION

In this chapter, I have attempted to map some historical roots of antinatalism within antiquity, including their course in the Middle ages, when they happened to be quite strongly stifled. Although the causes of such a decline are discussed more in detail within the next chapter, I am perhaps already able to confirm that, in spite of some explicitly antinatalistic passages of ancient texts and even the *Bible* itself, the antinatalistic themes had to wait for a long time for their radicalization, since antinatalism was a purely esoteric issue up to that time. A developed nihilism is, indeed, a phenomenon of the modern age.[108]

However, a boundary between the ancient and the mediaeval antinatalism, i.e. between the protohistory of antinatalism, and the modern age, should not be taken too strictly, since whereas life was still considered to be something valuable at least on a theoretical level in the ancient times, as I attempted to prove in this chapter, the situation began to change significantly already together with the advent of Christianity, rather than later in the modern times. In this respect, the modern age was therefore specific rather for its enriching of the escalated (originally ancient-Christian) dualism by a modern age in-

---

[103] Héloïse (2007, p. 75).
[104] Ibid. (p. 76).
[105] Otisk (2005, p. 42).
[106] Abaelard (1922, chap. VII).
[107] Otisk (2005, p. 42).
[108] Arendt (1998, p. 261); Bouretz (2010, pp. 612n.).

dividualism and for the seeds of Benatar's asymmetry argument, which gradually became to be (systematically) formed in the modern age.

According to Benatar, the existential issues in general remained peripheral or completely unreflected even untill the 19th century,[109] while according to Coates, in the 19th century only Schopenhauer and his follower Hartmann took a negative attitude towards life.[110] However, we try to prove, in this chapter as well as in the next ones, that either in course of antiquity or in course of the Middle ages such existential issues were definitely not entirely overlooked. Furthermore, in the introductory chapter of the second section of this book I argue that they have not stayed unnoticed even in the course of modern times. The claim that in the 19th century only Schopenhauer and Hartmann took a negative attitude to life, is being questioned by Markéta Poledníková and Karim Akerma in the same section.

Benatar, however, is not mistaken in claiming that the antinatalistic debate has taken on an entirely new dimension since the 19th century, for as far as I know, yet then the considerations regarding the possible nonexistence were connected to the asymmetry between good and evil for the first time, which, after many transformations, finally developed into Benatar's asymmetry argument. This asymmetry, at the time lacking an antinatalistic dimension, has nevertheless originated in the modern age. Therefore, the following sections are to discuss all of these turning points: the modern age, when more attention started to be paid to antinatalistic thoughts and the asymmetry between good and evil began to be (systematically) discussed; the 19th century, under which falls the first attempt at their synthesis, viz. the work of Arthur Schopenhauer, but also the 20th or the 21st century, when antinatalism has gradually been established, and when the main participants of the present antinatalistic discussion began to publish their main works.

---

[109] Benatar (2010, pp. 1n.); Magee (1978, pp. 77–81).
[110] Coates (2014, pp. 122, 219n.).

ARISTOTLE AND HIS EUDEMUS

INTRODUCTION

There is a brand-new publication dealing with antinatalism theme printed last year. It is a dictionary that describes plenty of terms, persons, works etc. related to antinatalism from every branch of human theoretical thinking, but especially from philosophy and religion. Akerma's *Antinatalismus: Ein Handbuch*[111] is complex and highly useful work, beyond of academical interest of one field and academical sphere itself.

But, when I was looking into the book, and seeking for Aristotle's entry rapidly, I was disappointed that this item was missing. Honestly, I am accustomed with situations, when I am looking for history of some new field, philosophy, social movement etc., Aristotle is there mentioned quite often as a founder, or at least as a significant contributor. Firstly then, the intention of this chapter is to contribute to the history of philosophical antinatalism with emphasis on Aristotle's influence, and, secondly, to take of partial analysis of Aristotle's work from this side of view.

It is a dictionary indeed, and not a detail-focused analysis of history of philosophy. Still, it is possible to recognize some aspects, emphases or importance of certain Ideas or philosophers, and take some advantage from it. In this case it is a fact that a person from the oldest ages there, if I saw it correctly, is Anaxagoras, well known as the *lord of the assembly,* and so there is an entry on *Anaxagoras' Anthropodizee.* Therefore, I presume that Akerma considers Anaxagoras to be the first man who spoke and wrote his ideas about worthless life and born-disaster. Other philosophers, including Aristotle, are for Akerma, apparently, insignificant.

But I do not want to be unfair to the Akerma's book. In the passage about Anaxagoras Aristotle's name is mentioned:

---

[111] Akerma (2017).

"While Sophocles, in his Oedipus at Kolonos, made the proclamation that the best thing is not to be born, Anaxagoras (so Aristotle in his Eudemian Ethics) raised the question as to why a man could choose better to be born than not to be born."[112]

It is understandable that Akerma used Anaxagoras for the head note and Aristotle was mentioned only in brackets. Anaxagoras is an earlier thinker then Aristotle is. But does it mean that his influence on his successors was more extensive and more important? Here, I must take some doubts about it. In fact, I must admit that this might not be the case because Aristotle's works were – thankfully – oftentimes preserved as a whole, and therefore they might finally have provided to Aristotle's followers and successors more ideas, passages and quotes, then Anaxagoras' pieces-fragments.

Nevertheless, this is not the answer for my question. The fact, that in case of Anaxagoras we have got a limited possibilities to take our chance with these fragments and place them in roots of every possible antinatalistic idea, says nothing about their influence itself. And here is the main point of change. Although it is not excluded that Aristotle could be influenced by Anaxagoras, his ideas, opinions, quotes and works were considerably more influential, in general, then just a few of Anaxagoras' quotations. It must be said, despite, that Anaxagoras received a compliment for his antinatalistic ideas directly from Nicolaus Copernicus himself.[113] Still, it is a rare case, incomparable with Aristotle's importance.

However, is it truly a fact that Aristotle influenced many thinkers with his antinatalistic ideas? Or rather, was Aristotle the quite important person in many branches, especially in philosophy, with his antinatalistic ideas? Indeed, had antinatalism influenced his way of thinking at all? In other words, this question could be said most gently: Were Aristotle's antinatalistic ideas as influential as the other parts of his philosophical system? For this question, the answer is a bit difficult. On the one hand, it seems to be a strong claim that Aristotle created some antinatalistic conception *per se*, or, more earnestly, that he created some antinatalistic conception at all. Several ideas are hardly a philosophical system after all. On the other hand, Aristotle was mentioned in the entry intentionally, and, despite of just a few antinatalistic ideas and lack of the concept of *antinatalism* in his work, he had, let us say, rightly fundamental influence for the next evolution of the concept and antinatalistic philosophy itself.

Arthur Schopenhauer with his pessimistic way of thinking, is mostly marked as the *father* of antinatalism:

"Schopenhauer's thought includes a strong expression of anti-natalism – both as compassion to the unborn and as refusal to prolong the misery of existence – a philosophical

---

[113] For more details see Blumenberg (1975. p. 17).

treatise arguing the case for anti-natalism has appeared for the first time only recently, just a few years ago."[114]

Parerga and paralipomena, his important work, for the birth of antinatalism, can be translated as *Miscellaneous.* Unlike in other more compact parts of the Schopenhauer's philosophical system, there are most importantly only some random questions on the topic. Nevertheless, Schopenhauer is taking here another authority than Anaxagoras or Plato, mostly quoted by Schopenhauer himself. There is Aristotle; the Aristotle who is for him a pure scientific, factual and logic philosopher.

For clarification, Schopenhauer did not refuse or dishonest Aristotle or his philosophy in this context. From this view he is opposite against it. He takes him in this matter quite often, although Plato's philosophy was honoured by Schopenhauer most frequently, and he was generally recognized by him. Aristotle was respected likewise others philosophers of the ancient times. However, in *Parerga and paralipomena,* in chapter XII, entitled *Additional Remarks on the Doctrine of the Suffering of the World,* there is the most important section, for establishing antinatalism, a realm between the paragraphs 149 to 156. In a very close realm of this range Schopenhauer quotes Aristotle two times. In chapter X, called *On the Doctrine of the Indestructibility of our True Nature by Death,* Schopenhauer quotes Aristotle's work *On the Soul* in §140:[115]

Aristotle *"right at the beginning, lets out incidentally his own opinion that the νοῦς is the real soul and immortal, which he supports with false assertions. He says that hating and loving belong not to the soul, but to its organ, the perishable part!"*[116]

Schopenhauer is refusing Aristotle's view, and here Plato's one also, when he strongly bases on not a truly immortal soul or its parts.

The second quotation is right at the beginning of chapter XIII, called *On suicide,* in §157, i.e. immediately after the most important passage §149 to §156. In this chapter Schopenhauer presents his not unfriendly attitude to a suicide, basically because suicide was honoured in Hinduism, although Schopenhauer did not encourage his readers to suicide and he did not exhort to commit this act. He takes it, truly, without emotions or fearlessly. In this context, he quotes Aristotle's interesting and double-edged opinion:

"It is true that Aristotle says suicide is a wrong against the State, although not against one's own person."[117]

---

[114] Coates (2014, p. 23).
[115] It refers to the De An. (I, 4).
[116] PAP (X, p. 277, §140).
[117] It refers to EN (V, 15).

The second part of this idea is the most important for Schopenhauer's philosophy. But is this the reason, why Schopenhauer valued Aristotle in case of antinatalism? Maybe, nevertheless Akerma's entry on Anaxagoras contains some clue to Aristotle as well. It is a shame that this link leads reader to Aristotle's work *Eudemian Ethics*. The truth is, that a work that is mostly and generally connected to this theme is Aristotle's early-academic dialogical work *Eudemus*. For the answer why this dialog is so important and influential, I must take a brief look to this dialog and quote a relatively large piece of this dialog.

Finally a short note about this dialog itself must be made. Just after that it will be possible to quote the fragment of Aristotle's *Eudemus* and consider some point of this text. The point, which I am talking about here, is Aristotle's idea depicted in this fragment, that a soul is immortal. Nevertheless, it is not simply immortal, it is evolving, improving, developing trough the time. Thus, I will finally consider three points of views on Aristotle's concept of a soul, which are important, or at least interesting, for the history of antinatalism, and for a philosophical analyse of Aristotle's position in this stream of current as well.

DIALOGUE EUDEMUS

Firstly, a brief introduction to the Aristotle's text has to be made, or more accurate, a research about the fragment of Aristotle's lost work *The Eudemus*. However, the notion *Eudemus* can mean two different things. One of these is the dialog itself. But, it can mean the person as well. Who was Eudemus, a man important enough for Aristotle to name his writing after him?

Surprisingly it is not Eudemus of Rhodes, a famous Aristotle's pupil, whose name was borrowed for the title. Eudemus of Rhodes, after whom *The Eudemian Ethics* is named, was an editor of Aristotle's texts, speeches or personal notes. His name is related to the many titles of works, which Eudemus of Rhodes wrote as a comment, or explanation of Aristotle's ideas. Not only *The Eudemian Ethics*, which is composed of parts of *The Nicomachean Ethics* and from few other short texts, belongs among them, but *Eudemus' Physics, Analytics* and *Categories* too.

The Eudemus, whom Aristotle had in his mind, was Eudemus of Cyprus. He was Aristotle's close friend from Plato's Academy. The immortality of soul was a study matter in those days. It was one of the top themes in lessons of the Academy and in Plato's teaching as well. Aristotle's teacher wrote down his philosophy about immortality of soul in his famous dialogue *Phaedo*. Otherwise, Aristotle's Eudemus is also famously known as *On the Soul*. In this dialogue Aristotle used a dream of Eudemus. Eudemus was frightened of death in the dream. He was looking for a consolation or a consolation-philosophy.

The second one is the so called *protreptic text* written not only by Aristotle, but by many authors inviting young men to their philosophy. Aristotle himself devoted to this idea his work *Protrepticus*, which is the main base of his *Metaphysics A* and *Posterior analytics* 19. The work *On the Philosophy* was a part of this genre as well, but not much from this exoteric dialogue remained available. A consolation was also a literal genre used abundantly. Namely the problem of a soul was treated in particular. *Phaedo* and *Eudemus* were treated as the main, equal texts about immortality of a soul later on in the schools of Neoplatonism.

In these texts Aristotle followed Plato's teaching about the elements of a soul. These elements must be in a mutual symmetry state. Then, and only then, there can be made conjunction between a soul and a body. There must be balance among these elements, a kind of symmetric, or even geometric system of their settings. But Aristotle denied the idea that it must be the harmony, which is a stream and a centre of this balance necessary for a soul.[118] In concordance with Plato, Aristotle insisted on the immortality of a soul either as a whole and as a part. His opinion was that a soul is ἐντελέχεια, a power providing motion and basical vital signs.

In Aristotle's classical philosophy (Lyceum era) there is a special new term εἶδος introduced by him. It means a form, a basic appearance of something. However, it is not just a relief of matter, it is an idea, the basic, immortal, absolute core of everything. Besides, it is not the ἰδέα of Plato, which means something like a soul or the God. Although εἶδος could be translated as a *shape*, the question pinned to the term hides this word into the bowels of the earth. Why is it shaped like that? Likewise, what shaped this thing just this way, what shaped me?

These questions are interesting, but answers on them must be a matter for another paper. This chapter is focused on antinatalism and questions related with it. Therefore, there must be another question, which can be related with this exoteric text. The phrase *shaped* could be translated as *created*, or more accurately, *born*. Indeed, there is no long way from the question *What shaped me?* to the question *Did I have to be shaped?* Hanging on Plato's metaphysical system, Aristotle, in *Eudemus*, considers the question whether life is better than death. Surprisingly, he claims, that death is better than living. Jaeger called this position a *naive pessimism*. For Aristotle's own good, this *naive* and *pessimistic* aspects were vanished from his latter philosophy. It was overcomed in that very moment, when Aristotle recognized the poor logical structure of thinking. Just the tough declaration of a soul as a psychosomatic phenomenon was made a way out of

---

[118] Cf. Ross (1952, pp. 19–22, frag. 7).

those dark thoughts of his youth. *Νοῦς*, a chief part of a soul, is not capable of coherent continuity between pre-existence and post-existence.

Thus, already in *Protrepticus*, Aristotle was concerned with life. It is possible to interpret the passage[119] PEP B18 In this way:

"When Pythagoras was asked [why he was born], he said, 'to be an observer of the sky', and he used to claim that he himself was an observer of nature, and it was for the sake of this that he had passed into his way of life. And they say that when someone asked Anaxagoras for what reason anyone might choose to come to be born and to live, he replied to the question by saying that it was 'to be an observer of the sky and the stars around it, as well as moon and sun,' since everything else at any rate is worth nothing."[120]

EUDEMUS (ROSS, FRAGMENT 6)

"Not merely now, but long ago," as Crantor says, the lot of man has been bewailed by many wise men, who have felt that life is a punishment and that for man to be born at all is the greatest calamity. Aristotle says that Silenus when he was captured declared this to Midas. It is better to quote the very words of the philosopher. He says, in the work which is entitled *Eudemus*, or *On the Soul*, the following:

"'Wherefore, O best and blessedest of all, in addition to believing that those who have ended this life are blessed and happy, we also think that to say anything false or slanderous against them is impious, from our feeling that it is directed against those who have already become our betters and superiors. And this is such an old and ancient belief with us that no one knows at all either the beginning of the time or the name of the person who first promulgated it, but it continues to be a fixed belief for all time. And in addition to this you observe how the saying, which is on the lips of all men, has been passed from mouth to mouth for many years.'
'What is this?' said he.
And the other, again taking up the discourse, said: 'That not to be born is the best of all, and that to be dead is better than to have.' And the proof that this is so has been given to many men by the deity. So, for example, they say that Silenus, after the hunt in which

---

[119] This passage is repeated in EE (1216a 11).

[120] *"Τοῦτο Πυθαγόρας ἐρωτώμενος, 'Τὸ θεάσασθαι' εἶπε τὸν οὐρανόν, καὶ ἑαυτὸν δὲ θεωρὸν ἔφασκεν εἶναι τῆς φύσεως καὶ τούτου ἕνεκα παρεληλυθέναι εἰς τὸν βίον. Καὶ Ἀναξαγόραν δέ φασιν εἰπεῖν ἐρωτηθέντα τίνος ἂν ἕνεκα ἕλοιτο γενέσθαι τις καὶ ζῆν, ἀποκρίνασθαι πρὸς τὴν ἐρώτησιν ὡς 'Τοῦ θεάσασθαι {τὰ περὶ} τὸν οὐρανὸν καὶ {τὰ}; περὶ αὐτὸν ἄστρα τε καὶ σελήνην καὶ ἥλιον,' ὡς τῶν ἄλλων γε πάντων οὐδενὸς ἀξίων ὄντων"* (Hutchinson and Johnson, 2015, p. 49).

Midas of yore had captured him, when Midas questioned and inquired of him what is the best thing for mankind and what is the most preferable of all things, was at first unwilling to tell, but maintained a stubborn silence. But when at last, by employing every device, Midas induced him to say something to him, Silenus, forced to speak, said:

'Ephemeral offspring of a travailing genius and of harsh fortune, why do you force me to speak what it were better for you men not to know? For a life spent in ignorance of one's own woes is most free from grief. But for men it is utterly impossible that they should obtain the best thing of all, or even have any share in its nature (for the best thing for all men and women is not to be born); however, the next best thing to this, and the first of those to which man can attain, but nevertheless only the second best, is, after being born, to die as quickly as possible.'

It is evident, therefore, that he made this declaration with the conviction that the existence after death is better than that in life."[121]

INTERPRETATION: THREE VIEWS ON A SOUL

This sub-chapter takes a brief look at the account of the three interconnected aspects of Aristotle's view on a soul in *Eudemus*. The first part of the sub-chapter considers one

---

[121] *"Πολλοῖς γὰρ καὶ σοφοῖς ἀνδράσιν, ὥς φησι Κράντωρ, οὐ νῦν ἀλλὰ πάλαι κέκλαυσται τἀνθρώπινα, τιμωρίαν ἡγουμένοις εἶναι τὸν βίον καὶ ἀρχὴν τὸ γενέσθαι ἄνθρωπον συμφορὰν τὴν μεγίστην τοῦτο δέ φησιν Ἀριστοτέλης καὶ τὸν Σειληνὸν συλληφθέντα τῷ Μίδᾳ ἀποφήνασθαι. Βέλτιον δ᾿ αὐτὰς τὰς τοῦ φιλοσόφου λέξεις παραθέσθαι. Φησὶ δὴ ἐν τῷ Εὐδήμῳ ἐπιγραφομένῳ ἢ Περὶ ψυχῆς ταυτί. 'Διόπερ, ὦ κράτιστε πάντων καὶ μακαριστότατε, πρὸς τῷ μακαρίους καὶ εὐδαίμονας εἶναι τοὺς τετελευ- τηκότας'.*

Νομίζειν καὶ τὸ ψεύσασθαί τι κατ᾿ αὐτῶν καὶ τὸ βλασφημεῖν οὐχ ὅσιον ὡς κατὰ βελτιόνων ἡγούμεθα καὶ κρειττόνων ἤδη γεγονότων. Καὶ ταῦθ᾿ οὕτως ἀρχαῖα καὶ παλαιὰ παρ᾿ ἡμῖν, ὥστε τὸ παράπαν οὐδεὶς οἶδεν οὔτε τοῦ χρόνου τὴν ἀρχὴν οὔτε τὸν θέντα πρῶτον, ἀλλὰ τὸν ἄπειρον αἰῶνα διατελεῖ νενομισμένα. Πρὸς δὲ δὴ τούτοις διὰ στόματος ὂν τοῖς ἀνθρώποις ὁρᾷς καὶ ἐκ πολλῶν ἐτῶν περι- φέρεται θρυλούμενον.' 'Τί τοῦτ᾿;' ἔφη. Κἀκεῖνος ὑπολαβὼν 'ὡς ἄρα μὴ γενέσθαι μέν' ἔφη᾿ ἄριστον'.

Πάντων, τὸ δὲ τεθνάναι τοῦ ζῆν ἐστι κρεῖττον. Καὶ πολλοῖς: οὕτω παρὰ τοῦ δαιμονίου μεμαρτύρηται. Τοῦτο μὲν ἐκείνῳ τῷ Μίδᾳ λέγουσι δήπου μετὰ τὴν θήραν ὡς ἔλαβε τὸν Σειληνὸν διερωτῶντι καὶ πυνθανομένῳ τί ποτ᾿ ἐστὶ τὸ βέλτιστον τοῖς ἀνθρώποις καὶ τί τὸ πάντων αἱρετώτατον, τὸ μὲν πρῶτον οὐδὲν ἐθέλειν εἰπεῖν ἀλλὰ σιωπᾶν ἀρρήκτως: ἐπειδὴ δέ ποτε μόγις πᾶσαν μηχανὴν μηχανώμενος προσηγάγετο φθέγξασθαί τι πρὸς αὐτόν, οὕτως ἀναγκαζόμενον εἰπεῖν 'δαίμονος ἐπιπόνου καὶ τύχης χαλεπῆς ἐφήμερον σπέρμα, τί με βιάζεσθε λέγειν ἃ ὑμῖν'.

"Ἄρειον μὴ γνῶναι; μετ᾿ ἀγνοίας γὰρ τῶν οἰκείων κακῶν ἀλυπότατος ὁ βίος. ἀνθρώποις δὲ πάμπαν οὐκ ἔστι γενέσθαι τὸ πάντων ἄριστον οὐδὲ μετασχεῖν τῆς τοῦ βελτίστου φύσεως ἄριστον ἄρα πᾶσι καὶ πάσαις τὸ μὴ γενέσθαι: τὸ μέντοι μετὰ τοῦτο καὶ πρῶτον τῶν ἀνθρώπῳ ἀνυστῶν, δεύτερον δέ, τὸ γενομένους ἀποθανεῖν ὡς τάχιστα.' Δῆλον οὖν ὡς οὔσης κρείττονος τῆς ἐν τῷ τεθνάναι διαγωγῆς ἢ τῆς ἐν τῷ ζῆν, οὕτως ἀπεφήνατο· μυρία δ᾿ ἐπὶ μυρίοις ἄν τις ἔχοι τοιαῦτα παρατίθεσθαι πρὸς ταὐτὸ κεφάλαιον: ἀλλ οὐκ ἀναγκαῖον μακρηγορεῖν" (Plutarch, Mor. 115b–e; Ross, 1952, pp. 18n., frag. 6, R[2] 40, R[3] 44, W 6).

syllogism from *Eudemus* and the base for following part is established at the same time. The second part takes a short survey of Aristotle's term *νοῦς*. It is an important concept for his philosophy of a soul, not only in *Eudemus*. *Νοῦς* is the basic term of Aristotle's philosophy in general, so much that this word can be found especially in his texts – in plenty uses with proper place within a theme of the chosen text. In the third part a difference between a personal and impersonal death of a soul is inspected. The question of a personal and impersonal death of a soul is inseparably linked with another Aristotle's *terminus technicus μνήμη* (*a memory*). These three points are the cornerstones for my conclusion.

Soul as *ἁρμονία*

A brief note about the above-mentioned Aristotle's frag. 7 has to be made. This fragment is interesting in many ways, but I anticipated that my interest will be focused on the relation between harmony and soul. Incidentally, one of the speciality of Ross' frag. 7 is that there are four preservations of it. There are quite large pieces from John Philoponus' *De anima*[122] and from Themistius' commentary[123] to Aristotle's *De anima* (407b 27–32) among them. The Preservations from Sophonias,[124] in his commentary to the same Aristotle's work is short but not quite transparent. In this preservation Aristotle's *Eudemus* is mentioned very briefly and, for the purpose for this paper, in an useless form. Nevertheless, there is one more preservation from Olympiodorus' commentary to Plato's *Phaedo*.[125] The syllogistic structure of this fragment makes it a brief and transparent advantage:

"Aristotle in the Eudemus objects as follows: 'Disharmony is contrary to harmony, but soul has no contrary, since it is a substance; the conclusion is obvious. Again, if the disharmony of the elements of an animal is disease, their harmony must be health, not soul (...).'"[126]

"The third argument is the same as the second in the Eudemus."[127]

Accordingly, the syllogistic structure of Aristotle's argument is:

P1: The harmony (*ἁρμονία*) has its own opposite in disharmony.
P2: A soul does not have any opposite.
C: A soul is not the harmony.

---

[122] Philoponus (De an. 141. 22, 30; 144. 21; 145. 21; 147. 6–10).
[123] Themistius (In De an. 24. 13.; 25. 23–25).
[124] Sophonias (In De an. 25. 4–8).
[125] Olympiodorus (In Phd. 173. 20, 30).
[126] In Phd. (173. 20).
[127] In Phd. (173. 30).

If harmony is equipped with the same set of characteristics as a soul, then harmony must be equal with soul, it must be a soul. Additionally, the harmony admits levels or degrees of its own quality. And Aristotle is the keen defender of Plato's teaching of *Phaedo:*

"'Would it not,' said Socrates, 'be more completely a harmony and a greater harmony if it were harmonized more fully and to a greater extent, assuming that to be possible, and less completely a harmony and a lesser harmony if less completely harmonized and to a less extent?'
'Certainly.'
'Is this true of the soul? Is one soul even in the slightest degree more completely and to a greater extent a soul than another, or less completely and to a less extent?'
'Not in the least,' said he.
(...)
'That one soul is no more or less a soul than another; and that is equivalent to an agreement that one is no more and to no greater extent, and no less and to no less extent, a harmony than another, is it not?'
'Certainly.'
'And that which is no more or less a harmony, is no more or less harmonized. Is that so?'
'Yes.'[128]

If a soul was the harmony, and the harmony had levels, then a soul would have to have them as well. Consequently, a soul can be, in this way, more or less a soul. This does not make a sense and leads to a paradox. A soul must be the substance, the primary and absolute substance, and the harmony can be its attribute only. The origin of Aristotle's logic, *Categories* especially, resonates here. The problem of substance is one of the big problems of *Categories* and its cornerstone of Aristotle's logic at all. There he defines a substance:

"Another characteristic of substances is that there is nothing contrary to them. For what would be contrary to a primary substance? For example, there is nothing contrary to an individual man, nor yet is there anything contrary to man or to animal. This, however, is not peculiar to substance but holds of many other things also, for example, of quantity. For there is nothing contrary to four-foot or to ten or to anything of this kind – unless someone were to say that many is contrary to few or large to small; but still there is nothing contrary to any definite quantity."[129]

[128] Plato (Phaedo, 93a–b, d).
[129] Cat. (3b 24nn.).

Soul as νοῦς

A soul is the primary substance of a body. Nevertheless, according to Aristotle, there are three types of a soul. Each human being has a vegetative, sensitive and rational soul. Certainly, the vegetative and sensitive souls are important, but animals and plants have got these souls as well. A soul that is only human is a rational soul, the so called νοῦς in Aristotle's works.

As we were able to see in the previous sub-chapter, a soul is a fundamental base of body. The question od *Eudemus* is, whether a soul can live without a body. And the answer is that it can, but only the part called νοῦς. Anything else disappears with a body.[130] Life without a body is, in this way, a natural state for a soul (νοῦς).

The νοῦς is the very important and at the same time very unclear[131] notion of Aristotle. It seems, that νοῦς is a part of the God's[132] soul in our body. Undoubtedly, there lies a reason why the νοῦς-soul is immortal and in lead of an aggregate of a soul – like the most general part. The quite apt quote from Aristotle's *Protrepticus* describe it in such way:

"So nothing divine or happy belongs to humans apart from just that one thing worth taking seriously, as much insight and intelligence as is in us for, of what is ours, this alone seems to be immortal, and this alone divine. And by being able to share in such a capacity, our way of life, though by nature unfortunate and difficult, yet so gracefully managed that, in comparison with other animals, and human seems to be a god. For 'intellect is the god in us' – whether it was Hermotimus or Anaxagoras who said so – and 'the mortal phase has a part of some god.' So one must either philosophy or say goodbye to living and go away from here, since everything else seems to be a lot of trash and nonsense."[133]

Νοῦς is a part of the Good in us. This is for Plato the Good, more accurately the Idea of Good. In *Eudemus,* Aristotle was dependent on Plato's teaching and philosophical ideas that these main ideas come to us from outside. There is an immortality of whole soul as the main idea of Aristotle. In the latter works where reedition was maid – probably by Aristotle himself – *Methapyhisics* and *De anima*, Aristotle was more restrained.

---

[130] De An. (403a 16).
[131] For the list of problems with Aristotle's νοῦς see Theiler (1983, p. 141, and esp. 142); Davidson (1992, p. 3); Salmieri (2008, p. 163, fn. 60) or Cassin (2014, pp. 492–500, and esp. 495).
[132] And it is possible that Aristotle had the Only One God in his mind.
[133] PEP (48. 9–21). "Οὐδὲν οὖν θεῖον ἢ μακάριον ὑπάρχει τοῖς ἀνθρώποις πλὴν ἐκεῖνό γε μόνον ἄξιον σπουδῆς, ὅσον ἐστὶν ἐν ἡμῖν νοῦ καὶ φρονήσεως· τοῦτο γὰρ μόνον ἔοικεν εἶναι τῶν ἡμετέρων ἀθάνατον καὶ μόνον θεῖον. Καὶ παρὰ τὸ τῆς τοιαύτης δυνάμεως δύνασθαι κοινωνεῖν, καίπερ ὢν ὁ βίος ἄθλιος φύσει καὶ χαλεπός, ὅμως οὕτως ὠικονόμηται χαριέντως ὥστε δοκεῖν πρὸς τὰ ἄλλα θεὸν εἶναι τὸν ἄνθρωπον. Ὁ νοῦς γὰρ ἡμῶν ὁ θεός, {εἴθ᾽ Ἑρμότιμος εἴτ᾽ Ἀναξαγόρας εἶπε τοῦτο}, καὶ ὅτι ὁ θνητὸς αἰὼν μέρος ἔχει θεοῦ τινος. Ἡ φιλοσοφητέον οὖν ἢ χαίρειν εἰπούσι τῶι ζῆν ἀπιτέον ἐντεῦθεν, ὡς τὰ ἄλλα γε πάντα φλυαρία τις ἔοικεν εἶναι πολλὴ καὶ λῆρος" (B 108–110).

In these works he admits, that there is not an obstacle for immortality of some part of a soul. However, immortality of a soul as a whole is rejected here by him.[134] In *Metaphysics Λ* merely *νοῦς* can (or may) be entire:

"Whether any form remains also afterwards is another question. In some cases there is nothing to prevent this, e.g. the soul may be of this nature (not all of it, but the intelligent part [νοῦς]; for presumably all of it cannot be)."[135]

3. Soul as *μνήμη*

"The continuity of consciousness depends on memory [μνήμη]; Whereas he later denies that νοῦς possesses this, in the Eudemus he tries to save it for the soul that has returned to the other world."[136]

Werner Jaeger, in this quotation, stresses the very important fact. A soul, in *Eudemus*, is tied to a memory. This is another Plato's influence. It is not a sustainable argument. Therefore, Aristotle, in the first chapter of *Metaphysics A*, linked memory to the origin of man's consciousness, i.e. to separated simple organisms and to the intelligent ones. Then, the *νοῦς* can be linked to a few of intelligent animals.[137] But, in *Eudemus* Aristotle points to an interesting phenomenon which he derives the theory of three states of soul's memory from. Jaeger continues the above-mentioned quotation:

"He [Aristotle] does this by enlarging Plato's recollection into a doctrine of the continuity of consciousness in all three phases of the soul's existence – its former existence, its life on this earth, and its life after death. Alongside the Platonic view that the soul remembers the other world he sets his thesis that it remembers this one. He supports this by an analogy. When men fall ill they sometimes lose their memories, even to the extent of forgetting how to read and write; while on the other hand those who have been restored from illness to health do not forget what they suffered while they were ill. In the same way the

---

[134] Cf. De An. (430a 13) and Met. (993a 1).

[135] *"Εἰ δὲ καὶ ὕστερόν τι ὑπομένει, σκεπτέον ἐπ᾽ ἐνίων γὰρ οὐδὲν κωλύει, οἷον εἰ ἡ ψυχὴ τοιοῦτον (μὴ πᾶσα, ἀλλ᾽ ὁ νοῦς πᾶσαν γὰρ ἀδύνατον ἴσως)"* (Met. 1070a 24–26). For the inseparability of the mental functions from the body compare De An. (403a 16nn.). For the difference between the *νοῦς'* and the other psycho-somatic functions see De an. (408b 18–30).

[136] Jaeger (1968, p. 51).

[137] While in Apo. (II, 19) the indication is merely implicit; the mention in HA (610b 22) is already quite explicit. Instead of *νοῦς*, however, the description in both passages discusses rather something very closely connected with *νοῦς*, which, in addition, occurs solely by some selected species of animals (e.g. bees: PA, 648a 5–8; deers: HA, 488b 15, 611 and 15n.; hares: HA, 488b 15 or cuckoos: HA 618a 25n.). In HA (VIII), nevertheless, Aristotle adds many other examples of intelligent animal behavior too. For study of this part of Aristotle's philosophy see the table of the intelligent acting of animals with corresponding passages in Coles (1997, pp. 287–324). For the opposite evidence that *νοῦς* is exclusive for humans, a God part in us see e.g. GA (736b) or Met. (1072b, 1074b 16 etc.). Some authors resigned on the resolution of this problem (see reasons in Gregorić (2007, pp. 91–98).

soul that has descended into a body forgets the impressions received during its former existence, while the soul which death has restored to its home in the other world remembers its experiences and sufferings (παθήματα) here."[138]

The phenomenon Aristotle described concerns remembering of suffering after death. The first state of life is the so called *proto-existence*. In this state we are consciousless, our memory is clear and full of afterthoughts from previous life. A soul is waiting for a new incarnation into a body and is remaining in its natural state. *"Life without a body is the soul's normal state (κατὰ φύσιν)."*[139]

Jaeger called this state *apriory* (he takes the German philosophical tradition into account – probably). Nevertheless, a soul, waiting for reincarnation, must forget the previous life before that. It must take a gulp from the Lethe river – the river of forgetfulness. Only then the next step can be proceeded.

In the second state of a soul-being life the soul is present in some body. This is not so important stadium of the soul-cycle. However, the fact that a soul cannot remember its previous life in the new incarnation, is very notable from an antinatalistic view, especially when we consider the third-state-connection.

Finally, there is the third state of Aristotle's soul-cycle. It is a *post-existence* of a soul. Significantly, at least from an antinatalistic point of view, Aristotle claims that a soul in the third stadium, i.e. after death, can remember a suffering (παθήματα) from its life. Moreover, it seems (e.g. in his example of illness) that Aristotle even says that a soul can forget the good, but not the suffering.

This being given, Aristotle could have considered suffering to be more significant or essential, more real, than anything good. The asymmetry argument works with quite similar idea, although this certainly was not the asymmetry argument of Benatar, as Kateřina Lochmanová stated in previous chapter.[140] It could be one of the soft-variants of the asymmetry argument, but not the Benatar's one yet. Nevertheless, Aristotle presents here an argument for asymmetry of good and bad. In this way Aristotle could be considered as an initiator of asymmetrical arguments in general.

CONCLUSION

In *Eudemus* Aristotle definitely and undoubtedly claims that a death is much better than a life. Moreover, his statement is that being born is very bad thing for all mankind.

---

[138] Jaeger (1968, p. 51).
[139] Id.
[140] See Benatar (1997, pp. 346n.; 2006, pp. 31–37; 2012, pp. 128–130; 2013, pp. 122n.; 2015, pp. 25–29).

Death is a great state, more noble and divine than life. Aristotle appeals to both sexes. After death, neither men nor women desire to be the best and they are no more a part of this greatness of nature (φύσις). But, despite the ideas expressed in *Eudemus*, in another lost dialogical work *On Good Birth* Aristotle argues that a good-birth can happen. Moreover, it seems that our parents (their qualities – accurately) can be well-born, or bad-born in us:

"I said, 'good birth is excellence of stock.'"[141]

"Good birth is excellence of stock (...) this is the function of an origin – to produce many results like itself. (...) But those whose ancestors have long been rich or good, should be well-born. The argument has its eye on the truth; the origin counts more than anything else. Yet not even those born of good ancestors are in every case well-born, but only those who have among their ancestor's originators. When a man is good himself, but has not the natural power to beget many like him, the origin has not in such a case the power we have ascribed to it."[142]

Aristotle's note about *power to beget* is hardly connected with *good*, or *good man*. There is a genetic-argument, though Aristotle did not know about gens – of course. But this passage shows that he was aware of the system and functions of gens without knowing of the term and modern teaching about them. The argument in his text shows to us that well-born is a very rare, hard one, and it fundamentally depends on a line of predecessors. The ratio between well-born and bad-born is very disproportionate indeed, and bad-born seems to be less rare and more frequent then well-born case. It is not surprising therefore, that Aristotle concludes: *"And in truth there is no difference between the low-born and the well-born."*[143]

Aristotle implicitly stated that life has always got its price, the bad one probably. And if it is true, it means that parents want to have a child because they are selfish and they meet their own needs. That fact is also reflected in the relationship between child and parents:

"Moreover, [there is also a difference between the love of parents and the love of children] in point of time: parents love their children as soon as they are born, but children love their parents only as, with the passage of time, they acquire understanding or perception. This also explains why affection felt by mothers is greater [than that of fathers]."[144]

---

[141] Ross (1952, p. 60, frag. 2, R^2 83, R^3 92).
[142] Ibid. (p. 61, frag. 4, R^2 85, R^3 94).
[143] Ibid. (p. 59, frag. 1, R^2 82, R^3 91).
[144] EN (1161b 30).

A child's love to its parents seems to be a very fragile bound and it must be gained:

"(...) While brothers love one another because they were born of the same parents: the identical relation they have with their parents makes them identical with one another. This is the origin of expressions like 'of the same blood', 'of the same stock', and so forth. Brothers are, therefore, in a sense identical, though the identity resides in separate persons."[145]

Anyhow, it is clear that Aristotle does not value a birth very well and definitely not as the most valuable, desirable event or even purpose of a life. It is not strange that Aristotle submits birth of children to a common-good, which means politics and social-life dimension. There are better things parents can give to their child than the birth itself, e.g. an education.[146] Anyway, Aristotle brings up his demand not only for sake of a family or a relationship between parents and their children; it is demand of πόλις,[147] which must determine the birth of children. Aristotle's requirement is a little bit curious, but underlyed by rich and quite long argumentation in his *Politics*:

"And it is also strange that although equalizing properties the writer does not regulate the number of the citizens, but leaves the birth-rate uncontrolled, on the assumption that it will be sufficiently levelled up to the same total owing to childless marriages, however many children are begotten, because this seems to take place in the states at present. But this ought to be regulated much more in the supposed case than it is now, for now nobody is destitute, because estates are divided among any number, but then, as division of estates will not be allowed, the extra children will necessarily have nothing, whether they are fewer in number or more. And one might think that restriction ought to be put on the birth-rate rather than on property, so as not to allow more than a certain number of children to be produced, and that in fixing their number consideration should be paid to the chances of its happening that some of the children born may die, and to the absence of children in the other marriages."[148]

---

[145] EN (1162a 8).

[146] Cf. Polách (2007, p. 11).

[147] *"The city is prior by nature to the household and to each of us"* (Pol. 1253a 19).

[148] *"Ἄτοπον δὲ καὶ τὸ τὰς κτήσεις ἰσάζοντα τὸ περὶ τὸ πλῆθος τῶν πολιτῶν μὴ κατασκευάζειν, ἀλλ᾽ ἀφεῖναι τὴν τεκνοποιίαν ἀόριστον ὡς ἱκανῶς ἀνομαλισθησομένην εἰς τὸ αὐτὸ πλῆθος διὰ τὰς ἀτεκνίας ὁσωνοῦν γεννωμένων, ὅτι δοκεῖ τοῦτο καὶ νῦν συμβαίνειν περὶ τὰς πόλεις. δεῖ δὲ τοῦτ᾽ οὐχ ὁμοίως ἀκριβῶς ἔχειν περὶ τὰς πόλεις τότε καὶ νῦν: νῦν μὲν γὰρ οὐδεὶς ἀπορεῖ, διὰ τὸ μερίζεσθαι τὰς οὐσίας εἰς ὁποσονοῦν πλῆθος, τότε δὲ ἀδιαιρέτων οὐσῶν ἀνάγκη τοὺς παράζυγας μηδὲν ἔχειν, ἐάν τ᾽ ἐλάττους ὦσι τὸ πλῆθος ἐάν τε πλείους. Μᾶλλον δὲ δεῖν ὑπολάβοι τις ἂν ὡρίσθαι τῆς οὐσίας τὴν τεκνοποιίαν, ὥστε ἀριθμοῦ τινὸς μὴ πλείονα γεννᾶν, τοῦτο δὲ τιθέναι τὸ πλῆθος ἀποβλέποντα πρὸς τὰς τύχας, ἂν συμβαίνῃ τελευτᾶν τινας τῶν γεννηθέντων, καὶ πρὸς τὴν τῶν ἄλλων ἀτεκνίαν. Τὸ δ᾽ ἀφεῖσθαι, καθάπερ ἐν ταῖς πλείσταις πόλεσι, πενίας ἀναγκαῖον αἴτιον γίνεσθαι τοῖς πολίταις, ἡ δὲ πενία στάσιν ἐμποιεῖ καὶ κακουργίαν"* (Pol. 1265a 38 – 1265b 12).

Finally, the main question must be: Was Aristotle an antinatalist? Here I must say a strict *no*, he was not. Firstly, in *Eudemus* his ideas were dependent on Plato's seniority and authority. Secondly, that time Aristotle was a young man who had not created a complex philosophy or some sediment opinions or ideas yet. In his later works he claimed clearly and repeatedly that life is more than a mere existence[149] and, more importantly, that to be is better than not to be.[150] Aristotle was a founder of antinatalism by *Eudemus*, or he influenced Schopenhauer's founding of antinatalism. Still, this is only one work with one fragment. Lot of another Aristotle's ideas, quotes, passages, fragments etc. show us the exact opposite.

---

[149] See e.g. De An. (415b 13).
[150] GC (336b 28).

ANTINATALISM IN EARLY CHRISTIANITY

INTRODUCTION

For most people, Christianity is evidently a natalistic religion. It is true that the official position of the Catholic Church, openly opposed to abortion and even to contraception, tends to confirm this preconception. Thus it is frequent in conversations on this subject with nevertheless intelligent and cultured people to surprise them by asserting that the original Christianity, that of the Gospels, of the New Testament and of the first centuries of the Church, was in fact permeated with antinatalistic tendencies, that is to say averse to the reproduction of the human species.

It is regrettable that few intellectuals have taken the time to examine this paradox and shed light on what is perhaps the greatest trickery in the world's history: the falsification of the evangelic message, clearly refractory to procreation, and its transformation by the Church in a familialistic and fertilistic propaganda, completely contradictory to the teaching of Christ and of the first Christian theologians, fervent laudators of virginity, and therefore... of non-reproduction.

Kierkegaard, who besides being a philosopher was also a theologian, is one of the rare thinkers to have revolted against this betrayal. Before examining antinatalism in early Christianity, it is therefore necessary to briefly deal with Kierkegaard's critique of Christian pronatalism. In 1854, he launches a crusade against the official Danish Church, and more generally against Christendom, which he deems to be in blatant violation of genuine Christianity, i.e. that of the Gospels. His sharpest weapon: the pamphlets published in the ten issues of the magazine *The Instant*. Among the targets of his anger: the professional clergy at the service of the State and remunerated by it, the collusion of the Church with the royalty, believers' gregariousness and superficialism, the oblivion of evangelic values, but also marriage, family, the enticements of fecund household life to which even the priests, being nothing else than functionaries, succumb.

Kierkegaard was indeed convinced that Christianity is radically incompatible with procreation. Thus did he confide to his *Journal* these unambiguous lines: "*It was obvious in the eyes of Christ that the Christian should not get married;"*[151] *"The reproduction of the species. Christianity wants to block it;"*[152] *"Giving birth to a child! But the child is born in sin after having been conceived by infringement, and this existence is a valley of tears;"*[153] *"No, the mistake is not that the priest be celibate... a Christian must be so;"*[154] *"God wants (...) that humans abandon this selfishness that there is in the fact of giving life;"*[155] *"I give thanks to God (...) that no living being owes me its existence;"*[156] *"Here is how one raises a child ... in Christianity: your father and your mother are two people who are agreeable to God; above all, this episode which has brought you to life, this prowess on their part, is something that has especially pleased God. Abominable lie! This exploit is, Christianly, a crime, in the eyes of God a crime, and the vileness of this crime is that those concerned do not suffer of it themselves, but that an innocent, by being born, be thrown into this institution of criminals that human existence is."*[157]

A few years later, the author of *Die Philosophie der Erlösung* (*The Philosophy of Redemption*), Philipp Mainländer, will in his turn emphasize Christianity's opposition to the perpetuation of the species: *"Perfect chastity was for him the inner core of Christianity, and the crucial step toward redemption.(...) Mainländer insists on nothing less than virginity because – in a world of uncertain birth control – this alone ensures that life does not perpetuate itself."*[158] In all likelihood, there is a huge hiatus between the discourse of the official Churches (Catholic, Orthodox or Protestant), all favorable to natality, and the original message of Christianity.

This chapter will therefore have for purpose to highlight the antinatalistic tendencies at work in the New Testament in general, in the Gospels in particular, and in the writings of the Church Fathers of the first centuries. I shall make beforehand a brief incursion in the Old Testament where also emerge statements hostile to procreation. Excerpts from Kierkegaard's *Journal* will punctuate this exploration of the shadow zone, of the scotomized part of the religion whose worshippers, often fond of fertility, remain, logically, the most numerous in the world.

---

[151] Kierkegaard (1961, p. 102). Translation from French by the author.
[152] Ibid. (p. 256).
[153] Ibid. (p. 257).
[154] Ibid.
[155] Ibid. (p. 260).
[156] Ibid. (p. 294).
[157] Ibid. (p. 352).
[158] Beiser (2016, p. 221).

DISGUST OF LIFE, PRAISE OF DEATH, AND DETESTATION OF BIRTH IN THE OLD TESTAMENT

Even in the Old Testament, yet placed under the sign of the famous injunction given by Yahweh to the human race: *"Be fruitful and multiply and fill the earth and subdue it,"*[159] some discordant voices, marked with the seal of antinatalism, have made themselves heard.

Job's tragic history is well known – he was the victim of a bet between Satan and Yahweh, the aim of which was to find out if the hardships and sufferings inflicted by Satan unto this believer would succeed in making him deny his faith in God the Creator. If he did not deny his faith, Job openly protested against the fact of having received life:

"Job opened his mouth and cursed the day of his birth. And Job said: 'Let the day perish on which I was born, and the night that said, A man is conceived. (...) Let that night be barren; let no joyful cry enter it. (...) Why did I not die at birth, come out from the womb and expire? (...) For then I would have lain down and been quiet; I would have slept; then I would have been at rest."[160]

If Job, overwhelmed with pains and outrages, deplores his birth on a personal level, the author of *Ecclesiastes* (*Kohelet*) broadens the perspective by proclaiming the vanity of all things and by considering that, given the injustices that strike the multitude, the fate most universally desirable is to be dead, or better still: not to be born:

"I saw all the oppressions that are done under the sun. And behold, the tears of the oppressed, and they had no one to comfort them! (...) And I thought the dead who are already dead more fortunate than the living who are still alive. But better than both is he who has not yet been and has not seen the evil deeds that are done under the sun. (...) A good name is better than precious ointment, and the day of death than the day of birth."[161]

For his part, Ben Sira, in his *Wisdom of Sirach*, will affirm the banality of suffering and misfortune, for *"all creatures, human and animal,"*[162] from birth to decease,[163] before greeting death as a welcome remedy for the wretch.[164]

---

[159] Gen. (1:28; 9:1).
[160] Jb. (3:1–13).
[161] Ecc. (4:1–3; 7:1).
[162] Sir. (40:8n.).
[163] Sir. (40:1).
[164] Sir. (41:2).

In its reflection on the seeming anomaly of the premature death of the righteous, *The Wisdom of Solomon* insists on the fact that it is a gift, a privilege intended by God, to die before one's time and thus go out in haste from the midst of wickedness.[165]

The prophet Jeremiah, who witnessed the destruction of Jerusalem by the Babylonians, will remain single and without children after having received the order to do so by God in person. Remarkably, the text suggests that everyone would do well to follow this wise advice rather than reproduce in a tragic context:

"The word of the Lord came to me: 'You shall not take a wife, nor shall you have sons or daughters in this place'. For thus says the Lord concerning the sons and daughters who are born in this place, and concerning the mothers who bore them and the fathers who fathered them in this land: 'They shall die of deadly diseases. They shall not be lamented, nor shall they be buried. They shall be as dung on the surface of the ground. They shall perish by the sword and by famine, and their dead bodies shall be food for the birds of the air and for the beasts of the earth.'"[166]

Saturated with sufferings, Jeremiah, in terms similar to those used by Job, will eventually revolt with violence against his birth:

"Cursed be the day on which I was born! The day when my mother bore me, let it not be blessed! Cursed be the man who brought the news to my father, 'A son is born to you', making him very glad. Let that man be like the cities that the Lord overthrew without pity (...) because he did not kill me in the womb; so my mother would have been my grave (...). Why did I come out from the womb to see toil and sorrow, and spend my days in shame?"[167]

If the disgust of having been born is unequivocally and repeatedly affirmed in the Old Testament, it is worth remembering that Yahweh himself repented of having created mankind and all that lives on Earth.[168] After the Flood that resulted from this salutary moment of lucidity, Yahweh, persisting in his pessimism, will confess that *"the intention of man's heart is evil from his youth."*[169] From this, it can be concluded that humanity is incurable, save by the cessation of procreation.

And this is indeed the conclusion Kierkegaard will reach: *"God who knows the roguery of 'man' [aims] to transform his character. Thus, He aims, above all, for the cardinal point:*

---

165 Wis. (4:7–17).
166 Jr. (16:1–4).
167 Jr. (20:14–18).
168 Gen. (6:5–13).
169 Gen. (8:21).

celibacy. Heterogeneity, that is what God wants, heterogeneity to this world. To die to the world instead of the joy of living; celibacy instead of marriage and childbirth."[170]

The Father having regretted having given birth to mankind, it was fairly logical that the Son had to come to teach this species – this *brood of vipers*[171] whose father is the devil[172] – the rudiments of the art of ceasing to reproduce, before definitively exterminating it in a gesture both soteriological and apocalyptical. This will be the purpose of the New Testament.

DEMOLITION OF THE FAMILY BY JESUS

Everyone knows to what extent the family, as in many cultures, is exalted within the Jewish culture. *Honor your father and your mother* is one of the Ten Commandments given to Moses by Yahweh, and the mere fact of cursing one's father or mother is punishable by death.[173]

Yet, as the Gospels unfold, Jesus demonstrates an astonishing contempt for the elementary signs of respect owed to parents. Even in his childhood, concomitantly with the episode of the debate in the Temple with the doctors of the law, one discovers a *runaway* Jesus deserting parental authority and completely indifferent to the anguish his long absence inflicts on Joseph and Mary.[174] At the beginning of his preaching, it is with unspeakable brutality that he recruits one of his disciples, recently bereaved and wishing to bury his father first: *"Follow me, and leave the dead to bury their own dead,"*[175] the Saviour replies to him, in a ruthless negation of all filial piety. After having expressed his disdain for the father figure, Christ will publicly attack the image of the mother – in the middle of a wedding, what's more. Thus during the Marriage at Cana, when Mary disturbs him to point out that the wine is lacking and gets for sole answer a contemptuous: *"Woman, what does this have to do with me?"*[176] It is an understatement to say that

---

[170] Kierkegaard (1961, p. 266). Translation from French by the author.

[171] Lk. (3:7).

[172] Jn. (8:44).

[173] Ex. (21:17).

[174] Lk. (2:41–50).

[175] Mt. (8:21–23).

[176] In the *Bible de Jérusalem*, an authoritative scientific edition widespread in the French-speaking world, the footnote commenting on this refusal opposed by the Saviour to the request of Joseph's wife reveals all the animosity contained in its literal meaning: *"Litt. 'Quoi à moi et à toi ?', Sémitisme assez fréquent dans l'AT. (...) On l'emploie pour repousser une intervention jugée inopportune ou même pour signifier à quelqu'un qu'on ne veut avoir aucun rapport avec lui"* (1992, p. 1531).ᵃ The website of The United States Conference of Catholic Bishops (USCCB) specifies for its part: *"Literally, 'What is this to me and to you?' – a Hebrew expression of either hostility or denial of common interest. [In Mark 1:24 and 5:7, it is] used by*

Jesus rebuffs Mary very coldly: he does not even call her *mother*, but simply *woman*, rejecting her with a single word into ontological banality and breaking linguistically – by the Logos itself – the ties of flesh supposed to unite them.

The episode of Cana was nevertheless instrumentalized by generations of priests and theologians in an attempt to demonstrate that Christ blessed marriage and fecundity. This dishonest interpretation is sarcastically swept away by Kierkegaard: *"The Wedding at Cana. Christendom's tenacious insistence to emphasize that Christ attended a wedding and provided wine (...) indirectly proves that people themselves have a suspicion that Christianity is contrary to marriage, and that is why this story is as important to them as their argumentationt based on it is ridiculous."*[177]

Far from praising nuptial rejoicings and married life, the Gospels show us, on the contrary, a fiercely anti-familialistic Christ, urging us to abandon everything – father, mot-

---

demons to Jesus."[b] The same website also tells us that the term *woman* is never used in the *Bible* to address one's own genitrix: *"Woman: a normal, polite form of address, but unattested in reference to one's mother."*[b] If it were necessary to prove that this way of talking to one's progenitress remains highly problematic, even nowadays, it would be sufficient to read this translation, incredibly mawkish and syrupy, given in the *International Children's Bible* (ICB): *"Jesus answered, 'Dear woman, why come to me?'"*[c] *Dear woman...* What a close call! Jesus was not far from saying: *"My beloved mother, it will be a pleasure to help you!"* Such euphemisms and twists of meaning are very symptomatic of the strategies put in place by the different Christian Churches to make Christ's message acceptable to the greatest possible number of people, who must in no way be encouraged to renounce traditional family values and the established state order. The very survival of these Churches is at stake: I will analyse this phenomenon of semantic distortion for adaptive purposes in more detail in the conclusion of this chapter.

a) *"Lit. 'What to me and to thee?', Semitism quite frequent in the Old Testament. (...) It is used to reject an intervention deemed inappropriate or even to signify to someone that one does not want to have any relation with them."* Translation from French by the author.

b) Read online:

http://www.usccb.org/bible/jn/2:4#51002004-b

https://web.archive.org/web/20170712164557/http://www.usccb.org/bible/jn/2:4

c) Read online:

https://www.biblegateway.com/passage/?search=John+2%3A1%E2%80%9311%3A1&version=ICB

[177] Kierkegaard (1961, p. 262). Translation from French by the author. A most ridiculous argumentation indeed, based only on the unsteadiest fringe of metonymic reasoning: Jesus accepts a banal invitation to a wedding feast where he reluctantly renders a derisory service, so he is in favour of procreation. What a brilliant demonstration.... Except that it would be just as absurd and tendentious to claim that Jesus blesses alcoholism because he provides several hectolitres of wine to an assembly that has evidently already drunk too much – since the jars are empty and the master of the banquet congratulates the bridegroom on serving the best wine when people are inebriated (Jn. 2:9n.) –; or that Christ condones debauchery, or even secretly indulges in it, because he accepts that a prostitute covers his feet with kisses and perfume (Lk. 7:37n.); or that he praises war and military abuses because he heals the child of a centurion (Mt. 8:5–13). On the contrary, if the episode of the wedding at Cana explicitly and indubitably demonstrates one thing, it is that Jesus does not feel any *filial* love for his mother and does not consider her particularly worthy of respect as such, not even hesitating to humiliate her in public. This kind of material is evidently of low pedagogical value and thoroughly unsuitable for a Sunday sermon given in front of pious families whose children might be tempted to behave in a very Christic way by not respecting their parents and later by refusing to reproduce, thus depriving the societal machinery of its most essential fuel.

her, and children – to follow him,[178] bringing dissension into homes and rising up children against parents. *"A person's enemies will be those of his own household,"*[179] *"they will be divided, father against son and son against father, mother against daughter and daughter against mother."*[180]

To those who wish to become his disciples, Jesus, in words of astounding violence, even sets as a precondition to hate the members of one's family and to despise one's own life, which is radically incompatible with the famous *Be fruitful and multiply: "If anyone comes to me and does not hate his own father and mother and wife and children and brothers and sisters, yes, and even his own life, he cannot be my disciple."*[181]

Repudiating once again the bonds of blood, the Messiah also affirms that his true family is that of his disciples,[182] the community of those who, like him, try to follow the path of holiness by living in accordance with the values of the Kingdom, in this love of God and of one's neighbor, which he proclaims to be the two cardinal Commandments.[183]

A certainty therefore emerges from the Gospels. Jesus is in no way the apostle of the biological family. The family he promotes is of spiritual type and his preaching clearly aims to break the bonds of flesh and blood in favor of those of the Spirit. The very essence of the coming of Christ is indeed to redeem Adam's sin, which has been passed down from parents to children since the Fall and the expulsion from Eden.

The surest way to put an end to the omnipresence of evil and original sin is, of course, to put a stop to reproduction. Adam is the father of all humans; Jesus, the New Adam, will be the father of none, offering himself up as an example to entire mankind. From this will arise the concept of *Imitatio Christi*, which will spread to the whole of Christendom as an ideal to be attained. It goes without saying that if all those who claim to be Christians lived like Christ and imitated him by remaining single, virgin, and thus without children, humanity would become extinct very quickly, which is a highly desirable eventuality, as St. Augustine will assert. I am coming back to this in the last subchapter.

JESUS' INFINITE RESPECT FOR CHILDREN

This love of one's neighbor, which Christ celebrates, also includes, naturally, the weakest of the weak, the children. Here again, Jesus takes an opposing stance to society

---

[178] Mt. (19:29).
[179] Mt. (10:36).
[180] Lk. (12:53).
[181] Lk. (14:26).
[182] Mk. (3:32–35).
[183] Mt. (22:36–40).

and reverses the commonly accepted values: it is not the male adults who occupy the top of the hierarchy, but definitely the children, the already born children, of course, for nowhere does Christ call for the making of new ones: on the contrary, as we shall see, he blesses the barren women and threatens the pregnant ones.

These already born children, he expresses true kindness towards them, he valorizes them to the highest degree and is mindful of protecting them. After having declared, in an exemplary way, that they are the greatest in the Kingdom of Heaven,[184] he severely dissuades people from causing them to sin,[185] which amounts to harm them, and warns: "*See that you do not despise one of these little ones.*"[186] To a mother whose daughter was unwell, he enjoins, as if he was suspecting some parental incompetence: "*Let the children be fed first, for it is not right to take the children's bread and throw it to the dogs.*"[187] Quite revolutionary words and attitudes, diametrically opposed to the parental violence towards children that was nevertheless tolerated by the ancient tradition – education by the rod and the whip included,[188] and even death by stoning in case of recidivist indocility.[189]

Christ, on the contrary, does not mistreat children, he heals them from their ills,[190] embraces them, blesses them[191] and asks us to receive them as if we were receiving Him in person![192] As one can guess, it is therefore imperative to cause no harm at all to children – which is strictly incompatible with the fact of bringing them into the world, since evil is omnipresent here below: the devil is the "*Ruler of this World*"[193] and "*the whole world lies in the power of the evil one.*"[194]

If the Gospels portray a Christ hostile to any form of child abuse and, at a pinch, implicit proponent of adoption (receive children in his name), they do not show us in any case Jesus as a zealot of procreation. One sentence, totally diverted from its original meaning, has nevertheless caused much ink to be spilled by natalistic priests: "*Let the children come to me.*" Let us read the text: "*And they were bringing children to him that he might touch them, and the disciples rebuked them. But when Jesus saw it, he was indignant and said to them, 'Let the children come to me; do not hinder them, for to such belongs the kingdom of God. Truly, I say to you, whoever does not receive the kingdom of*

---

[184] Mt. (18:1–4).
[185] Mt. (18:6).
[186] Mt. (18:10).
[187] Mk. (7:27).
[188] Prv. (13:24; 23:13); Sir (30:1; 30:7–12).
[189] Dt. (21:18–21).
[190] Mt. (9:18–25; 17:14–18); Jn. (4:46–53).
[191] Mk. (10:16).
[192] Mt. (18:5); Mk. (9:37).
[193] Jn. (12:31).
[194] 1 Jn. (5:19).

God like a child shall not enter it.' And he took them in his arms and blessed them, laying his hands on them."[195]

Kierkegaard, once again, ferociously scoffs at Christendom's fallacious use of these evangelic verses and reminds us that Christ's vocation is not to godfather all babies who are born, but to save our species by diverting it from procreation:

"Let the little children come to me (...) To interpret this passage by saying, as millions and trillions of people have said: 'Now we only have to give birth to little children... for Christ said: let the little children come to me': this is either bestial stupidity or effrontery. In Christendom Christ has been made a good fellow, one who offers wine at banquets, almost as if Christ had come to the world not to save a lost humanity, but to serve as godfather to all the children of the earth. The case however is very simple: to save our species, it means: this species is lost, we have only too much of it, the question is to be saved by getting out of the species, and therefore we must start by blocking our species."[196]

Coming back to Mark's text, let us take note of this passage: *"Whoever does not receive the kingdom of God like a child shall not enter it."* It is also found in Matthew, in an even clearer formulation: *"Unless you turn and become like children, you will never enter the kingdom of heaven."*[197] Yet, what does it mean *to turn and become like children?* At first reading, one might think that Jesus invites us to regain the simplicity of heart, humility, or the spirit of openness, receptivity and wonderment that is supposed to characterize children. In a deeper exegesis, one can also remember that a child, until puberty, is a being unable to reproduce. Thus it is perhaps to this unmarried, single, chaste, and sterile condition inherent to childhood that the Messiah enjoins us to return if we wish to enter the Kingdom of Heaven. This reading will be strongly corroborated by other passages of the New Testament, as we will see in the next chapter.

PRAISE OF INFERTILITY AND OF VIRGINITY IN THE NEW TESTAMENT

The two main protagonists of the New Testament, Mary and Jesus, are closely associated to virginity, and therefore to non-procreation. The Virgin Mary or Blessed Virgin is supposed to have given birth to only one child, of divine essence. The conception of Jesus was the work of God himself, without Mary having had sexual intercourse, and

---

[195] Mk. (10:13–16).
[196] Kierkegaard (1961, p. 264). Translation from French by the author.
[197] Mt. (18:3).

her *son* is nothing less than a person of the Holy Trinity, therefore, again, God himself. Hence the epithet Mother of God (*theotokos*) which was given to Mary by several Fathers of the Church. The doctrine of Mary's perpetual virginity even affirms that she did not lose her virginity while giving birth to Jesus.

In short, far from celebrating animal motherhood, the Gospels valorize, through Mary, a *magical* form of procreation, by no means biological, but plainly theological, and that makes sense solely in the framework of the Economy of Salvation according to which the Christ-Logos becomes incarnate and offers himself as a sacrifice only to redeem Adam and Eve's original fault. Thus, there is nothing more ridiculously paradoxical than to use the figure of the Blessed *Virgin* to justify motherhood or to encourage any carnal fecundity on the part of believers. What Christianity exalts, it is the virtues of spiritual *fecundity*, namely: the ethics of love, altruism and forgiveness, ethics through which are transcended, rightly, our most condemnable instinctual impulses.

The second protagonist, Jesus, the willfully sterile Saviour, marvelously exemplifies the refusal to procreate which deeply pervades the Gospels. Born of a Virgin, he will himself remain perfectly virgin and hence will not have even the shadow of a child. His celibacy marks a radical rupture with traditional Judaism where marriage was a social obligation, including for prophets. In the Old Testament, one can however find a few unmarried prophets unencumbered with children, such as Jeremiah or Elijah, but it was the exception rather than the rule.

But Jesus is going to proclaim loudly and clearly the virtues of celibacy and sterility, not only by breaking the fatality of family ties, as exposed in previous but one chapter, but also by urging those who believe in him, and are able to understand his message, not to reproduce. Thus in this famous passage of the *Gospel according to Matthew* – which immediately precedes, note it well, the one in which Christ affirms that the Kingdom of Heaven belongs to those who are similar to the prepubescents.[198] Not everyone can receive this saying, but only those to whom it is given. For there are eunuchs who have been so from birth, and there are eunuchs who have been made eunuchs by men, and there are eunuchs who have made themselves eunuchs for the sake of the kingdom of heaven. Let the one who is able to receive this receive it.[199]

This praise of voluntary castration for soteriological purposes is strengthened by less known verses of the Gospels in which Christ invites us to cut off our hand or foot, or to tear out our eye, if these organs are for us an occasion to sin.[200] It is obvious that the organ most susceptible to incite us to sin is precisely the one that we need to make children, and that it is implicitly targeted in this call to get rid of the corporal parts that may cause our doom.

---

[198] Mt. (19:13n.).
[199] Mt. (19:11n.).
[200] Mt. (18:8n.).

Origen, one of the leading fathers of biblical exegesis, will take this invitation very seriously and will have his testicles cut off, which mightily demonstrates that the early Christian theologians had very well understood that this new religion had come to *block our species*, according to Kierkegaard's formula. This exhortation to perpetual continence and to non-reproduction will likewise be perfectly understood and put into practice by many Christians in the early centuries of our era, before its consecration by the canon 33 of the Synod of Elvira (*circa* 303) which formally forbids the bishops, priests and deacons to beget children.[201]

As a proponent of celibacy and voluntary sterility, Jesus incites his disciples to abandon everything, including their families, in order to follow him, thus founding a paradigmatic community where men and women stand side by side without thinking of marrying and conceiving children, all of them being enamoured with the call of the Lord and the Kingdom of God. This ideal assembly, composed of individuals who forsake procreation, it will be the Church (*ekklesia*), an earthly analogue of the Kingdom of Heaven where marriage is abolished:

"The sons of this age marry and are given in marriage, but those who are considered worthy to attain to that age and to the resurrection from the dead neither marry nor are given in marriage."[202]

Moreover, *that age*, the Kingdom, is not only very near,[203] but is already here, already among of us.[204] Understanding this lesson therefore truly implies renouncing reproduction. Because it will be in the end of time as in the days of Noah: *"They were eating and drinking and marrying and being given in marriage, until the day when Noah entered the ark, and the flood came and destroyed them all."*[205]

The Christian phantasy of the destruction of this world and of the extermination of humanity unfolds *par excellence* in the *Apocalypse of John*, where the virgins, the non-procreators, are once again extolled. After having equated the Devil with the Dragon, the Serpent, the horned Beast, the frogs, the locusts, that is to say with ancient fertility symbols, John describes the chosen ones in these terms: *"No one could learn that song except the 144.000 who have been redeemed from the earth. It is these who have not defiled themselves with women, for they are virgins; these follow the Lamb wherever he goes."*[206] Virginal like the Lamb, a prepubescent and sterile creature, to which the Evangelist compares the Saviour.

---

[201] Brown (1995, pp. 255n.).
[202] Lk. (20:34n.).
[203] Lk. (21:31–36); Mk. (1:14n.).
[204] Lk. (11:20; 17:21).
[205] Lk. (17:26n.).
[206] Apoc. (14:3n.).

Paul too will stand up as an advocate for sexual abstinence, chastity, celibacy and virginity. One must not overinterpret the concession he made, half-heartedly, to marriage: it is only a last resort (*better to marry than to burn*) in order to avoid debauchery, it is not an obligation.[207] Paul on the contrary drastically devalues the flesh,[208] he even invites us to crucify it ("*Those who belong to Christ Jesus have crucified the flesh with its passions and desires*"),[209] and repeats his exhortations to renounce marriage,[210] even within the framework of marriage – for those who succumb to it: "*Let those who have wives live as though they had none.*"[211]

Putting the last nail into fertility's coffin, Paul proclaims that it is a good thing to remain a virgin,[212] and that he wishes everyone be like him.[213] Celibate, without sexual intercourse and therefore without children. These are very clear statements, and they seal the New Testament: the ideal would be that everyone renounces procreation! Besides, it is very revealing that the key characters around which the New Testament is structured are considered to be virgin or unmarried, such as John the Baptist (the Forerunner), Mary, Jesus, John the Evangelist (putative author of the *Apocalypse* and Christ's favorite disciple) and lastly Paul of Tarsus (the Apostle to the Gentiles). This solid chain of *continents* (*encratites*) which conveys the holy teachings and stretches through the whole New Testament brilliantly manifests the antinatalistic dimension of Christianity.

CONDEMNATION OF MOTHERHOOD BY JESUS

In the Old Testament, the *Book of Wisdom* (or *Wisdom of Solomon*) already affirmed the superiority of virtue over carnal fecundity,[214] and celebrated both sterile women and eunuchs.[215] This proclamation of virtue's superiority over procreation, Jesus will endorse it, while shattering at the same time the enthusiasm of a motherhood devotee:

---

[207] 1 Cor. (7:1–9).
[208] Rom. (7:4n.; 7:22–25; 8:2–13); Gal. (5:16–21; 6:7n.).
[209] Gal. (5:24).
[210] 1 Cor. (7:8; 7:27; 7:37n.).
[211] 1 Cor. (7:29).
[212] 1 Cor. (7:25n.).
[213] 1 Cor. (7:7).
[214] Wis (4:1).
[215] Wis (3:13n.).

"A woman in the crowd raised her voice and said to him, 'Blessed is the womb that bore you, and the breasts at which you nursed!' But he said, 'Blessed rather are those who hear the word of God and keep it!'"[216]

Salvation lies therefore in the adherence to spiritual values, not at all in childbearing. Even more dissuasively, Christ exalts sterility, including voluntary sterility, and incites, considering the cataclysms to come, to show compassion towards children, of course by not bringing them into the world, since the already born children deserve that one weeps over their fate:

"There followed him a great multitude of the people and of women who were mourning and lamenting for him. But turning to them Jesus said, 'Daughters of Jerusalem, do not weep for me, but weep for yourselves and for your children. For behold, the days are coming when they will say, Blessed are the barren and the wombs that never bore and the breasts that never nursed!'"[217]

Even more violently, when evoking Jerusalem's forthcoming destruction, as a prefiguration of the end of time, the Saviour specifically threatens the candidates for maternity: better to renounce becoming pregnant! This is true for the days of *great distress*, and *a fortiori* for the days of disaster described in the Apocalypse, but since we do not know when these will occur,[218] and that in these dark hours *"children will rise against parents and have them put to death,"*[219] the wisest decision is obviously to opt quickly and definitively for non-reproduction: These are days of vengeance, to fulfill all that is written. Alas for women who are pregnant and for those who are nursing infants in those days![220] For there will be great distress upon the earth and wrath against this people.[221] Furthermore, Christ had very persuasive antinatalistic words, as when he said of Judas: *"Woe to that man by whom the Son of Man is betrayed! It would have been better for that man if he had not been born."*[222] Since no one chooses to be born, the Messiah clearly makes us understand in this statement that it is better to refrain from begetting, because begetting is to take the incalculable risk of begetting damned ones. Thus, this *better not to have been begotten* concerns not only Judas, but also, by extension, all those who will be thrown into hell at the Last Judgment. Now, the Gospels warn us:

---

[216] Lk. (11:27n.).

[217] Lk. (23:27–29).

[218] Mt. (24:36); Mk. (13:32n.).

[219] Mk. (13:12).

[220] Other translation, from the *Disciples' Literal New Testament* (DLNT): *"Woe to the ones having a child in the womb, and to the ones nursing in those days."*

[221] Lk. (21:22n.).

[222] Mt. (26:24).

many called, few chosen,[223] only a few will be saved, the door of Salvation is narrow, and it will be necessary to strive to enter.[224]

In short, faced with the eventuality of giving birth to evil individuals doomed to damnation, Christ recommends here the zero risk policy. This is congruent with his crucial commandment: *love thy neighbour*, for it is true that begetting a child who risks spending eternity in the torments of Hell is not the sign of an immoderate love for one's offspring. Saint Jerome too will adopt, as the next sub-chapter shows, this wise precautionary principle. In the introductory chapter of the second section of this book it will be exposed how this principle has gradually begun to be promoted in the modern times.

To conclude, let us turn once again to Kierkegaard, who as a good theologian was fully convinced that a good Christian is a Christian who does not procreate:

"If the world, as [Christianity] teaches, is a sinful world that lieth in wickedness, then eo ipso the one who from a Christian standpoint is a good citizen, is, if I dare say so, the one who does not perpetuate this sinful race."[225]

ANTINATALISM OF THE CHURCH FATHERS

As a very valuable complement to this sub-chapter, I can only recommend the reading of Peter Brown's book[226] to measure how much the dawn of Christianity was permeated by antinatalism, which flourished even in the writings of numerous early theologians or Church Fathers. Among these personalities refractory to procreation and/or who powerfully praised virginity, deserve to be mentioned authors such as: Tertullian, Origen, Cyprian of Carthage, Methodius of Olympus, Athanasius, Gregory of Nazianzus, Basil of Caesarea, Gregory of Nyssa, Ambrose, Chrysostom, Jerome, or Augustine. I stop here: the list would be too long.

It is nevertheless important to reproduce here some very meaningful reflexions, such as those made by Jerome who, after having underlined, in his *Against Jovinianus*, that *"marriage replenishes the earth, virginity fills Paradise,"*[227] appeals to the precautionary principle evoked at the end of the previous chapter: *"Shall a joint-heir of Christ really*

---

[223] Mt. (22:1–14).
[224] Mt. (7:13n.); Lk. (13:23n.).
[225] Kierkegaard (2017, p. 413).
[226] Brown (1995).
[227] Jerome (1893, p. 360).

long for human heirs? And shall he desire children and delight himself in a long line of descendants, who will perhaps fall into the clutches of Antichrist?"[228]

For his part, in his treatise *On Virginity*, Gregory of Nyssa condemns reproduction, in the sense that it only perpetuates corruption and death: *"The bodily procreation of children (...) is more an embarking upon death that upon life for man. Corruption has its beginning in birth and those who refrain from procreation through virginity themselves bring about a cancellation of death by preventing it from advancing further because of them."*[229]

In his own work *On Virginity*, John Chrysostom will also associate death and fertile marriage, while insisting on the necessity to renounce having children to give oneself a chance for Salvation: *"Marriage, this mortal and servile garment (...) is the consequence of disobedience, of curse, of death. Where is death, there is marriage; remove one, the other disappears."*[230] *"The true generous ones, the lovers of light (...) fly towards the heights and get close to the Heavens, having abandoned everything here below, marriage, wealth, worries and everything which, ordinarily, attracts us to the earth. However, do not believe that this permission to marry, granted at the beginning [of human history], is for the rest of time an obligation which prevents us from abstaining from marriage. For [God] wants us to renounce it."*[231] *"You are still talking to me about flocks of sheep and herds of oxen, of marriage and children? (...) Virginity is far superior to marriage."*[232] *"So we must deploy all our efforts down here, he who has a wife to be as if he had none, and he who indeed has no wife to practice with virginity all the other virtues, so that we do not have, at the end of this life, to consume ourselves in useless lamentations."*[233]

The most famous Doctor of the Church himself, Augustine of Hippo, will point out in his book entitled *Of Holy Virginity* that: *"It would be utterly foolish to undergo this burdensome tribulation of the flesh, which the Apostle presages for those about to marry, by indulging in marriage in this day and age, when no service is done to Christ's future coming by begetting offspring for him through the progeny of the flesh."*[234] It would be fortunate if the contemporary ecclesiastical dignitaries, so quick to encourage fecundity, deeply meditated this statement because, at the time when it was written, at the beginning of the 5th century, the planet was burdened with only 200 million human beings, instead of 7.8 billion in this Anno Domini 2020...

To dispel all doubts about the intrinsically antinatalistic, and even extinctionistic, dimension of Christianity, let us leave the crucifying last word to this same Augustine,

---

[228] Jerome (1893, p. 384).
[229] Gregory of Nyssa (1999, p. 48).
[230] Chrysostom (1966, p. 143). Translation from French by the author.
[231] Ibid. (p. 151).
[232] Ibid. (p. 385).
[233] Ibid. (p. 395).
[234] Augustine (2001, p. 83).

who, in his work *On the Good of Marriage*, explicitly wished that everyone refrained from procreating in order to precipitate the end of the world!

"I know what people are murmuring: 'Suppose,' they remark, 'that everyone sought to abstain from all intercourse. How would the human race survive?' I only wish that this was everyone's concern so long as it was uttered in charity, 'from a pure heart, a good conscience, and faith unfeigned;' then the city of God would be filled much more speedily, and the end of the world would be hastened. For what else is the Apostle clearly urging when he says, speaking on this issue: 'Would that all were as I myself am?' [i.e. celibate and continent]."[235]

Kierkegaard was therefore not wrong in waging war on the false Christians of his time, who, among other betrayals of the evangelic message, scandalously burnt incense before the joys of marriage, family and perpetuation of the species. It is not certain, incidentally, that the Christians of the 21st century have fully found the way back to Christ's teachings, and it is even less certain that they are eager to make themselves eunuchs for the sake of the Kingdom of Heaven.

CONCLUSION

Destruction of the family, disdain for the elementary marks of respect due to parents, praise of virginity, of celibacy, continence, chastity, barrenness and voluntary sterility, to the point of making oneself eunuch for the Kingdom of Heaven, exhortation to do no harm to children, call to not take the risk of giving birth to future damned ones, admission that the devil is the prince of this world, affirmation of virtue's superiority over carnal fecundity, threats addressed to pregnant women, phantasy of an apocalyptic destruction of this world: the canonical Gospels and the New Testament, corroborated by the writings of the early Church Fathers, display an antinatalism, if not an anticosmism, of the most consistent kind.

This antinatalism also manifests itself, and sometimes very radically, in the corpus of Christian texts described as apocryphal. It must be kept in mind that these *Christian* apocryphal writings were composed by people who considered themselves as *Christians*, for the use of people who also considered themselves as *Christians*. Therefore, these texts, later rejected by the official Churches, shed light on the manner in which the message of Jesus and his apostles was spontaneously perceived by the first com-

---

[235] Augustine (2001, p. 23).

munities of the faithful. And this message was rightly perceived as hostile to procreation.

A wonderful example of this perception is given by *The Gospel according to the Egyptians*. Unfortunately, this Gospel has been lost, but some fragments have survived thanks to Clement of Alexandria. They abruptly summarize Christ's mission (to put an end to reproduction) and are a prelude to Gregory of Nyssa's reflexions (to abolish death by abstaining from procreation).[236] They also provide a comforting answer to Paul's tragic, but very human, question in his *Epistle to the Romans*: "Wretched man that I am! Who will deliver me from this body of death?"[237] The remedy for death proposed by *The Gospel according to the Egyptians* is indeed the only possible one – not to give life:

"*Salome asked, 'How long will death prevail?' the Lord replied, 'For as long as you women bear children.' (...) The Savior himself said, 'I have come to destroy the works of the female.' By 'the female' he meant desire and by 'works' he meant birth and degeneration.*"[238]

This rejection of procreation by adherence to the values of the Gospels will also be preached by Tatian, a Christian apologist of the 2nd century, whose trajectory is not without resemblance to that of Kierkegaard, since, disappointed by the Church of his time, he broke with it and became the leader of the *Encratites* (from the Greek *enkrateia*, *continence*), these *Christians* radically opposed to marriage and reproduction of the species.

Many early Christians understood that fidelity to Jesus' message implied perpetual sexual renunciation.[239] Among these, a relatively unknown ascetic, Hieracas of Leontopolis, deserves particular attention for the clarity of his interpretation of evangelic soteriology: "*[Hieracas] taught that marriage was indeed permitted in the time of the Old Covenant, but that since Christ it is forbidden to all his disciples. Enkrateia is the only truly new thing He has brought; it is, in other words, the essential of His preaching; it is only through purity and continence that one reaches the Heavenly Kingdom.*"[240]

This distinction between Old Law (natalistic) and New Law (antinatalistic) perfectly corresponds to Chrysostom's exegesis, who too asserted that if marriage was allowed at the beginning of mankind, God now wants us to renounce procreation.[241] This reading of Christianity will also be that of Marcion, who will push it to its paroxysm by excluding the Old Testament from the holy scriptures. In his wake, many Gnostics, considering

---

[236] Cf. supra (chap. 6).
[237] Rom. (7:24).
[238] Ehrman (2003, p. 18).
[239] Brown (1995, pp. 56n., 120–123, 216).
[240] Roldanus (1977, p. 341). Translation from French by the author.
[241] Cf. supra (chap. 6).

themselves as Christians, will become the torchbearers of *encratism* and rejection of procreation.

This close connection between antinatalism and Christianity (or at least subjective feeling of being Christian and/or belonging to Christian lineage) will be perpetuated over the centuries through Manichaeism, Priscillianism, the Bogomils, the Cathars and the Shakers, without forgetting the Skoptsy who understood the evangelic message in the manner of Origen and castrated themselves for the sake of the Kingdom of Heaven. One will note that perpetual continence and renunciation of procreation have also been affirmed in the official Christianity through asceticism, eremitism, monasticism, and also through clerical celibacy in Catholicism.

Likewise, the concept of *Imitatio Christi* is a fervent appeal, addressed to every Christian, to live in accordance with the example given by the Saviour – and thus to abstain from procreating, as abstained from it Christ himself – this paradigmatic encratite, since of divine essence.[242] There is therefore no doubt on the fact that renunciation of marriage and procreation is consubstantial to Christianity. But there is still to suggest some hypotheses on the paradoxical disavowal of the original Christian antinatalism by the Churches when they became official and dominant. The main reason is of course sociological and strategical, not at all exegetical or theological.

Saint Paul laid the foundations for what would become the Church's classical doctrine of marriage: the ideal is to remain a virgin and not to reproduce, but for the weak who are unable to answer this call, marriage is preferable to debauchery. This indulgence towards marriage, more or less manifested by the Church Fathers, in spite of their hyperbolic praises of virginity and continence, is easily explained by a concern for realism and *realpolitik*. Adaptive strategy, to put it in Darwinian terms. It is obvious that renouncing procreation is an unpopular demand *par excellence*, and which arouses a lot of animosity against it, as everyone can still see today.

The refusal to procreate was even more unacceptable in Roman Antiquity. Thus, the emperor Augustus, by a tragic irony more or less at the same time as Jesus's birth, promulgated strict laws against celibacy. Indeed, every self-respecting empire needs soldiers, craftsmen, peasants and fertile women to survive: it was therefore a civic duty to abundantly produce new citizens. Rome's persecutions against Christians, as early as the first centuries, are notorious. Probably tired of running to martyrdom, the Church could only engage in a double game: *better to celebrate marriages than to burn*, to paraphrase Paul. Opportunism and diplomacy which would become fatal to the evangelic ideal of non-reproduction.

The gradual transformation of Christianity into a state religion under Constantine and Theodosius (380) could only exacerbate the Church's complaisance towards fertile

---

[242] On *Imitatio Christi* and virginity's salvific dimension in Christianity as well as in other religions cf. Giraud (2006, pp. 38–40, 120, 125–127).

marriage. The laws enacted by Theodosius in 382 against *encratism*, making it punishable by death, probably represent the key moment of the fall of Christendom into natalism.[243] Moreover, blessing procreation ensures to massively increase the number of worshippers, all the more so since a *Christian* couple who founds a large family generates many new believers who will in their turn, through their own children, exponentially increase the herd of Christ's soldiers.

Kierkegaard was deliciously ironic about the strategy consisting in erasing the high evangelic demands in favour of a simple celebration of family life:

"Christianity's view of life is high and therefore may easily be an offense to the multitude of men. If on the other hand Christianity amounts only to begetting children, it becomes as popular and comprehensible as possible."[244]

In short, the fact of displaying a natalistic ideology was an obvious adaptive advantage for the Church, and this remains true today. Exhorting people to renounce procreation is incompatible with any society concerned about its survival. One knows what an atrocious fate was reserved for Mani, another famous advocate of non-procreation. The *vox populi* and the belly's tyranny always have the last word. Nothing more utopian than to ask the primate *Homo Sapiens* to have the wisdom and kindness to cease reproducing. And yet it is precisely this audacious request that the genuine Christianity makes to us, as these Kierkegaard's lines published in *The Instant* once again show:

"Christianly it is egoism in the highest degree that because a man and a woman cannot control their lust another being must therefore sigh, perhaps for seventy years, in this prisonhouse and vale of tears, and perhaps be lost eternally."[245] *"The world into which the parents introduce the child is a sinful, ungodly, wicked world. (...) Lamentation, anguish, wretchedness, awaits everyone that is born."*[246] *"I am unable to comprehend how it can occur to any man to unite being a Christian with being married."*[247] *"The obligation is: the imitation of Jesus Christ."*[248]

There is nothing to add. The natalistic stance of the official Christian Churches is probably the greatest trickery in the world's history: a disastrous heresy and a nameless betrayal. This is an ideal moment to read again the excerpt of the *Gospel according to*

---

[243] Priscillian, a Christian encratite, put to death in 385, will be the first *heretical* martyr to fall under the blows of State Christianity. No need to dwell on the millions of deaths that *Christian* churches will subsequently have on their conscience. Christ will judge if these crimes are compatible with his cardinal commandment: *Love thy neighbor.*
[244] Kierkegaard (1946, p. 215).
[245] Ibid. (p. 223).
[246] Ibid.
[247] Ibid. (p. 213).
[248] Ibid. (p. 280).

Matthew quoted in chapter 5: *Woe to that one by whom the Son of Man is betrayed! It would have been better for that one not to have been born."* To conclude on a humorous note, it is therefore obvious that for all the *Christians* who betray Jesus Christ by glorifying procreation, it would have been better not to be born.

Ite in pace, glorificando vita vestra Dominum.

HISTORY
OF ANTINATALISM

AUTHORS:

Kateřina Lochmanová

HISTORY OF ANTINATALISM:

From Modern Age to Present

(pp. 91–109)

Markéta Poledníková

SOLOVYOV AND HIS GODMANHOOD:

Antinatalism in Russia

(pp. 111–124)

Karim Akerma

KURNIG AND HIS NEO-NIHILISM:

The First Modern Antinatalist

(pp. 125–145)

HISTORY OF ANTINATALISM:
FROM MODERN AGE TO PRESENT

INTRODUCTION

The previous section of this book has been dedicated to a period which, in relation to antinatalism, might be called a protohistoric one. Some sporadic antinatalistic statements have already occurred, but it has not been lent an ear to them sufficiently and, above all, it has not yet been the issue of antinatalism in a narrow sense, supplemented by argumentation based on an asymmetric relationship between good and evil, together with a proposal for a concrete solution.

All of this gradually started to change together with the advent of modern times, partly since the antinatalistic debate has been resumed, partly since the asymmetry of good and evil has begun to be thematized, and partly since this two lines of thought started to be interconnected together including also a proposal for concrete solution as late as in the 19th century. The antinatalistic debate has gradually become so rich that, consequently, its exhaustive description has become to be almost impossible. Thus, we do not try to achieve such a goal neither within this chapter nor in the following ones, we are attempting to capture all the qualitatively new elements instead, which finally culminated into the theory systematically expressed in a book by David Benatar, and to document some reflection of these elements even in works of authors who are usually not considered to be connected with antinatalism.

Thus, after rather a brief introduction into the rise of antinatalistic spirit in the modern times I intend to deal solely with a history of Benatar's asymmetry argument within this chapter. I have borrowed the conclusion of this argument from Benatar, that it would be more advantageous for each individual never have been born, in case they suffered even a slightest damage during their life, along with the assumption that such a harm would almost certainly occur.[249] Then I aim to map some historically older versions and justifications of this conclusion.

---

[249] *"My argument does not apply to those hypothetical cases in which a life contains only the good and no*

THE MODERN AGE

At the end of the introductory chapter of the previous section I stated that during anti-quity, as well as even more pronouncedly during the Middle ages, all the just arising antinatalistic ideas were confronted with too strong an opposition to be able to break through sufficiently. Although it may sound somewhat curious, the cause could be, fol-lowing Hannah Arendt's opinion, grounded in the fact that people of that times did not believe they could or even should be happy in this world. According to her, the requirement for personal happiness has been claimed by the only one sort of human, *homo laborans*, i.e. a man living in the milieu of at modern-days initiated and gradually hypertrophied glorification of work. *Homo faber*, who is a minority one today, nor a yet more rare *homo agens*, has not been so ambitious yet, at least as far as this world is concerned.[250] In the mythic outset, the desire for happiness was considered to be an unacceptable haughtiness, ὕβρις,[251] and so yet from the beginning of the modern times started to hold true, that a right to seek personal happiness "(...) *is as indisputable as the right to life, and it is even identical to it.*"[252]

Even if there were some exceptions in this respect, they included mainly philosophers, who could hardly be considered as typical representatives of common sense.[253] A new general tendency was thus represented as late as by John Locke, since yet in that time the interpretation of a desire for happiness as an absolutely unconditioned, universal attribute of all people[254] has become so deeply rooted that it finally was reflected in the US Declaration of Independence as well.[255] Among the modern-age authors who shared this view also occured for example Leibniz,[256] Rousseau,[257] Diderot,[258] La Met-trie[259] or Holbach.[260] Comenius claimed even that not only are we all desperate for hap-

---

evil. About such an existence I say that it is neither a harm nor a benefit and we should be indifferent bet-ween such an existence and never existing. But no lives are like this. All lives contain some evil" (Benatar, 2006, p. 29). We would also vainly look for lives corrupted by just one negligible prick by a pin: "*(...) There are no lives even nearly this charmed"* (ibid., p. 49).

[250] Arendt (1998, p. 134).

[251] Benjamin (1991, p. 128).

[252] Arendt (1998, p. 108).

[253] Philosophers as, randomly, Plato (Euthyd. 278e nn.; Prot. 358 c n.) or Cicero (Hortensius, fr. 36, Müller) and within the Middle ages for example Boëthius (CF III, II, 1–14) thus used to act against, rather than aye the common sense. Neither a general tendency of philosophers to remain childless (Pelcová, 2004, p. 109) had been typical for the earlier times.

[254] Röd (2004, pp. 488n.).

[255] Hanock (1776).

[256] L (630; 632).

[257] Röd (2004, pp. 488n.).

[258] Ibid. (p. 252).

[259] La Mettrie (1970, p. 180).

[260] Röd (2004, p. 286).

piness, but also for its endlessness.[261] A desire to live, on the contrary, is according to these authors conditioned, since reason allows us to constantly reevaluate it.[262]

Not even the religious optimism which, owing to Saint Augustine's influence, finally prevailed in the Middle ages, has continued to function as before. While yet Augustine assumed that the difference between eternal bliss and eternal suffering is just a difference between two distinct degrees of a good and that the amounts of the saved are incomparably higher than the amounts of the condemned, as soon as John Calvin presented his compact and consistent version of predestination theory, its tragic nature was revealed in all its nakedness.[263] The subsequent shift in the basic ethical categories of good and evil is perhaps most illustratively demonstrated by Shakespear's dramas.[264] As soon as such a fertile soil was prepared for antinatalism in all directions, the new, more pronounced boom of antinatalistic mood was after all a mere question of time.

Today, however, it may yet seem somewhat surprising that, besides the popular enlightened optimism, antinatalistic ideas began to echo even from the mouths of some main protagonists of the enlightenment, whether it was Voltaire, who used to urge other philosophers on trying to "(...) *employ themselves in rendering a few individuals happy, than in inciting the suffering species to multiply itself*"[265] or Montesquieu, according to whom "*we should bewail people when being born and not after their death.*"[266] Not so much philosophers soaked by the enlightenmened optimism thus used to hold the opposite, pronatalistic position within modern times as rather philosophers standing towards it to a large extent in opposition, particularly Jean Jacques Rousseau. For the reason why Rousseau appreciated the agrarian states so highly consisted in their population density: the wealth of a state is manifested not by material goods, but by the number of its inhabitants,[267] he also considered his own designs to be feasible wherever people will be born.[268] While he criticized childless people, since he considered procreation to be an obligation,[269] he himself had got five children and, although he later condemned such an attitude, they all ended up in an orphanage.[270]

Parallelly to this, also an argumentation, which is being of a main interest in this chapter and of which Benatar's asymmetry argument is a current developmental stage, has its roots mostly within the modern times. Even in the context of the modern times, how-

---

[261] Paneg. (IX, 31; likewise VII, 8; III, 2). "*Mallet non esse quam sibi male esse,*" i.e. "*anyone rather prefers not to be than to be miserable*" (Paneg. VIII, 3).

[262] For example Comenius (Paneg. IX, 31).

[263] Sully (1877, p. 50).

[264] Koldinská (2013, p. 13).

[265] Voltaire (1997, pp. 134n.).

[266] Montesquieu (1989, p. 116).

[267] OC (111, 904).

[268] Rousseau (1979, p. 35).

[269] Ibid. (pp. 44nn.).

[270] Krecar (1926, p. 10).

ever, it could be considered as asymmetric or tutioristic at the most. Under tutiorism[271] I mean an ethic-methodological direction whose priority is the elimination of threats. Tutiorists, in general, consider the risk of evil, irrespective of its likelihood, to be so severe that it is necessary to avoid it at all costs. On the contrary, as far as the good is considered, they are no longer so uncompromising, the effort to achieve the good is subordinate according to them, the vision of good should never be an obstacle in the effort to avert evil. Tutiorists therefore anticipate a key antinatalistic assumption: as for Benatar, the relationship between the good and evil is somewhat asymmetric for them, attributing a much greater weight within that asymmetry to the evil (like Aristotle), not to the good (like Epicurus). Although mainly Jansenists, especially Blaise Pascal, are usually presented to as the originators of this direction, within this chapter, I am trying to supplement such an exposition by a similar approach of another modern philosopher, namely Leibniz.

Leibniz, as well as René Descartes, has usually been regarded to be a typical adversary of the tutioristic approach,[272] for while the tutiorists handle even the least probable threat whatsoever as an absolutely certain one, rationalistic approach of Descartes and Leibniz condemns probability knowledge as irrelevant, since from a rationalist point of view probability has nothing in common with certainty.[273] That is why Leibniz never extended his principle of sufficient reason towards a principle of probable reason, although, unlike Descartes,[274] he was interested in probability.[275] In fact, even Descartes, although he considered tutioristic approach as merely a provisional solution, admitted the tutioristic rule, that it is primarily needed to avert the greatest possible evil by rational means.[276] Before passing to the question of Leibniz's tutioristic dimension, it is necessary first to outline the modern age context of the emerging theory of probability, tutiorism emerging out of it and the related conception of Blaise Pascal.

---

[271] The term is derived from a latin watchword of tutiorists: *In dubio tutius est eligendum*, that is *When in doubt, choose the more certain* (Vřešťál, 1909, p. 222).

[272] Leibniz has also usually been regarded to be a typical adversary of pessimistic approach. However, he was acutely aware that optimism itself was counterintuitive. He frequently conceded that our world seemed not to be the best one. Nevertheless, a more in-depth consideration proves the opposite, according to him (Strickland, 2006, p. 2).

[273] Jonas (1992, p. 81). *"Like Descartes, the other famous rationalist, Leibniz was looking for something solid to ground one's reasoning. Clearly stern deductive reasoning, which led Descartes to the absolute certainty of his fundamentum inconcussum, is very different from a probabilistic way of thinking which revolves around the notions of uncertainty and induction"* (Vries, 2010, p. 8).

[274] Descartes had *"no truck with the nascent concept of probability"* (Hacking, 1975, p. 45).

[275] *"With these assumptions in mind it is unsurprising that Leibniz, the intellectual father of the 'principle of ground', never spoke of probable grounds"* (Vries, 2010, pp. 8, 14).

[276] Röd (2001, p. 74). For example, the preference of moderate opinions was, among others, justified by the fact that eccentricities may be fully correct, but also fully wrong, while moderate views are no more than partially incorrect (Descartes, AT VI, 22n.).

The modern theory of probability began to develop in the second half of the 17th century almost simultaneously with the principle of sufficient reason, even more, it was born just 17 years before Leibniz in 1671, in *Theoria motus abstracti*, for the first time mentioned the principle of sufficient reason, as the year 1654, when Blaise Pascal was in correspondence with Pierre Fermat, is regarded to be the new probability concept formation year.[277] Such a newly developed approach was immediately applied within theological context in form of tutiorism, not only by Pascal, but also by other Jansenists,[278] who, by their extreme tutiorism, called antiprobabilism or rigorism too, justified the necessity of strict following all church regulations. Only absolute certainty about the invalidity of ecclesiastical regulations therefore justifies their violation. The church regulations thus *de facto* hold unconditionally,[279] for even the very least doubt about validity of other than ecclesiastical principles is a reason for their condemnation, no matter what advantages would otherwise emerge from following them.

So much to the modern age context of the subsequent philosophical outcome of Pascal's tutioristic considerations known as a Pascal's wager, which results into a conclusion that it is much more beneficial to believe in God, or at least act in the manner of believers, than not to believe. It is far better to prefer the risk of a fallacious belief than God's punishment for sinning. An impartial rationally thinking individual would therefore hypothetically prefer the first of these variants, for the benefit of a relatively care-free life of atheist is not sufficiently desirable face to face with the threat of an eternal suffering in hell.[280] The threat of eternal damnation is, as well as the threat of regulations' invalidity, regardless of its realization probability, so serious, that it is simply to be avoided at all costs.

According to MacLean, the Pascal's wager only revived an old apologetic argument indeed (by Jesus or Saint Jerome, as previous chapter shows), but Pascal's decision to quantify the advantageness of betting on God,[281] however, identifies his reflection with Leibniz's suggestion. Leibniz also stated that, especially when making practical decisions, a careful numerical consideration of the reasons for and against, which are usually to be found equally on both sides, is necessary. However, this is not sufficient according to Leibniz, for it is necessary not only to sum up all the reasons for and against on both sides, after that it is also necessary to balance these reasons in the right way.[282]

Thus, even Leibniz admits that by far not all cons should be assigned the same weight in the decision making; a fact that a good many of antinatalists realized while elaborating their pessimistic evaluation of life and which, at the same time, also answers the

[277] Vries (2010, p. 9).
[278] Vřešťál (1909, pp. 221n.).
[279] Opatrný (2015, p. 49, fn. 45).
[280] Pascal (1923, pp. 153–156).
[281] MacLean (2017).
[282] Leibniz (GP VII, 188; L 260); Thiercelin (2008, p. 258).

question of why Benatar regards suffering of existing individuals to be much more un-desirable than their joy of life is on the contrary to be desirable and than the loss of opportunity to exist is undesirable for never existing people. In fact, however, Leibniz claimed much more than just that some variants should be assigned a higher weight in decision making than others. In addition, he also agreed that even a weakly probable option might by its value-weight outweigh a more probable one.

An example of such an option is a variant A, the probability of which is 5 units and the qualitative value of which is 4 units. By the term *quality (bonitas)* Leibniz meant what we would call today *benefit*.[283] According to Leibniz, this variant conveys in its product a variant B with a probability value of 6 units and a qualitative value of 3 units, since 20 (i.e. 5 * 4) is more than 18 (i.e. 6 * 3):[284] *"It follows one should follow A more than B even if it is less probable. Thus a good person will avoid the smallest risk of sin even if a great advantage is proposed."*[285] Moreover, he claimed, that *"the fear of a great pain determines more strongly than the expectation of a pleasure."*[286]

Translated into antinatalistic diction it follows from Leibniz's considerations that the possibility to forestall the highest possible suffering (whether in hell or, let us say, in a concentration camp) prevails over the possibility of living a relatively satisfied life, even if the realization of such suffering would not be probable enough. Of course that Leibniz himself did not arrive at such an antinatalistic conclusion,[287] just as neither Descartes nor Pascal did. Leibniz pursued other purposes, the same as Pascal did, since his reflection continues by words: *"(...) Indeed no greater evil can bring them to renounce being a good person."*[288] Moreover, in the context of reflections on another topic, he eventually reached a symmetrical conclusion that the absence of good is equally an evil as is the absence of evil, on the contrary, good.[289]

However, the aim of this chapter is to prove that it is not difficult to encounter in course of history some personalities sharing grounds of Benatar's asymmetry argument (not necessarily the entire argument itself). Indeed, considering Leibniz's reflection's resemblance to Pascal, just a short step is separating it from antinatalism, since antinatalism

---

[283] Meyns (2017, p. 245, fn. 51).
[284] *"(...) Probabilities are to be followed, when the ratio of the probable effects is greater than [that of] the reciprocal, or if it is much more probable for act A to have a better effect than B, than for B [to be better] than A. Or if the product of the multiplication of the probability with goodness is greater with A than [with] B"* (A VI, 1, 71).
[285] Ibid.
[286] *"La crainte d'une grosse peine l'emporte sur quelque plaisir"* (GP VI, 308, §324). Translation by Lucas (1956, p. 131).
[287] The reason, why Leibniz definitely could not arrive at the very antinatalistic conclusion is simple: pro-creation does not result into creation of an entirely new being according to him, as well as death does not result into its perishing, since it would violate the principle of continuity (GP IV, 481).
[288] A (VI, 1, 71).
[289] *"Minus bonum habet rationem mali"* (DM 3, p. 56; GP III, 33, 574; L 567, 622; see also Grua 1952, pp. 212n.).

could be considered as a kind of generalization or completion of the Pascal's wager. For while Pascal attempted to avoid the threat of eternal damnation by devoutness, the target of antinatalism is to avoid (among others) the same threat, but somewhat more efficiently. Even if everybody would be able to achieve salvation for himself (which is, moreover, questionable),[290] the antinatalists assume that many of us, even if through their own fault, will actually not reach it despite. It would be more effective, therefore, not to conceive such people from preventive reasons, for never existing people avoid eternal damnation with certainty.[291] Regardless of whether or not also earthly bliss is entirely *in our hands*, it analogically applies even to this case, that many of us, even if through our own fault, will not achieve it, so from preventive reasons it would also be preferable not to conceive such people at all.

As another one of the personalities sharing the Benatar's asymmetry argument can be considered John Locke, according to whome by far not every absent good causes desire comparable to the desire to avert evil. For the absence of pleasure in itself need

---

[290] Whether or not prospective descendants get to heaven or hell is to a large extent a question of upbringing, but, because of human (or perhaps God's as well) freedom, upbringing is definitely not omnipotent. As already mentioned in previous chapter, it is written in the *Bible*, above all, that "(...) the gate is wide and the way is easy that leads to destruction, and those who enter by it are many. (...) The gate is narrow and the way is hard that leads to life, and those who find it are few" (Mt., 7:13n.). Jesus responds a question: "Lord, will those who are saved be few?" this way: "Strive to enter through the narrow door. For many, I tell you, will seek to enter and will not be able" (Lk., 13:23n.). Among the Christians, as members of the most numerous religious community in the world, only about a third of the world's population are those who could be saved. Only a third of all the people living on the Earth can be counted as Christians at least in the sense that they believe that the core of the Christian doctrine is true. The remaining two-thirds deny at least one of its basic pillars. The era when it used to be claimed that everyone is a Christian at least in the sense as, at certain times, it used to be claimed that everyone is a royalist, a republican, or a communist, has not yet come (Chesterton, 2004, p. 37). It is also necessary to distinguish between a mere superficial Christianity and the very Christianity as an inward faith, and it is also possible to take into account a Protestant belief about the ill-deserveness of salvation (Himma, 2010, pp. 179, 197) as well as the possibility that it is accessible exclusively to the monks (McGrath, 1999, p. 20), which reduces the amounts of potentially saved ones the more. Moreover, if a devout life is to be a mere means to get salvation, then it is unattainable as well, so that those who seek it on the basis of a consideration similar to this one, have got no chance either (Jonas, 1992, pp. 39n.). However, from the extreme-tutioristic point of view, the question of the life after death is irrelevant, for even an eternal absolute posthumous bliss would not be able to overweight the suffering experiences in course of life, for evil, in any quantity and anyhow probable, is many times more grave than good. It is therefore understandable why in 1690 the pope Alexander VIII. forbade such an escalated tutiorism (Vřešťál, 1909, p. 222), especially when it resonated mainly by Jansenists. Benatar, however, got by with a moderate tutiorism – the eternal absolute posthumous bliss is not a sufficient motive for anyone's comming into existence simply because the never existing one would never miss such a bliss. The relevant motivation, therefore, is solely the absence of suffering, and this is what is guaranteed for the never-existing individual with an absolute certainty. But neither moderate tutiorism lasted a long time among Catholics (Vřešťál, 1909, p. 222).

[291] "The avoidance of suffering in hell – even when avoided because the person remains non-existent – is a moral good, whereas the lack of pleasure because of non-existence is not a moral bad" (Bawulski, 2013, p. 332). This kind of argumentation was probably not the case of Jesus' (either Saint Jerome's) argumentation yet (ibid, p. 342, fn. 29).

not to be painful, while the presence of pain is always painful.[292] Edmund Burke also regarded pain, i.e. the evil, to be far more serious than pleasure, i.e. the good: *"The ideas of pain are much more powerful than those which enter on the part of pleasure. Without all doubt, the torments which we may be made to suffer, are much greater in their effect on the body and mind, than any pleasures which the most learned voluptary could suggest, or than the liveliest imagination, and the most sound and exquisitely sensitive body, could enjoy."*[293] The highest degree of pleasure is thus never able to cope with the highest degree of pain.

THE NINETEENTH CENTURY

Within the 19th century, pessimism developed into almost a mass movement, since never before such amounts of thinkers were so long and so intensely concerned with such questions.[294] Even the 19th century philosophers themselves were convinced that the nineteenth century pessimism stood for a new developmental phase, for they considered themselves to be a modern kind of pessimists, philosophical or systematic ones in contrast to the traditional pessimism.

A good many of explicitly antinatalistic statements could be find especially by Arthur Schopenhauer. Schopenhauer foremost asked whether *"If the act of procreation were neither the outcome of a desire nor accompanied by feelings of pleasure, but a matter to be decided on the basis of purely rational considerations, is it likely the human race would still exist? Would each of us not rather have felt so much pity for the coming generation as to prefer to spare it the burden of existence, or at least not wish to take it upon himself to impose that burden upon it in cold blood?"*[295] The ethical justification of the intention to bring someone into the world purely for the purpose of this person's being present here would be according to Schopenhauer so highly questionable, that only a few of us would be willing to accept such a cardinal responsibility. Schopenhauer even likens such a thought-out procreation, which was an ideal of a good many of church fathers according to him, in comparison with a lust-driven procreation to a plotted act commited by a cold-blooded killer in comparison with a murder in affection.[296] How could we

---

[292] Locke (1999, p. 234, prop. 31).

[293] Burke (1823, p. 86).

[294] Given that, in addition, in the 19th century the traditional pessimism were connected to the asymmetry between good and evil for the first time, it was probably just the 19th century when started to hold true that *"whether Leibniz was too optimistic (...) is no longer a question for academic dispute or literary wit, but one on which the very survival of civilization depends"* (Wiener, 1951, p. LI).

[295] Schopenhauer (2004, p. 9).

[296] Id. (1926, pp. 269n.).

even be proud of us when our own conception was such a serious crime, our birth is subsequently a punishment, our life is filled with labor and death is inevitably coming, which is the motive that also Kierkegaard has developed besides Schopenhauer.[297]

Regardless of whether Schopenhauer should, based on above stated, be considered as the first (systematical) antinatalist whatsoever, for that is still a subject of discussion and it is not a question of this chapter, it seems that right to him belongs the primacy in connecting the asymmetry between the good and the evil with reflections about the possibility of one's own non-existence. His predecessors considered either solely benefits of one's own non-existence (in addition to some ancient authors a more recent philosopher Peter Wessel Zapffe also took it into account this way); or on the contrary, when claiming the asymmetry between the good and the evil, they got by without considering one's own non-existence (modern age authors Blaise Pascal, René Descartes, John Locke or Edmund Burke as well as Thomas Hobbes, which is mentioned in next sub-chapter likewise John Rawls from the 20th century).

It was just Schopenhauer, however, who for the first time explicitly connected the conclusion, that it would be better never to be born, with the claim that it is not necessary for the evil to prevail during someone's life in order to this assumption be valid. He was convinced that no amount of good is able to outweigh the power of evil. Even if evil needs not to predominate in terms of quantity, it nevertheless prevails in terms of quality. The intensity of experiences such as murder, rape, torture and similar cruelties are simply beyond comparison with the intensity of good experiences, whatever we put for them.

The question whether the good or the evil prevails in the world, thus appeared to Schopenhauer to be somewhat unnecessary, since the very fact that evil exists is sufficient for never being born to be more advantageous. In short, the predominance of evil in the world is not necessary in terms of his argumentation, for the good never overweights it. Even if there were a hundred times less evil in the world than it actually is, its mere existence makes life worthy of lamentation, not exultation: *"For that a thousand lived in happiness and pleasure would never do away with the anguish and death-agony of a single one; and just as little does my present well-being undo my past suffering,"*[298] which is a motif to find also in Dostoyevsky's *The Brothers Karamazov*.[299]

Even though Schopenhauer did not yet escalate such a disproportion into Benatar's conclusion that life is to be refused even on the basis of a single unpleasant pin-prick, so that his asymmetry was not yet as distinctive as the Benatar's one, he at least enables us to free ourselves from considerations about the quantitative ratio of good to evil.[300]

---

[297] Schopenhauer (2007, p. 6); Kierkegaard (1968, p. 113).
[298] Schopenhauer (1964, p. 386).
[299] Dostoyevsky (1981, chap. 4).
[300] Janavay (1999, p. 332); Coates (2014, p. 153).

This, however, did not prevent him from having recourse to such reflections, while the result of such a balance is disturbing: the evil prevails.[301] Schopenhauer, moreover, used to interpret the good negatively, as a mere absence of suffering and thus he thereby exacerbated their asymmetry.[302]

Such as Schopenhauer's, also Olga Plumacher's argumentation was close to the Benatar's one,[303] since she also pointed out that antinatalism does not contradict the assumption that people are generally rather happy than unhappy. The key question is according to her whether a happy life really represents an advantage compared to non-existence, and where the boundary between life predominantly happy versus predominantly unfortunate lies; since from a philosophical point of view, existence, i.e. a state of a non-zero suffering could never be of a higher value than non-existence, i.e. a state of a zero suffering.[304]

However, even regarding the 19th century it is not true that the asymmetric relation between good and evil would appear as intuitive to all thinkers without exception. Henri Poincaré, for example, in his *The Value of Science* (whose publication falls yet to the beginning of the 20th century) claimed that no suffering can ever make us forget the enjoyable experience of tasting the first apple in our life, for the good marks in memory much more than the evil, not *vice versa*. Even if this, in itself, could be regarded as just a confirmation of the Pollyanna principle validity, the focus of all efforts to eliminate suffering lacks the very sufficient reason above all according to him: Why to resort to such a radical solution, especially when it is a negatively, not positively defined ideal? Along with some antinatalists, however, also Poincaré admitted that the most reliable way to prevent suffering lays in annihilation of existence.[305]

THE TWENTIETH CENTURY

The first systematical attempt to link all the points mentioned above belongs to the twentieth century: the negative evaluation of life together with the claim and even an attempt to explain the asymmetric relationship between good and evil for the first time resulted into a seriously intended proposal of a concrete solution: the demand for a complete extinction of mankind. Since Schopenhauer's solution did not counted on

---

[301] For example Schopenhauer (2004, p. 3).
[302] Ibid. (p. 2).
[303] For becoming familiar with Olga Plumalcher the author owes to Vlastimil Vohánka.
[304] Plumacher (1879, p. 82).
[305] Poincaré (1907, p. 11).

the possibility of human extinction yet,[306] while neither Solovyov nor Kurnig did consider the asymmetry principle yet,[307] there is no choice but to deny their primacy in this respect in favour of the author who, however, started to publish on the subject of antinatalism as late as at the very end of the 20th century, namely David Benatar. None of their predecessors within the twentieth century discussed all of these elements simultaneously: Hans Jonas and John Rawls did not concluded that it would be desirable to extinct, John Narveson was not certain of it, Rawls, in addition, did not even endorse life with suffering, as well as neither Nerveson nor Hermann Vetter did, whereas the last of the selected authors, Peter Wessel Zapffe, did not deal with the asymmetry of good and evil according to my opinion. Vohánka, however, holds another opinion,[308] which forced me to discuss him within this chapter as one of Benatar's asymmetry argument forerunners too.

Certain asymmetry between good and evil has been assumed, among others, by John Rawls' method of a *veil of ignorance*,[309] which subsequently became a mainstream basis of Anglo-American philosophy for the duration of an entire generation. After all, Rawls' intention was indeed to create a theory "*(...) based on a generally accepted moral intuition,*" which "*(...) does not rely on controversial attitudes in ethics.*"[310] Rawls argued that if people were offered the opportunity to freely choose a social order into which they would subsequently be born without having any idea about how concretely would all the social positions be distributed among them, they would rather try to prevent evil than maximize the good. They would, for example, refuse a caste system that guarantees some cardinal privileges for the highest class' members at the expense of others, especially the lowest class' members. The prospects of the highest casts' members are simply insufficiently motivational for them, for there is a threat, that they themselves will not belong to one of them. They would therefore rather prefer a somewhat egalitarian system which is able to at least minimize, if not completely eliminate, the hardship threat possibly of the lowest casts, classes or the least successful groups.

Although this Rawls' theory has nothing to do with antinatalism at the first glance, there are two pivotal implications for antinatalism derivable from it. The first of them, the

---

[306] Schopenhauer (1909a, pp. 517n.).

[307] As for Solovyov, "*(...) certainly he would (...) disagree with the assumptions necessary for the asymmetry argument to be correct. The absence of the good is definitely wrong,*" as Markéta Poledníková claims in next chapter (p. 121). As for Kurnig, he "*(...) does not explain more in detail why the 'nasty death catastrophe' that ends every existence cannot be compensated for by a fulfilled life,*" as Karim Akerma claims in next but one chapter (p. 140).

[308] Vohánka (2015, p. 60; 2019, p. 75, fn. 1).

[309] Rawls (1999, chap. 24, pp. 118–122).

[310] Gray (2003, p. 102). Rorty even claims that although a mass democracy is perhaps merely a purely European invention, the idea of a democratic utopia resonates all around the world. In each cultural tradition we would encounter stories about the cruelty of privileged people capitulating face to face the oppressed lower stratum (1995, p. 204).

question of whether people under the veil of ignorance would tend to choose rather no society than one of those offered, set up Benatar. For that is precisely what Rawls' statement implies, according to him: people are in favor of such a variant that would relieve the most disadvantaged, that means those who do not flourish within society. According to an antinatalistic assumption, however, as opposed to non-existence, none of existing people flourishes enough. Whichever society we thus choose, everybody would be severely disadvantaged, though to a varying degree. Since, according to Benatar, noone of us is so lucky to be able to truthfully claim that he is content,[311] the only desirable option seems to be the society which does not exist.

The second implication could be labeled as a tutioristic, although in Rawls' case relatively moderate one, since the evil that people in accordance with Rawls' presuppositions try to minimize is imminent with fairly a high probability. For it can be argued that the preference of an egalitarian system is not owing to the fact that all the benefits of some privileged persons are not good enough for them, but to the fact that the privileged persons even within the caste system usually do not account for more than just a minority of society, so that the likelihood that anybody would belong to it is scarce. It is thus possible to detect the implicit moderate-tutioristic conclusion from this Rawls position too, which also Benatar later assumed, that the vision of maximal individual profit is far from being appealing enough to cope with the threat of maximal suffering of the same individual. In short, the profit, i.e. something good, does not have the same value as the hardship, i.e. something bad. Although the application of this Rawls' asymmetry on the question of possible non-existence was carried out yet by Benatar, the fact that tutiorism is advocated through it makes out of it another segment of a historical matrix of Benatar's asymmetry argument.

As already mentioned, Rawls' intuition kept on resonate among thinkers. Hayry, for example, has based his argumentation on it[312] and also Keller testifies that without the warranty of at least a minimal living standard for the most disadvantaged citizens, i.e. without the elimination of evil, people would never accept the idea of equality.[313] Rawls's reflections seem most intuitive if a caste system is offered as an alternative to democracy, where any social mobility is almost excluded. For if we replaced it by a capitalistic hierarchy instead, people could easily rethink their preferences simply on the basis of hope guaranteed by social mobility, if they believe that capitalism is capable to ensure equal opportunities for all, or at least to provide sufficient opportunities specifically for them. But this would draw attention away from the core of the problem,

---

[311] "I have not argued, nor need I have argued, that all lives are so bad that they are not worth continuing. I have argued instead that all lives contain substantial amounts of whatever is thought bad" (Benatar, 2006, p. 88).
[312] Hayry (2004).
[313] Keller (2008b, p. 81).

from the question of whether it is primary important to eliminate evil, to a political question of which social order is able to guarantee it most effectively, which is neither the subject of this book nor of this chapter.

It seems that the asymmetry between good and evil has been explicitly interweaved with non-existence by Hans Jonas as well. Although the conclusion reached by Jonas fundamentally differs from Benatar's one, they both posed the same question: whether, with respect to the asymmetric relationship between good and evil, we should not better let the entire society spontaneously die out. Jonas' answer, however, unlike Benatar's one, was negative, since Jonas considers the claim that society should continue to exist to be indisputable. He thus conveyed the impression that there is no need to convince anybody about it, even though he regarded such an issue as the most serious basis for all ethics.[314]

The only circumstance able to justify unleashing of a war is thus, according to Jonas, a threat of the highest possible evil at all, namely a complete extinction of mankind, at the grass-roots level then the extinction of a particular state, which is sometimes just impossible to be prevented other way than by a defensive war. As in case of reasoning performed by Rawls, also Jonas' reflection seems to be quite intuitive, a similar intuition was shared for example by the leader of the American Republican senators, Cabot Lodge. Lodge's reflection was as follows: noone of the European powers will engage in a war in order to enforce the League of Nations' resolutions, since, broadly speaking, states, whose *life-sustaining interests* are not at risk, are used to avoid warring. Lodge's reflection were of course based on his own experience, and it ought to be remarked that the interests and safety of Europeans were definitely not indifferent for him: *"Would the US go to war to protect Britain's frontiers in India or Japan's in Shantung? Of course not. Any agreement America made with Britain and France must be based on the mutual accomodation of vital interests. Then it would mean something."*[315]

If we move Jonas' unfounded fear[316] of human extinction aside for a moment, it is hard to overlook that the formal structure of his reflection is nohow different from a Rawls'

---

[314] Jonas (1992, p. 62). Jonas correctly predicted that philosophers will surely look for a theoretical foundation of the assumption that people should go on existing. But such an esoteric, highest confirmation of the imperative of eternal conservation of all species, whether carried out by means of rationality or not, is somehow surprisingly, not necessary according to him, since the consensus on the need to maintain continuity of generations is, in his view, pretheoretical, instinctive and universal (1979, p. 42). *Das Prinzip Verantwortung* itself, however, concurrently arose as a reaction to reflections of Günther Anders, who "(...) *rejected all attempts to derive a justification for a special right for humanity to exist,"* although it in itself does not justify leaving mankind at the mercy of destiny according to him (Samuelson, 2008, p. 32).

[315] Johnson (1984, p. 32).

[316] Jonas explicitly resigned from a theoretical justification of the assumption that we should feel obliged to enable something to come into existence, that would otherwise never originate at all, for such a target would be achievable only with a great difficulty and without the help of religion it would be even impossible (1992, p. 36).

one and hence also from what is called tutiorism. The desire for good is in both cases uncompromisingly displaced in favor of the struggle against evil. At a first glance, it seems that Jonas deals exclusively with the highest possible evil at all, for mankind should, according to him, exist unconditionally, no matter how much happiness or suffering, good or evil would be associated with that. The effort to avert the threat of extinction takes precedence over everything else, including the pursuit of good, and abolishes otherwise inalienable bans and rules.[317] However, reasons supporting the effort to prevent such a crisis at all costs, which means even at a cost of suffering, conclude, a bit paradoxically, suffering connected with such a situation as well: *In any event, one should try as much as one can prevent the advent of emergency with its high tax of suffering or, at least, prepare for it."*[318]

Nor should it be surprising, therefore, that Jonas explicitly referred to Pascal and his wager, he even called his own tutioristic ethical imperative in Pascal's manner a wager principle. Endangering of the future existence of mankind was considered to be a totally inadmissible vabang wager in his view,[319] just as Pascal previously considered any behavior inconsistent with demands of faith to be an unacceptable gamble. Not Jonas' tutiorism itself, therefore, but rather the fact that even such a very pronatalisticaly-oriented author as Jonas has shared the identical intuition with antinatalists, is a considerable breakthrough.

Yet Jonas contributed to the treasury of antinatalistic thoughts, apart from the above mentioned, also by something innovative, namely by the attempt to explain the asymmetric relationship between good and evil. Within the introductory chapter of previous section I claimed that already the ancient philosopher Epicurus attempted to give such an explanation, but he focused merely on looking for reasons why the value of good exceeds the value of evil. Jonas, however, attempted to justify the opposite question of why the value of evil exceeds the value of good, the reason for which is according to him that the evil is more immediate, more urgent, and no one looks for it, it is easily attainable, and rarely called into question. The more difficult attainability of good could be in contrast caused by its infinitely more difficult comprehensibility, for the knowledge of good is often accessible merely by an indirect route through evil. We are usually not certain enough about what we want, while we are sure enought about what we do not want.[320]

Also Olga Plumacher argued by the much more difficult attainability of the good, but her argument was not asymmetrical yet, since she justified such an unreachableness by

[317] Jonas (1979, p. 43).
[318] Ibid. (p. 41).
[319] Šimek (2014, pp. 71n.).
[320] Jonas (1992, pp. 63n.).

the prevalence of the evil in the world. For natural and artificial circumstances producing pain are available, according to her, always and everywhere, while the circumstances that produce joy to overcome them are limited and difficult to reach.[321]

Based on conclusions like that, Jonas therefore supplemented his explanation of the asymmetry of good and evil by an appeal that *"the doom prophecy must be listen to more than the prophecy of prosperity."*[322] A simple failure probability review in case of an unknown experiment of a cardinal importance must for example never assume prosperity, for such a single variant faces an infinite amount of other more or less unsuccessful options. Or, in Benatar's words, *"it is much easier for things to go wrong than to go right."*[323] Of course, there is often more than just one single attempt, but that does not apply to the most significant and irreversible decisions we make,[324] among which, let us add, the choice whether to be or not to be undoubtedly belongs to. The evolution forestalls us by its reactions to our actions, while we are not able to make long-term forecasts, so that we are caught under the pressure of time. Therefore, we need to avert the apocalyptic threat and do not hope for any chilliastic fulfillment,[325] against an utopian dream of perfect humanity, Jonas thus emphasizes an imperative of prudence.[326] Let us add that similar tutioristic statements are also to be find by a number of other authors, not any differently than Jonas, Keller comments on the idea of a sustainable life: *"It is not a promise of future prosperity, that is, of some kind of immeasurable, though from technical reasons provisionally unattainable luck. It is not a vision of the great good that is waiting for us somewhere. It is quite a prosaic challenge not to waste time on dreaming of the future good, but yet at present to confront lots of smaller and bigger evils instead, that reduce our chances for a truly dignified life."*[327] Neither Petrů with his tutiorism is running late: *"A risky operation might only be legitimized by an urgent situation. However, I guess that mankind already is in such an urgent and over a long period*

---

[321] Plumacher (1879, p. 78).

[322] Jonas (1992, p. 71). Jonas was inspired by Hobbes in this respect (Bouretz, 2010, p. 622). However, while Hobbes dealt with an individual's fear of his own violent death, according to Jonas we are also obliged to be interested in an up to now merely theoretical fortune and misfortune of the future generations (Jonas, 1992, p. 65).

[323] Benatar (2015, p. 49). For example, people usually do not expect to win in a lottery, while winning the lottery is considered to be a sudden stroke of luck: *"The universe goes along, and one's life goes along, without winning lotteries"* (Suits, 2010, p. 270). Aristotle (Phys., 197a 31nn.) pointed out something similar: starting with Pythagoreans, the evil was identified with limitlessness, while the good with limitation. It is easy to miss a goal (EN, 1106b 30–35).

[324] Jonas (1992, p. 70).

[325] Ibid. (p. 63).

[326] Bouretz (2010, p. 622). This is as well in a stark contrast to Benatar, who referring to Schopenhauer argued that *"it is always irrational to prefer to come into existence. Rational impartial parties would choose not to exist and the upshot of this is zero population"* (Benatar, 2006, p. 182).

[327] Keller (1995, p. 46).

unsustainable situation." Therefore, it is necessary to try to solve the situation *"even at the expense of self-destruction, since we are endangered by (self)destruction anyway."*[328] Just a small step is missing from there toward Benatar's solution, since Benatar also believes that humanity will inevitably disappear as a result of the entropical decomposition of the universe.[329] Such a step could be (except for Benatar) awarded to Hermann Vetter (and apparently to John Narveson too), as the following quotation proves:

"In any case, it is morally preferable not to produce a child. This requires that in any individual encounter, and by any institutional activity (...) people should be discouraged from having children. If such tendencies are successful enough, the number of men on earth may begin to decrease, and if such development continues long enough, the human race will disappear. This, however, would not at all be a deplorable consequence according to Narveson's and my own opinion: the existence of mankind is not a value in itself. On the contrary, if mankind ceases to exist, all suffering is extinguished perfectly, which no other human endeavour will be able to bring about. On the other hand, of course, all happy experiences of men will disappear. But this, according to Narveson's conclusion, would not be deplorable, because no human subject would exist which would be deprived of the happy experiences."[330]

Narveson, which Vetter refers to, however, admitted that procreation could be a necessary tool to minimize suffering caused by the extinction itself: *"Is it ever one's duty to have children? I can think of only one case where it might. If it can be shown that the populace will suffer if its size is not increased, then it seems to me that one could perhaps require efforts in that direction, and punish those who could comply but do not. But I am inclined to think that such a situation is exceedingly rare."*[331]
Just for sake of completeness I remind that Vohánka[332] sees a germ of Benatar's asymmetry argument also within a statement of the Norwegian writer Zapffe for *the Aftenposten* daily, where Zapffe claims that a nonexistent person bothers about nothing and noone misses them. Therefore, none of us would have better been born if we had been offered such a choice.[333] Zapffe's reflection, however, rather resembles some ancient lamentations, and therefore rather stands for a regressive than progressive element in

---

[328] Petrů (2016, p. 218).
[329] Benatar (2006, pp. 194n., 209).
[330] Vetter (1971, pp. 302n.).
[331] Narveson (1967, p. 72).
[332] Vohánka (2015, p. 60; 2019, p. 75, fn. 1).
[333] Zapffe (1959, p. 63). Zapffe's primacy lies in something else. According to Coates, he is the first philosopher whatsoever, who saw the solution of human predicament in non-breeding, and hence the first explicit antinatalist whatsoever (2014, pp. 245, 261). However, Karim Akerma is questioning this opinion in the next but one chapter.

the development from the history of the asymmetry argument to its explicit explication by Benatar.

To treat Zapffe's reflection as an asymmetric one, it would be necessary to add that his consideration applies not only to those who are essentially unhappy, suffering or dissatisfied, but also to those who are sometimes happy as well, prosperous or satisfied. The claim that people of the first type would rather never be born is comparatively intuitive, or maybe logical, though definitely not necessarily true. But why those who would miss this way also some lighter moments that life brings to them would refuse their coming into existence too? It was only Benatar to give a response for this question, since his argumentation applies not only to such a half-happy people, but even to those, who are happy almost all the time,[334] and it even doubts the unambiguousness of choice of those who are absolutely blessed, if anyone like this actually exists. Despite all the previous attempts, thus, nobody until Schopenhauer, Plumacher, Jonas, Narveson, Vetter and Benatar, but not Zapffe, came with an original asymmetric argument concerning good versus evil in relation to existence versus non-existence.

CONCLUSION

The aim of this chapter was to map the history of the Benatar's asymmetry argument. I distinguished three breakthroughs: a modern age period, when parallelly with enlivening of the antinatalistic reflections, a new speculation about the tutioristic asymmetry of good and evil began; the nineteenth century, when those two previously separated lines of thought were interconnected for the first time, and the twentieth or twenty first century, when (among others) Benatar incorporated his tutioristic asymmetry into his article entitled *Why It Is better Never to Come into Existence* (1997), respectively into his later book *Better Never to have been* (2006).

Hermann Vetter could be regarded as the last one of the Benatar's predecessors in this respect, for after him it was only Benatar who noticeably dared to apply his conception of asymmetry between good and evil to a reflection about the non-existence possibility: "*I think that there could be much less suffering and yet procreation would remain unacceptable,*"[335] while his own justification for such a conclusion could be likened to

---

[334] "*However, any defect that was sufficiently minor to pass the life worth starting test would also be minor enough for us to be able to embrace the conclusion that no harm was done to the child who was brought into existence with that defect. Of course, I think that there are no such cases – because I think that no lives are worth starting. Those who think that at least some lives are worth starting need to decide where they set the bar and then accept the implications*" (Benatar, 2015, p. 21).

[335] Id. (2006, p. 13).

one of the directions that he himself comments on within *Better Never to Have Been*, namely to (anti)frustrationism.[336]

Antifrustrationists deduce the tutioristic conclusion that it is predominantly necessary to avoid unsatisfied desires from the assumption that there is no value difference between a satisfied desire and the absence of such a desire. For example, when we "paint the tree nearest to Sydney Opera house red and give Kate a pill that makes her wish that the tree nearest to Sydney Opera House was red,"[337] our actions are equivalent to not doing anything. Or, in Benatar's words: the state where a non-existent individual is not endowed by longing for a happy life is no less valuable than the one where an existing individual actually experiences his longed-for life. The state of non-existence is therefore no less desirable than the one of a happy life, but the existing people are, in addition to the possibility of living a happy life, at the same time exposed to a considerable risk of frustration, the risk of having unfulfilled desires. That is just the reason why we should prefer to avoid childbearing, since partly their satisfied desires would not be better than the absence of such desires and partly they will also be endowed by some unsatisfied desires, which would otherwise not threaten.

Benatar thus wiped out any value difference between the state of absent desire and the state of fulfilled desire at a much more general level than the antifrustrationists, since he did not even distinguish the state of nonexistence from the state of a happy life,[338] for in both cases there is nobody who could be truthfully declared to be unhappy, which is the only thing that matters from the point of view of his argumentation. The fact that the non-existent people consequently ultimately miss their occasion to be happy in the course of their life is irrelevant, since they do not regret such a loss. In short, it is at all costs necessary to avoid the threat of evil in the form of the existence of someone unhappy for the sake of an absolute certainty about non-realization of such an evil. The opposite choice, though popular, seems to be somewhat ineffective according to antinatalists: "*(...) While good people go to great lengths to spare their children from suffering, few of them seem to notice that the one (and only) guaranteed way to prevent all the suffering of their children is not to bring those children into existence in the first place.*"[339]

All Benatar's argumentation in favor of the asymmetry of good and evil (including all the affiliated asymmetries and tables illustrating them) is therefore based on a value

---

[336] The concepts of *frustrationism* and *antifrustrationism* are synonymous, though it is kind of confusing (Benatar, 2015, p. 39, fn. 12; 2006, p. 54).

[337] Fehige (1998, pp. 513n.).

[338] "*Absent pleasures that do not deprive are 'not bad' in the sense of 'not worse'. They are not worse than the presence of pleasures. It follows that the presence of pleasures is not better, and therefore that the presence of pleasures is not an advantage over absent pleasures that do not deprive*" (Benatar, 2006, p. 42).

[339] Ibid. (p. 6).

judgment emerging no later than in the modern age era by the Jansenists, namely by Pascal (maybe inspired by Jesus or Saint Jerome and a bit resembling Leibniz), but also by Descartes, Hobbes, Locke and Burke, that it is primarily necessary to avoid evil (i.e. on tutiorism) or, alternatively, that evil leaves a stronger impression in our memory than good does (as already Aristotle claimed). Within the 19th century Schopenhauer and Plumacher brought this idea back, as well as within the 20th century especially John Rawls, Hans Jonas, John Narveson and Hermann Vetter did. In short, in Benatar's view suffering happens to be so undesirable that not even a much higher amount of good would outweigh it, much less since a non-existent person does not regret the absence of such a good.

By some of the Benatar's followers, the tutioristic asymmetry has been further strengthened, for example by Kenneth Einar Himma, who condemns cases where a person X causes injury to a person Y without being sure that causing such a harm would with a logical necessity result into some kind of benefit for the person X, which would finally infinitely outweigh such an injury. [340] Evil is just, according to Benatar, his followers and some of his predecessors too, so undesirable that nothing is able to overweigh it except for an infinite amount of good, but compared to the non-existence state, not even the infinite amount of good is able to manage it.

---

[340] Himma (2004, p. 252).

SOLOVYOV AND HIS GODMANHOOD:
ANTINATALISM IN RUSSIA

INTRODUCTION

The ideas of Vladimir Sergeyevich Solovyov, a Russian philosopher of the second half of the 19th century, are still attractive not only for many historians of philosophy and theology. They can also serve well as case studies for research in multiple fields of systematic philosophy. A study of this kind, situated at the boundary of the history of philosophy and the anachronous studies of contemporary problems, is going to be offered in the following pages. I am going to argue that some features of ideas of contemporary antinatalists could be found in the work of Solovyov, although I am going to consider his position to be antinatalistic in a broader sense of the word. The author of the contemporary antinatalistic conception, David Benatar, sometimes refers to certain philosophers such as Schopenhauer or Flaubert as to his predecessors, although they did not identify themselves as antinatalists and neither did Solovyov. However, if Benatar interpreted Schopenhauer's and Flaubert's ideas as antinatalistic, I find very interesting to do it in similar way with Solovyov's ideas.[341]

The main aim of this chapter is to defend the claim that we can label Solovyov as an antinatalist, yet only in a broader sense of the word. As follows, the secondary aim is to argue once more that Christian antinatalism is not only possible (in agreement with what Benatar claims),[342] but even a very *suitable* standpoint.

The course of this chapter is going to be the following: First, I am going to concisely explain my interpretation of the concept of *antinatalism in a broader sense of the word* on the one hand and *antinatalism in a narrow sense of the word* on the other. In the second section, I am going to introduce those parts of Solovyov's philosophy that are necessary to get familiar with in order to understand the subsequent interpretation. By those parts I mean Solovyov's philosophy of history and its related concept of godman-

---

[341] Hereby I warmly thank to Radim Chvaja, who helped me to bring this chapter into the world.

[342] *"My arguments are not as incompatible with religious thinking as many people might think"* (Benatar, 2006, p. 16).

hood (*bogochelovechestvo, богочеловечество*),[343] as well as the resulting axiology demonstrated in Solovyov's *Three Conversations,*[344] which is a work situated on the boundary between literature and philosophy.

In the third and the most extensive part, I am going to focus on specific themes of Solovyov's philosophy that are, in my opinion, related to the topic of antinatalism. Such topics are: conceiving a child, bringing the next generations to the world, or also, a requirement of an ascetic life, which is an assumption for achieving eternity. During that part, I am also going to compare Solovyov's standpoint with Benatar's. This also means, at a more general level, comparing antinatalism in a broader sense of the word with antinatalism in a narrow sense of the word, as I defined them previously.

ANTINATALISM IN THE BROAD AND IN THE NARROW SENSE OF THE WORD

As Coates states, antinatalism has become more and more popular in recent times, while the antinatalistic movement is increasing its power and popularity as well. However, different authors understand it differently: some of them distinguish between Christian and atheistic antinatalism, others identify its predecessor in Buddhism. Not all of them consider antinatalism to be a current movement, for someone it is rather just a *concept* that we can attempt to apply on systems of thinkers who died long time ago.[345]

It seems to me that for clear conceptual work, it will be better to distinguish two types of antinatalism. On the one hand, we can think of antinatalism as in narrow sense of the word while on the other hand, we can understand it in the broader sense. The representative of the former is especially David Benatar who indeed invented the contemporary conception. Another author who falls into this category is Christian thinker Martin Smith, who wrote *No Baby No Cry.*[346] The narrow-sense antinatalism is considered wholly as a philosophical conception or at least a worldview where the idea of extinction of mankind is the central theme. This is to be achieved by ending childbearing, in other words, by ending the production of the next generation. Furthermore, philanthropic goal hidden behind the requirement of extinction is also important for the definition of the term. The goal is to decrease the suffering in the world to zero. It

---

[343] For more about this term and metaphysical concept see Solovyov (1902 or 1926).
[344] Id. (1903, pp. 453–582).
[345] Coates (2014, pp. 234, 319).
[346] Smith (2013).

seems that antinatalism in the narrow sense is characterized also by Benatar's asymmetry argument[347] as well as by claiming that life has no (absolute) meaning.[348] And it is this type of antinatalism, which has emerged in recent years, has been growing into a movement that gains supporters not only among philosophers.

Antinatalism in the broader sense of the word shares with the former mainly the rejection of the procreation of children, or more precisely the refusal to bring the new generations to the world. Moreover, philanthropic goals are also of considerable interest in this type of antinatalism. Nevertheless, what could be different is the identification of what *philanthropic* means. It does not need to be the extinction of mankind, especially if the aforementioned assumptions, which I have described as fundamental to Benatar, are invalid. The philanthropic goal may be, for example, reduction of the population, which should lead to a better quality of life. In this case we could talk about *temporary* or *incomplete* antinatalism. However, antinatalism can have other goals that may be surprisingly different, as I try to show later in next but one sub-chapter.

It is also necessary to say that the thinkers we can include in the group of antinatalists in this broader sense may not stress the idea of rejection of bringing life into the world nor understand it as a central within their philosophical systems. With the conception defined in the latter way, we can say that antinatalism is not only a matter of recent years, but we can find it in the theories of many older thinkers. Benatar himself refers to several of them by quoting their statements at beginnings of his chapters.[349] These statements of Benatar confirm it is not surprising that people experiencing the misery think of death. And from here it is just a step to wish never to be born. It is understandable that similar considerations appeared in the history hundreds to thousands of years ago.[350] However, Benatar (and Schopenhauer before him) worked on this topic systematically.

At the beginning, let me mention one quotation from the work by a Czech philosopher and writer Ladislav Klíma, whose prince Sternenhoch suffers[351] in the novel and at one moment speaks similarly as antinatalists: he would rather die immediately after birth.[352] I chose this quotation mainly because Klíma was in many ways inspired by Schopenhauer, although he did not, unlike his prince Sternenhoch, share Schopenhauer's pessimism. Klíma, among other things, was one of the first authors who reflected Solovyov's *The justification of the Good:*[353]

---

[347] Benatar (2006, p. 30).

[348] *I do not have in my mind any partial meaning etc.* (Ibid., p. 82).

[349] Ibid. (pp. 18, 60, 93, 163).

[350] For example, in plays of ancient author Sophocles (Ibid., pp. 18, 212).

[351] The novel itself is called *The Sufferings of Prince Sternenhoch* (Klíma, 2000).

[352] Apparently, he does not get the idea never to be born yet.

[353] Klíma (1993). See also Solovyov (1918 and 2010).

"Blessed is the one who breathes his last after the first few blows, still more blessed the one who, by a single swish of the scourge as thick as a beam, meets his end – ideally, right after birth."[354]

Now, when I suggested how antinatalism could be (and should be) understood, I will deal with Solovyov's contribution to the broader conception. However, at first I will introduce his philosophy in a nutshell.

SOLOVYOV'S PHILOSOPHY OF HISTORY, CONCEPT OF GODMANHOOD AND AXIOLOGY

Vladimir Solovyov is generally considered a first Russian philosopher.[355] This primacy is attributed to him because he was, among other things, the first Russian thinker who created highly systematic and very comprehensive conception with original elements. He is also author of an original conception of philosophy of history. He connected some selected Darwin's ideas with Christian teaching. Nevertheless, it is necessary to mention that Solovyov's attitudes towards Darwin were rather negative and he disagreed with his conception as a whole.[356] Similar synthesis was made 20 years later by Pierre Teilhard de Chardin, who is better known in Western Europe. However, he did it probably completely independently of Solovyov.

I introduce Solovyov's conception of history because, through it, we can easier understand his axiology and ethics as well as some certain parts of his work that I interpret as antinatalistic. According to Solovyov, history is a part of the cosmological process, specifically the part that begins with the emergence of the human species. He accepts that evolution formed and shaped the human species and it was preceded by a long process; the development of organic life from inorganic matter, then the evolution of more complex organisms from simpler ones etc. However, the cosmological process is not completed by the emergence of man, rather it continues by historical development that lies in improving man morally and ends in the moment when man becomes perfect. He called this state godmanhood.[357] At this moment, the kingdom of heaven and

---

[354] Klíma (2000, p. 79).

[355] This statement is valid only when we distinguish between term *Russian philosophy* and *philosophy on Russian territory* (Feber and Petrucijová, 2015, p. 6).

[356] For example, the process of evolution is not blind, according to Solovyov, but it has its own teleological goal.

[357] It should be mentioned that it is the opposite of the superman state. Solovyov, in fact, argues against Nietzsche's conception of supermanhood. Contrary, he wants humans to become similar to the God through humble following of Jesus Christ.

immortality for man's body and soul occur, not for the individuals but for humanity as a whole (the condition is to achieve the all-unity; *vseedinstvo; всеединство*).

The process of improvement requires an active contribution from a person, however, it is not possible to determine when mankind achieves perfection and therefore, we cannot demand perfect morality so far. We cannot judge the imperfect person for not being able to fulfill all the standards like we would expect from the fully developed godman. Solovyov explicitly changes the Christian formula *be perfect* to *become perfect*.[358] Therefore, we cannot judge man for not being perfect, but we can condemn them for not trying to improve. Solovyov claims: "*(...) other people's actions in this sphere we may not judge – we may only judge their principles.*"[359] He deals with the issue of perfection in many parts of his work. I choose this quote mainly because *in this sphere* refers to the topic that I am going to deal with in the next sub-chapter: the area of sexual love and shame.

To the same extent, of course, we can judge moral behavior, according to Solovyov, but this is connected with his concept of determinism and punishment only as a remedy or prevention. However, I am interested in other consequences resulting from the distinction between perfect and imperfect. I mean the consequences for axiology.

Solovyov distinguishes between actual and absolute values, this distinction is very important for him – he even devotes one whole book to it (namely *Three Conversations*). However, we can find this distinction in many other places in his work – especially in his book *The Justification of the Good* – because it is an important distinguishing element in his interpretation of morality and moral philosophy.

He demonstrates the differences between absolute and actual on several examples. One of them is a war. Solovyov deals with the war theme in *Three Conversations*, but also in *The Justification of the Good*, where there is one chapter named *The Significance of War*.[360] When we speak about war, we generally understand it to be an evil. The character of General, however, introduces few examples from his own experience, where war should be considered to be a good – and other participants of the discussion agree with him.

Nevertheless, General's truth is partial and, therefore, valid only for a particular situation. It is important to realize that war cannot be absolutely good, or be good *in itself*. In other words: this *true* does not apply in an ideal situation and in perfect conditions. However, as long as perfection is not achieved, certain situations require compromise, and war may be a good in some cases such as defense against an attack. It follows

---

[358] Solovyov (1918, chap. 2.8.5, p. 168).
[359] Ibid. (chap. 1.2.6, p. 53).
[360] Ibid. (pp. 385–408).

then, that war can never be good in absolute sense, but it can only serve as an actual good. And in a similar way we can, of course, think of other examples:

"(...) Neither of them take the good in its essence, or as it is in itself, but connect it with acts and relations which may be either good or evil according to their motive and their end. In other words, they take something which is good, but which may become evil, and they put it in the place of the Good itself, treating the conditioned as the unconditional."[361]

As we can see, the distinction between good and evil is not so simple. If it were easy to distinguish between them, Solovyov would probably not need to write his *Three Conversations*. In this work, he shows not only the absolute good and the actual good, but also the supposed good and the supposed evil. The supposed evil is a good that we wrongly identify as evil, and on the contrary, the supposed good is an evil hidden behind the mask of good.[362] Demonstration of the latter is *The Short Tale of the Antichrist*.[363] The character of Antichrist is considered a superman in the beginning of the novel. The problem is that his goodness is only the supposed one because he does not follow Jesus Christ. Hence, this good is revealed as evil in the end, it brought only death to man.[364]

The idea of development is so important for Solovyov that he does not describe only the current state neither future visions, but he deals with past development of humankind and its institutions. It is necessary to distinguish whether he speaks of absolute values, an ideal state, or whether he is judging any fact in the historical or imperfect state. If we read inappropriately, we may find that Solovyov contradicts himself because the truth (or goodness) of other content may take on different situations. Thus, with the understanding of Solovyov's philosophy, we can move on to his particular thoughts connected with antinatalism. We will see how antinatalism stems from Solovyov's specific ethical principles.

---

[361] Solovyov (1918, Preface to the First Edition, part V, pp. XXVIIIn.).
[362] For detailed interpretation of this distinction see Tenace (1993).
[363] This story is part of *Three Conversations* (Solovyov, 1903, p. 556).
[364] The relationship of good and evil is similar in Dostoevsky's *The Brothers Karamazov* (1981). Dostoevsky's Grand Inquisitor represents the type of antichrist and his legend demonstrates the same difference between good and evil.

FROM ETHICAL NORM TO ANTINATALISM

Let us now focus on Solovyov's ethics. He summarizes it in his work *The Justification of the Good*, which consists of three parts: *Good in human nature, Good from God* and *Good through the history of mankind*. Marina Kostalevsky accurately names the issues of those three parts:

"The first part examines the question of natural human morality, that is, organic and imperfect, the second part discusses the perfection of good in God, and the third part is devoted to the process of perfection (or the concordance of the imperfection in human nature with the perfection of God) as the goal of life."[365]

This quotation, in my opinion, sums up perfectly what I described in the first sub-chapter, namely the distinction between eternal and temporal, absolute and historical, perfect and imperfect, and a distinction between the corresponding values. I should mention that the improvement that I spoke of as a kind of norm here lies mainly in the aiming to the God, or in following Christ in particular. However, it is only a general formulation. Solovyov develops his ethics, which is anchored in this Christ following, in detail. Among other things, he explains how the idea of the good determines us, how one knows what norms to follow in his life or what the human dispositions for it are. He examines these issues in the first part of his *The Justification of the Good*.

In the part named *Good and human nature*, Solovyov describes three emotions, the foundations of morality in particular, that are given to a person and which help them to recognize what is good and what is not.[366] There are three foundations: shame, pity (or compassion), and religious feeling. As follows, there are moral principles derived from each of these three emotions: principle of ascetism, principle of altruism, and the religious principle. We can achieve good life only when we follow them simultaneously. It is the emotion of shame that finally lead us to a topic that is of special interest to us. This moral foundation governs us to live ascetically in many aspects of our lives.

But Solovyov argues that material nature is not the subject matter of shame. Rather, what matters is that our bodily needs should not control the spiritual part of us.[367] This is mainly about the *nutrition and reproduction*.[368] I am focusing on the latter point as Solovyov rejects the physical love based on it. This fact itself does not mean that we are dealing with antinatalism. However, it aims towards antinatalism in the case of Solo-

[365] Kostalevsky (1997, p. 171).
[366] The only problem is that we do not know how to perfectly follow them yet. This is one of the explanations of why we do not always act morally.
[367] Solovyov (1918, chap. 1.2.1n.).
[368] Ibid. (chap. 1.2.5, p. 49).

vyov. Nevertheless, comparing this Solovyov's approach with Benatar's we can argue that they are opposite to each other. It is because sex that does not lead to procreation is, according to Benatar, rather positive than negative due to its increase of pleasure in the world.[369]

Solovyov, however, does not bind the request for the abandonment of sexual life not only with shame and asceticism, but partly with pity (or compassion), altruism, and with religiousness because, according to him, it is "(...) *destructive of human love and life (...),*" and thus, "(...) *we must adopt the path that leads to its limitation and abolition.*"[370] The reason why physical *love* is wrong is not only the fact that, according to Solovyov, it destroys true love, but also that it supports the cycle of life and death. And death is one of the worst manifestations of evil.

According to Solovyov, the cycle of life and death, the alternation of generations, is "*bad, empty infinity.*"[371] The task of this cycle is to preserve the genus, not the individual. In Solovyov's opinion, however, it is not dignified for human being because they are a *super-animal* and even *super-natural* person:

"(...) *To be merely a means or an instrument of the natural process by which the blind life-force perpetuates itself at the expense of separate entities that are born and perish and replace one another in turn. Man as a moral being does not want to obey this natural law of replacement of generations, the law of eternal death. He does not want to be that which replaces and is replaced. He is conscious – dimly at first – both of the desire and the power to include in himself all the fulness of the infinite life.*"[372]

Thus, Solovyov does not reject only the bodily act itself, as well as the resulting procreation, but he rejects the bodily act *because*, among other reasons, it leads to bringing children into the world. Older generations, according to him, are replaced by new generations, childbirth brings death that is the evil and suffering. Therefore, participating on this perpetuation of birth and death is immoral. The rejection of bringing new generations into the world is made in order to decrease suffering, which we can consider to be an antinatalistic idea. Nevertheless, the goal is not the extinction of mankind that would completely end all hardships as Benatar argues. The aim is to reach the immortality (eternal life) that keeps man from the biggest suffering by protecting them from death. As I mentioned in the previous sub-chapter, this immortality concerns soul as well as body, it is the doctrine of the resurrection.[373]

---

[369] Benatar (2006, p. 126).
[370] Solovyov (1918, chap. 1.2.6, p. 53).
[371] Ibid. (chap. 2.7.3, p. 138).
[372] Ibid. (chap. 2.7.4, p. 138).
[373] Id. (1926).

Solovyov, however, in accordance with Christian teaching, admits that children are good for mother and father,[374] in some ways also for society, and finally for children themselves (which the strict antinatalist would certainly disagree with[375]): *"(...) And is of course also good for those who receive the gift of life."*[376] Klíma criticizes this (ostensible, as we will see later) contradiction in Soloyvov's philosophy. He says: *"(...) The childbirth is both evil and good at the same time."*[377] I explained in the previous sub-chapter why something could seem to be both good and evil simultaneously in Solovyov's conception. Klíma misinterpreted Solovyov because he did not distinguish between the values of childbearing in absolute terms and values that procreation could gain during the human history.

Solovyov himself was aware of this paradox in his philosophy: *"There is a great contradiction here, a fatal antinomy, which must be recognised even if there is no hope of solving it."*[378] However, finally he found the solution:

"This is the solution of fatal antinomy: the evil of child-bearing may be abolished by child-bearing itself, which through this becomes a good. (...) But the evil, of natural way for man only be put right by man himself, and what has not been done by the man of the present may be done by the man of the future, who, being born in the same way of the animal nature, may renounce it and change the law of life."[379]

Hereby Solovyov argues that, until (and unless) we are perfect, childbirth is good. The reason is that, by doing that, we bring a new people into the world who can[380] move toward achievement of godmanhood and overcome the cyclic law of nature by which an *"(...) earthly nature builds up life upon dead bones – for ever, but in vain."*[381] Solovyov offers yet another slightly different explanation:

"If the Divine Wisdom, according to its wont, brings forth out of evil a greater good and uses our carnal sins for the sake of perfecting humanity by means of new generations, this, of course, tends to its glory and to our comfort, but not to our justification. It treats in exactly the same way all other evils, but this fact cancels neither the distinction between good and evil nor the obligatoriness of the former for us."[382]

---

[374] Solovyov (1918, chap. 2.1.5, p. 141).

[375] Benatar (2006, p. 97).

[376] Solovyov (1918, chap. 2.1.5, p. 141).

[377] Klíma (1993, pp. 115n.).

[378] Solovyov (1918, chap. 2.7.6, p. 141).

[379] Ibid. (chap. 2.7.6, p. 141).

[380] Instead of us, if we are not able.

[381] Solovyov (1918, chap. 2.7.4, p. 139).

[382] Ibid. (chap. 1.2.6, p. 54).

Thus, on the one hand, procreation is the evil when we treat it in absolute sense of the term, on the other hand, it could be actual good in certain situation. (Or, in other words, the Divine Wisdom creates the good from the evil.) The hierarchy of values is, however, obvious because the absolute good will always exceed all supposed goods, which may turn to evil under certain conditions: *"Marriage is approved and sanctified, child-bearing is blessed, and celibacy is praised as 'the condition of the angels'."*[383]

Solovyov is willing to admit several generations to achieve the desired goal because the godmanhood can only be achieved in development that is highly time-consuming.[384] Similarly, Benatar is willing to admit several generations to achieve the extinction of human species without excessive pain. In other words, Benatar is also willing to admit some evil to avoid greater evil that are, according to him, generations of old childless people without anybody who can take care of them while the suffering of those generations increases.[385]

Nonetheless, Solovyov had to cope with the objection that other Christian writers proposing a life of asceticism as valuable had already faced. Their opponents had claimed that such an ascetic life must necessary lead to the extinction of mankind, rather than to godmanhood and immortality. Masaryk made subsequent notion to this issue: *"Finally, he is criticized, that his doctrine disagrees with the Bible – although it agrees with some of Church Fathers. Solovyov actually draws the conclusions that E. von Hartmann came to. Solovyov calls for total sexual abstinence, but the extinction of mankind would not be contrary to his standpoint."*[386]

Solovyov himself considers this objection to be foolish and explains that, as long as generational perpetuation is necessary, it will not happen that all people will quit producing offspring. Conversely, when mankind as a whole reaches the ideal of ascetic life, the historical process will complete itself and kingdom of heaven will come consequently.[387] To be sure, I would like to add explicitly here that asceticism is not the result of the transformation of the human state into the state of godmanhood, but rather its assumption, which means that it is realized before eternity is reached. Solovyov comments this objection as follows:

"So long as the change of generations is necessary for the development of the human kind, the taste for bringing that change about will certainly not disappear in man. (...) As

---

[383] Solovyov (1918, chap. 1.2.6, p. 53). The original wording (with connector *but*) is clearer: *"Брак одобряется и освящается, деторождение благословляется, а безбрачие превозносится как «ангелское житие"* (id., 2010, p. 139).

[384] However, Solovyov is not able to determine how much time it takes.

[385] Benatar (2006, p. 184).

[386] Masaryk (1996, p. 198). Translation by the author.

[387] However, asceticism is not the only one condition.

if any one, in surrendering to the desire of the flesh, had ever thought of safeguarding thereby the future of humanity!"[388]

There is an apparent inspiration in Schopenhauer as well as the same sense of sarcasm. As already stated, Schopenhauer says: *"If children were brought into the world by an act of pure reason alone, would the human race continue to exist? Would not a man rather have so much sympathy with the coming generation as to spare it the burden of existence?"*[389] Whereas Schopenhauer's statement ends pessimistically, Solovyov's philosophy does not, although he remains critical.

So far, we can sum up Solovyov's attitude to be antinatalistic at the following points in a nutshell. He considers procreation itself to be an evil because it results in death and suffering. Elimination of this suffering is the reason to reject procreation. However, he is willing to admit mankind to reach the all-unity and godmanhood through the cycle of generations under certain conditions. It should be mentioned, nevertheless, that antinatalism seems to be a part in comprehensive work on ethics only, rather than the central idea of his work. It is namely because the condition of ascetic life is one of many others.

Even the goals are not shared among Solovyov and Benatar. However, this claim depends on the level of generality in formulation of these goals. While Benatar is arguing for extinction, Solovyov assumes that the kingdom of heaven will come, although both of them develop their argumentation framed into philanthropical intentions. Nevertheless, the argumentation of both of them is based on different assumptions. First of all, Solovyov argues against questioning the meaning of life but certainly he would also disagree with the assumptions necessary for the asymmetry argument to be correct. The absence of the good is definitely wrong. Solovyov uses it to explain the existence of the evil in the world. Although this Solovyov's explanation is in fact more complicated, we can claim, simply put, that the absence of the good is equal to the evil.[390]

This imaginary equation should be valid even in the case of non-existence of mankind or, better to say, in the case of non-existence of someone who would experience the good. And the non-existence of mankind, life as a whole itself in particular, would be evil as well. However, thinking about a Christian writer, it should not surprise us.[391] It should not be surprising, indeed, that Solovyov even defends the meaning of life, in the absolute sense of the word, and finds it in God. However, he uses some interesting

---

[388] Solovyov (1918, chap. 1.2.6, p. 54).

[389] Schopenhauer (2005, p. 7).

[390] We must be aware that Benatar operates in his asymmetry argument with different concepts: the absence of pleasure on the one hand and the absence of suffering on the other hand. To disprove his asymmetry would be more complicated. However, for Solovyov pleasure or absence of pain in this sense are not the goal, he could not agree with asymmetry argument.

[391] Solovyov is undoubtedly a Christian thinker, and so are all the Russian philosophers in the sense I mentioned (Feber and Petrucijová, 2015, p. 7).

arguments and examples to support his conclusions. I find it useful to mention them here because when examining those arguments we encounter similar issues as Benatar or Schopenhauer did.

According to Solovyov, suicides prove the meaning of life, and not only in case of those *practicing* suicides who really kill themselves, but also in case of those who theorize about it while never committing it. Those *practicing* suicides do not think of killing themselves because of the fact, that life is meaningless, but rather because they have not discovered the real meaning of life. Instead, they were trying to achieve the supposed meaning. This supposed sense brought them unhappiness only, which in turn led them to commit suicide. Those, who have never committed suicide but only think about it, contradict themselves when they claim that life is meaningless while they still remain alive. This, however, proves that life has a meaning.

Solovyov also responds to possible objections, one of which is the objection that some kind of instinct keeps those suicidal *theorists* out of killing themselves. Solovyov replies that it does not matter whether it is an instinct or something else. He claims that if it makes our life desirable or if it can overcome pessimism, then it also denies the understanding of life as misfortune and evil. Hence, the *phenomena* of human psychology such as the Pollyanna Principle[392] would not be an argument for extinction of humankind. Conversely, he would consider them to be the arguments for preservation of human species as well as life in its whole.

In dialog with himself, Solovyov introduces another objection. Even if we were to count those instincts as a kind of pleasure, still it will be true that there is more misery than happiness in human life. His answer consists of two parts: First, these values are incalculable and incomparable. Second, even if they were not incomparable and the misery outbalanced the happiness in our life, it would not question the meaning of life because it is not about the pleasure as such. It should be said, however, that Solovyov operates only with the concept of *life, which is not worth living,*[393] but this should be understandable in the discussion of suicide. In the case of man who has already been born, it does not make any sense to discuss the concept of *life worth beginning.*

Different goals and assumptions indicate that Solovyov cannot be considered to be an antinatalist in the narrow sense of the word. However, I suggest that he is an antinatalist in the broader sense or that, at least, we can find significant antinatalistic elements in his philosophy. I am aware of the fact that to classify Solovyov in such a way is determined by my own definitions of two conceptions of antinatalism introduced in the previous but one sub-chapter. Hence, I attempted to make that distinction to be suitable and acceptable.

---

[392] Psychologists describe the Pollyanna Principle as a psychological phenomenon that causes our inclination toward optimism (Benatar, 2006, pp. 64–67).

[393] Solovyov (1918, p. XVII); Benatar (2006, pp. 37, 40).

CONCLUSION

In this chapter, I briefly introduced antinatalism *in the broader sense and in the narrow sense* of the word. The representative of the former is primarily David Benatar. The first aim of my argumentation, then, was to show that the 19th century Russian philosopher Vladimir Sergeevich Solovyov could be considered to be an antinatalist, however, not in the same sense as Benatar is. Hence, I characterized Solovyov's philosophy on a very general level in order to explain those parts of his teaching that concern the topic of antinatalism and thus to be able to assess whether it is really antinatalism.

I suggested why Solovyov should be considered to be an antinatalist. The reason is that he rejects to bring new generations into the world because this causes perpetuation of life and death, while death is a kind of suffering. He also, similarly to Benatar, admits the birth of several generations to avoid undesirable consequences resulting from the premature or rapid *implementation* of antinatalism in society. However, the goals of both thinkers are different. While Benatar's goal is to make human species extinct, Solovyov believes in eternity – and this is probably the biggest difference between them as well as the reason to refer to Solovyov as to antinatalist in the broader sense of the word.

The second aim of this chapter was to show how it is possible to be antinatalist while believing in God, in man and in absolute meaning of life simultaneously. Solovyov being undoubtedly a Christian thinker is primarily confirmed by his claim to follow Christ, his belief in the kingdom of heaven and Good, but also his conviction that evolution and the universe itself is a teleological phenomenon. I argued that antinatalism could be not only conceivable for a Christian thinker but, in Solovyov's view, it is even the only possible approach. Nonetheless, Solovyov himself would probably not classify his own approach in the abovementioned way. Therefore, doing this we have to specify under what kind of antinatalism we subsume him. Without doing this we are misinterpreting and overgeneralizing.

However, it is important to remember that although Solovyov's and Benatar's objectives are at first glance different, they in fact are the same. We can generally express them as philanthropic goals: the elimination of suffering. Both loved a man. Benatar loves the *existing* people. He expressed it not only in his dedication, where he talks about his brothers.[394] Solovyov was a well-known philanthropist who consistently applied his moral philosophy in his life. Not only was he ascetic, he was also an altruist who gave away everything he had.

---

[394] Benatar means that the existing people are beloved, although existence cause harm to them: "*(...) To my brothers, each of whose existence, although a harm to him, is a great benefit to the rest of us*" (2006, pp. V, 223.)

Let us summarize the most important point that we should remember from his philosophy for our philanthropic endeavors: You cannot *"take something which is good, but which may become evil,"* and *"put it in the place of the Good itself, treating the conditioned as unconditional."*[395]

---

[395] Solovyov (1918, Preface to the First Edition, part V, pp. XXVIIIn.).

KURNIG AND HIS NEO-NIHILISM:
THE FIRST MODERN ANTINATALIST

INTRODUCTION

There is a good reason to assume that if one subtracted the metaphysics of will from Schopenhauer's proto-antinatalistic philosophy, some non-metaphysical antinatalism would ensue. Therefore, one might suspect that after the decline of Schopenhauer's metaphysics of the will, a modern antinatalist might have taken up the respective systematic place. As a matter of fact, there is at least one such philosopher. He wrote under pseudonyms such as Quartus and finally published his antinatalistic writings under the pseudonym of Kurnig. Some indications in Kurnig's writings suggest that he made a living as a medical doctor.[396] Otherwise we know very little of him except for the following remarks according to which he was a well-travelled man: In Bethlehem he saw the places where Jesus was active. He visited mosques in Africa and Turkey. On Ceylon, in India, China and Japan he stood still in front of Buddha's image.[397] One more personal attribute which Kurnig reveals to his readers is his atheism.[398]

It was only in November 2019, more than a year after having finished my study on Kurnig, that I read Francis Ronsin's book on the topic of the birth strike, thus becoming aware of what follows: *"A German named Kurnig spreads very original propaganda throughout Europe, from Heilbronn am Neckar, based on what he calls Neo-Nihilism and the total rejection of procreation. Since 1896, he has distributed a first brochure in French: Nouvelle appréciation de l'instinct sexuel (pessimisme, jurisprudence, psychiatrie), in which he claims to be inspired by Schopenhauer's work and, in particular, by his chapter on the metaphysics of sexual instinct. Kurnig's efforts to influence thought in France would continue for several years. Having founded an international educational consul-*

---

[396] See Kurnig's self-referential quotation of Byron: *"(...) I have shown kindness to men (...)"* (Kurnig, 1903, p. 51, fn.) as well as his many references to the medical profession.
[397] Ibid. (p. 51, fn.).
[398] Cf. ibid. (pp. 84n.).

ting centre in Heilbronn, he published a new manifesto: Neo-Nihilism-Anti-Militarism-Sexual Life (End of Humanity), which he distributed free of charge in a large number of copies, particularly among French teachers. (...) As for the synthesis he attempts to establish between nihilism and the rejection of childbirth, his work has most certainly influenced some French neo-Malthusians (in particular Marie Huot)."[399]

To my knowledge Kurnig is the first thinker who dedicated a whole book to antiprocreationism. In his time the term *antinatalism* was not yet in use as a label for the ethics of non-procreation. Kurnig defends an outspoken antinatalism, which – in the wake of Schopenhauer's ethics of compassion – aims at nothing less but a complete depopulation of the world. While it is true that Kurnig's thinking is deeply rooted in Schopenhauer's philosophy, as evinced by numerous quotations from Schopenhauer, his antinatalism is non-metaphysical. At the same time it also features an optimistic touch inasmuch as it presupposes growing insight: *"With increasing intelligence, mankind comes to realise that, all in all, suffering far outweighs pleasure, that it must stop procreation and must do so as soon as possible. Thus: NEO-NIHILISM."*[400]

Kurnig's optimism resides in his assumption that mankind on the whole displays increasing intelligence over the course of history. Since Kurnig published his *Neo-Nihilism* around the turn of the 20th century, before the First World War, we must in hindsight say that his optimism was exaggerated.

In what follows I want to make the reader familiar with a thinker who is extremely difficult to access. Not only because he published under a pseudonym – but also because his writings seem to have been out of print for a long time with only a few copies available second hand or in libraries. In addition to this, his *Neo-Nihilism* is printed in Gothic script, which even members of the German language community have difficulty reading.

Let me first present the philanthropic character, the modernity, and the radicality of Kurnig's antinatalism through a series of quotations.

To those who – in the face of human suffering and the inevitable death experience – expressly adhere to procreation, Kurnig replies:

"You think you're saying and doing something pretty strong, beautiful, full of character, don't you? But do you know what it is? Weakness of character and ignorance. I mourn the creatures you bring into the world who could not defend themselves when you created them, who otherwise would have protested out loud against your action. Since it all boils down to suffering and destruction. Our race serves nothing and exists only as a result of

---

[399] Ronsin (1980, p. 118).
[400] Kurnig (1903, last page).

those who, like you, do not examine things thoroughly. Life is suffering; to abstain from procreation is philanthropy and duty."[401]

Since his view amounts to self-annihilation of mankind, and many will associate this with violence, Kurnig anticipates the accusation of defending a violent view by saying: *Not by violent means (murder, war and the like), but peacefully, let mankind disappear from our globe.*"[402] Kurnig accuses optimistic philosophers of both the present and past of not thinking through "*(...) a topic of supreme importance such as an existence that is forced upon man. This alone is enough to condemn their erroneous philosophizing. They live, as it were, in a fatal circle, in the stupor of eternal procreation.*"[403]

The determination with which Kurnig defends antinatalism is evidenced in the following quotations: "*The silence of some of us may not confuse us. Because of external circumstances many are not allowed to admit that they are pessimists and, therefore, not prepared to have children.*"[404] "*It is better to accept martyrdom in whatever form – which is connected to non-procreation – than to procreate.*"[405] To those who experienced hardships in their lives because they never had children, Kurnig offers the following consolation: "*Never to have procreated – this be your consolation when you die.*"[406]

Even though Kurnig may well have been the first thinker ever to dedicate a whole book to antinatalism it makes sense to speak of predecessors.

ANTINATALISTIC PREDECESSORS

While it is true that Kurnig is the first outspoken modern antinatalist I know of,[407] there may be earlier ones and other antinatalists still to be discovered. Perhaps they published in foreign or non-European languages; perhaps they were hushed up early on. As is the case for the history of ideas in general, language barriers constitute a considerable problem also for the history of antinatalism. Most contributions to antinatalism are of recent date, written in the English-speaking world with authors who sometimes appear to read no other languages than English and who are thus cut off from non-English contributions to proto-antinatalism and antinatalism in past and present.

---

[401] Kurnig (1993, p. 84).
[402] Ibid. (p. 51).
[403] Ibid. (p. 73).
[404] Ibid. (p. 126, fn.).
[405] Ibid. (p. 57).
[406] Ibid. (p. 92, cf. p. 139 and 156).
[407] Cf. my short presentation published on 1 June 2015 in the online magazine tabula rasa (Akerma, 2015); see also Akerma (2017, pp. 396nn.).

A good case in point is the Norwegian philosopher Zapffe (1899–1990), who features as the first modern antinatalist in Ken Coates' intriguing account of rejectionist philosophies and antinatalism: *"But it is Zapffe who must be credited as being the first rejectionist to come up with the idea of anti-natalism as the way out of existence for humans."*[408] In discussions on the internet Zapffe's voluminous book *Om det tragiske* (*On the Tragic*) is sometimes heralded as antinatalism's yet unexploited Holy Grail. Upon closer inspection, however, the book contains but a few truly antinatalistic statements.[409] Since Kurnig and Zapffe have a common denominator, and are both responding to a given demand, towards the end of this chapter I will present English translations of some of Zapffe's antinatalistic utterances from *Om det tragiske*.

In his reflections on modern antinatalism Coates continues with the following remark: *"Although Zapffe was also an anti-natalist, Benatar is unique in his focus on procreation and in his strong advocacy of anti-natalism on philosophical grounds."*[410] Since Kurnig has dedicated a whole book to antinatalism, what Coates says about Benatar also applies to Kurnig. It will apply to Kurnig until maybe someday we discover an as of yet unknown or hushed up thinker who anticipated Kurnig's antinatalism. While the protohistory of antinatalism can be traced back well into antiquity and other worldly religions, even Kurnig's antinatalism is not solitary. He aligns himself with Schopenhauer. Although he has other antinatalistic predecessors as well, he does not seem to be familiar with them:

Pseudo-Humboldt

In 1861 a previously unknown author published the alleged memoirs of Alexander von Humboldt (1769–1859). I quote from the presumptive forgery: *"'I am not cut out to be a family man. I also believe that marriage is a sin, and the production of children a crime.' Whoever marries with the intention to procreate is 'a sinner because he gives life to children without being able to give them the certainty of happiness.'"*[411]

Edmond (1822–1896) and Jules (1830–1870) de Goncourt

The Goncourt brothers are not only namesakes for the *Prix Goncourt,* the most famous French literary prize, they are also early visionaries of a two-pronged ebbing away of mankind:

"How is it that in no epoch of history, in no place on earth, a sect of wise men has been formed with the aim of making human life die out in the face of the cruelty of its evils?

---

[408] Coates (2014, p. 245).
[409] Cf. Akerma (2017, pp. 664nn.).
[410] Coates (2014, pp. 264n.).
[411] Humboldt (1894, pp. 209n.).

Why is it that this end of mankind by abstention from procreation has not been preached? – Or, for the more hasty, by exploring and inventing in public chemistry laboratories possibilities for the most gentle suicide, where a combination of exhilarating gases would be taught that made a bout of laughter out of the transition from being to nonbeing?"[412]

Further down I will show that the Gnostics were such a *sect of wise men* propagating non-procreation. In the Humboldt memoires as well as in the Goncourts' journal one encounters an outspoken form of antinatalism. These utterances are, however, piecemeal and unsystematic. What Kurnig achieved – who may never have read *Humboldt* or de Goncourt – was to offer antinatalism as a moral device in order to end suffering.[413]

THE STRUCTURE OF THE BOOK NEO-NIHILISM

In a short text on a frontispiece Kurnig writes in November 1901: *"In view of the lively interest that Neo-Nihilism has already aroused in wider circles, I consider it my duty to offer my formerly published views (sometimes under deviating pseudonyms) to the thinking reader this time collected in a new form."* In 1903 *Der Neo-Nihilismus* was published in a second increased edition. Its subtitle reads *Anti-Militarism – Sexual Life (End of Mankind)*.

The book consists of two parts, with the second part being subdivided into three major sections. Part one (pp. 1–46) is called *Anti-Militarism: A Look into the Pedagogical Anarchy of the Present Day*. This part had formerly been published under the pseudonym of Quartus. Part two of Kurnig's Neo-Nihilism is subdivided into the following three major sections:

1   Sexual Life and Pessimism (pp. 49–92)
     [Here Kurnig makes clear that there is no contradiction between a sexual life and the abstention from procreation. Remarkably he does so way before the invention of reliable and accessible modern contraceptives.]

---

[412] *"Tous les systèmes, toutes les religions, toutes les idées sociales se sont produits ici-bas. Comment ne s'est-il pas formé, à aucune époque de l'histoire, à aucune place de la terre, une secte de sages pour laisser mourir la vie devant la férocité de ses maux? Comment n'a-t-elle pas été déjà prêchée cette fin de l'humanité, non seulement par l'abstention et la procréation, mais encore pour les plus pressés, par la recherche et l'invention du plus doux suicide, par l'institution d'écoles publiques de chimie, où serait enseignée une combinaison de gaz exhilarant, qui ferait un éclat de rire du passage du être au non-être?"* (Goncourt and Goncourt, 1868, p. 279). Translation by the author.

[413] Not only does Kurnig leave out of account animal suffering, he even ridicules the vegetarian diet of a critique (see Kurnig 1903, last part, pp. 17n.). For the relation between antinatalism and vegetarianism see Akerma (2014).

2   Sexual Life and Pessimism: New Contributions to Kurnig's Neo-Nihilismus – Dialogues and Fragments (pp. 95–161)
     [Kurnig here designs a number of dialogues in which different people discuss various aspects of his philosophy. He takes on an external perspective on his own teachings having the dialogue partners discuss Kurnig's views as if Kurnig were a stranger.]

3   The Pessimism of Others (pp. 165–192)
     [Here, Kurnig offers a list of pessimistic quotations.]

After page 192, the pagination starts anew offering a collection of criticism and Kurnig's replica on pages 1 to 24. This is followed by a short chapter entitled *Geogenie: Materials for a Description of the Earth's Origin in a Neo-Nihilistic Perspective.* Arranged as an essay for the first time by Kurnig on pages 25 to 30.

SCHOPENHAUER'S PROTO-ANTINATALISM

Throughout his antinatalistic writings Kurnig borrows from Schopenhauer.[414] But there is a clear cut with regard to the modernity of Kurnig's antinatalism. Even though we can provide a series of quotations suggesting that Schopenhauer was an early antinatalist, this is only valid with some reservations. Schopenhauer's antinatalistic utterances are overarched by his metaphysics of the will. One may, therefore, speak of Schopenhauer as a proto-antinatalist. The following quotation comes close to modern antinatalism though even here Schopenhauer's antinatalism is still embedded in his metaphysics of the will:

"Voluntary and complete chastity is the first step in asceticism or the denial of the will to live. It thereby denies the assertion of the will which extends beyond the individual life, and gives the assurance that with the life of this body, the will, whose manifestation it is, ceases. Nature, always true and naive, declares that if this maxim became universal, the human race would die out; and I think I may assume, in accordance with what was said in the Second Book about the connection of all manifestations of will, that with its highest manifestation, the weaker reflection of it would also pass away, as the twilight vanishes

---

[414] For an assessment of Schopenhauer's proto-antinatalism cf. *Schopenhauer als Verebbenstheoretiker/ Schopenhauer as theorist of mankind's ebbing away* (Akerma, 2000, chap. 11).

along with the full light. With the entire abolition of knowledge, the rest of the world would of itself vanish into nothing; for without a subject there is no object."[415]

In view of this quotation the question arises of why Schopenhauer did not espouse non-procreation more outspokenly? It looks as if there are two major answers to this question [(1) and (2)]:

1 Unlike Kurnig, Schopenhauer may have been of the opinion that non-procreation requires an overall renunciation from sexual activity which could be achieved only by marshalling all one's willpower. Against this background Schopenhauer may have treated the call to abstain from procreation in the same manner as he treated suicide: suicide as well as abstention from procreation can rightly be considered as extreme expressions of the will rather than a dismissal of the will. Kurnig, by contrast, is of the opinion *"that the cruelty of child production should be fought with determination and, as Kurnig has made clear, without sacrificing sexual pleasure."*[416]

Kurnig is justified in saying this since *preventive intercourse* or *facultative sterility* was not only widely practised at his time but also supported by a series of devices.[417] Particularly noteworthy is Wilhelm Mensinga's (1836–1910) invention of the occlusive pessary (a rubber cap with an elastic rim that seals the cervix and protects against pregnancy) which he tested before publishing the results of his anti-procreational research in 1882 under the pseudonym of C. Hasse in his *Über die facultative Sterilität vom prophylaktischen und hygienischen Standpunk [On Facultative Sterility from a prophylactic and hygienic point of view].*[418] Against this backdrop Kurnig seems entitled to say: *"Everything depends on good will; if you only want to satisfy the desire without procreating, then you will certainly succeed in the majority, the vast majority of cases."*[419]

2 Within the frame of these metaphysics of the will a second argument against antinatalism has been put forward by Eduard von Hartmann (1842–1906); subtextually it may have been anticipated and been present in Schopenhauer too. Hartmann was opposed to antinatalism since, according to him, evolution would

---

[415] Schopenhauer (1909a, pp. 486n.). Schopenhauer's presentation is prefigured in a strain of Gnostic thinking, namely in the Valentinian speculation as depicted by Hans Jonas: *"For if not only the spiritual condition of the human person but also the physical condition and very existence of the universe are constituted by the results of ignorance and as a substantialization of ignorance, then every individual illumination by 'knowledge' helps to abolish again the total system sustained by that principle"* (Jonas, 1963, p. 175).

[416] Kurnig (1903, p. 126).

[417] For an overview cf. e.g. The Family Planning Association (2010).

[418] See Mensinga (1882).

[419] Kurnig (1903, the last part, p. 5).

sooner or later bring about a new human-type being. Whereupon misery would begin anew.

Both interpretations as to why Schopenhauer did not espouse antinatalism are not too convincing since, with man having died out, all manifestations of the will would vanish – the will would *cease* as Schopenhauer says. Ultimately the fact that Schopenhauer does not espouse antinatalism remains a riddle.

CAUTIOUS OPTIMISM, ART, AND EXODUS FROM EXISTENCE

In his *Antimilitarismus* (first published in 1894 under the pseudonym Quartus, being part of Kurnig's edition from 1903) Kurnig explains his cautious optimism: had there been no progress, people would still burn witches. Against the background of moral progress Kurnig envisages a more peaceful confederation of states. Doing this, however, he has the following reservation undermining all full-fledged optimism. Even if there were to be a confederation of states, "*mankind will never achieve the blissful life once dreamed of by the Greeks. Rather, the most important thing will remain to be: getting through with as little pain and suffering as possible. Thus we are to procreate as little as possible in order to keep as small as possible, and to continually diminish, the number of sufferers. (...) The study of philosophy and the cult of beauty (in art) is the only means that will be able to warrant mankind relatively lasting satisfaction. And it will prepare mankind for an exodus from existence, as imagined by the saints in the religious sphere.*"[420]

BUDDHISM, HINDUISM, AND EARLY CHRISTIANITY AS MODELS

In line with Schopenhauer, Kurnig finds a model for his antinatalistic moral theory in original Christianity as well as in Asian religiosity. With respect to Brahmanism and Buddhism Schopenhauer had poignantly observed: "*The innermost kernel and spirit of Christianity is identical with that of Brahmanism and Buddhism; they all teach a great guilt of the human race through its existence itself, only that Christianity does not proceed*

---

[420] Kurnig (1903, p. 42).

directly and frankly like these more ancient religions: this does not make the guilt simply the result of existence itself, but makes it arise through the act of the first human pair."[421] In Schopenhauer's account of genuine Christianity, marriage is only a compromise and a concession to the sinful nature of man while celibacy and virginity are set up as the higher consecration.[422]

Let me first present Kurnig's thoughts on genuine Christianity followed by an account of his thoughts on Asian religion. This is against the chronological order, but, according to Kurnig, the Christian doctrine has already lost its antinatalistic impetus whereas, in his assessment, Buddhism and Hinduism will help to foster a modern spirit of depopulation.

Christianity

When Kurnig praises the sceptical spirit of early Christianity as regards reproduction, he is well aware of the following: "*One of my objections to Christianity has always been that it is not always clear enough about the repudiation of child production.*"[423] In its beginnings it was widely assumed that: "*After Christ mankind would soon cease to exist.*"[424] Then a departure from the pessimistic spirit of original Christianity occurred: "*The Jewish optimistic spirit and desire to have children became dominant.*"[425] Because of this Kurnig is in a position to confront his Christian contemporaries with a central finding of David Friedrich Strauss (1808–1874), who is also mentioned by Schopenhauer in Chapter XLVIII – entitled *On the Doctrine of the Denial of the Will to Live* – of his *The World as Will and Idea*.

Strauss published his sensational work *The Life of Jesus: Critically Examined* in the years 1835–36 and made the following remark in his *The Old Faith and the New* (published in 1872): "*So we must confess: we are no longer Christians.*"[426] Because Christianity – which originally was pessimistic and sceptical about reproduction against the background of an imminent end of the world – had long since been coloured optimistically by the subliminal continuing effect of Jewish beliefs, there were actually no more real Christians who, according to Luke, would have to endorse the following: "*The people of this age marry and are given in marriage. But those who are considered worthy of ta-*

---

[421] Schopenhauer (1909b, p. 410). For a confirmation of the view held by Schopenhauer cf. David Graeber in his book *Debt* where he summarises the kernel of the holy scriptures of the Brahmanas in such a way "*that human existence is itself a form of debt. (...) To live in debt is to be guilty, incomplete. But completion can only mean annihilation*" (2011, p. 1205).

[422] Cf. Schopenhauer (1909b, p. 426).

[423] Kurnig (1903, p. 56, fn.).

[424] Ibid. (p. 129).

[425] Ibid. (p. 130).

[426] Strauss (1872, p. 130).

king part in that age and in the resurrection from the dead will neither marry nor be given in marriage."[427]

In the accurate diagnosis of Kurnig (in all this borrowing from the account in chapter XLVIII of Schopenhauer's *The World as Will and Idea*) there is not much left of early Christianity's sceptical spirit with respect to procreation. In chapter XLVIII of his *The World as Will and Idea* Schopenhauer says: "*For not only the religions of the East, but also true Christianity, has that ascetic fundamental character throughout which my philosophy explains as the denial of the will to live; although Protestantism, especially in its present form, seeks to conceal this.*"[428] By and large adopting Schopenhauer's analyses, Kurnig points out that Christianity has lost its antinatalistic aspirations.

Asia as a Harbinger of a Complete Depopulation? – The Vedic Contradiction

While Christianity has long since lost most of its antinatalistic impulse, Kurnig believes that he is entitled to welcome the harbingers of a future depopulation of the earth in the guise of contemporary Buddhists and Hindus. In his replica to a review in *The Pionier* on 22 September 1897, he writes: "*(...) The vast majority of the earth's inhabitants pay homage to the pessimism of a gentle depopulation of our globe.*"[429] Here, Kurnig seems to commit the cardinal error of not distinguishing between Hindu priests or Buddhist monks, with the latter living in celibacy, on the one hand and their lay followers on the other, who rarely intend on giving up having descendants. Contrary to Kurnig's view, a considerable amount of Hindu teaching is even strongly pronatalistic. According to the Laws of Manu the begetting of a son is a religious duty the fulfilment of which contributes to the salvation of the father's soul.[430]

Elsewhere Kurnig describes what I would like to call the Vedic Contradiction. Far from paying homage to mankind's ebbing away, Buddhists and believers of Hindu religions follow a maxim that Kurnig himself has exposed as problematic: "*Beget a child such that it may be redeemed from existence – in other words, one is supposed to do something in order to make it undone.*"[431] In fact, a Buddhist – provided he does not believe in a persisting soul substance – would have difficulties in raising objections against Kurnig's irony: Inasmuch as Buddhism does not conceive of a persisting soul, there can be no pre-existing soul for which it would be an advantage to become incarnated.

A Hindu, however, who believes in reincarnation, might reply to Kurnig: While it is true that the Hindu parents are responsible for the fact that a person has to die, one must also consider that a human incarnation is an important stage for souls in order to find

---

[427] Lk. (20:34n.).
[428] Schopenhauer (1909b, p. 424).
[429] Kurnig (1903, p. 16).
[430] Cf. Reynolds and Tanner (1983, p. 42).
[431] Kurnig (1903, p. 135).

salvation. In sum it is probably safe to say that for the vast majority of Hindus und Buddhists throughout history a pronatalistic impetus resides in the belief that a prevented birth is a prevented rebirth.

KURNIG'S NEO-NIHILISM AS MODERN GNOSTICISM

Had Kurnig labelled his position *antiprocreationism* (by recourse to the word *procreation*, which he uses a lot) rather than *neo-nihilism*, we would then have a term today, which describes more clearly or more exclusively the meaning of the actually established term *antinatalism*, which played a role in population policy before it came to designate a moral theory.[432] In this context, I would like to mention the antinatalistic French thinker Annaba.[433] He used the term *antiprocreationism* rather than *antinatalism*. In 2008 Annaba looked back on 40 years of antiprocreationistic statements: *"For forty years you've been laughing at/my antinatalistic imprecations."*[434]

Kurnig, however, went for the term *neo-nihilism*: *"Neo-Nihilism is destined to become (...) the domain of reconciliation between the nihilistic elements in the teachings of Buddhism and Christianity on the one hand – and the optimistic spirit of culture on the other (...)."*[435] If Kurnig sees a positive tendency in human cultural development, he is optimistic in yet another respect. Against all the empty talk that life is just as it is, he formulates with the greatest justification: *"The pessimist does not admit that the tragedy of human life on earth is something unavoidable (...)."*[436] This is where the second strain of optimism resides within Kurnig's pessimism.

In spite of this, however, the term *neo-nihilism* is somewhat unfortunate inasmuch as Kurnig himself says about the anarchists and, in part, the nihilists[437] that they are almost

---

[432] Before the concept of *antinatalism* was used to designate a moral theory it had been used by historians such as Gisela Bock in her contribution *Antinatalism, Maternity and Paternity in National Socialist Racism* (1994). In her text Bock scrutinizes nazi antinatalism as being directed first and foremost against women and especially women of Jewish and Gypsy origin, many of whom became sterilized. There is a second usage of the concept of antinatalism – prior to designating a moral theory. It is in the domain of research on development policies from the 1970s and 1980s where we find the concept of *antinatalism* being used to discuss such topics as an antinatalistic population policy in a series of developing countries.

[433] Cf. Akerma (2017, pp. 85n.).

[434] *"Depuis quarante ans vous vous vous gaussez/De mes imprécations antiprocréationnistes"* (Annaba, 2008, p. 34).

[435] Kurnig (1903, last part, p. 24).

[436] Ibid. (p. 102).

[437] Cf. Ibid. (p. 109).

conservative in comparison with his teaching, since they are content with palliative so-cial changes: *"Anarchists, socialists, nihilists, optimistic philosophers – all content them-selves with palliatives."*[438] In fact, for Kurnig the sentence could be coined, following Marx: The critics only wanted to change the world in various ways, however – the point is to sublate it.

As shown above, Kurnig himself was well aware of the fact that he cannot appeal on Christianity as a non-ambiguous role model for his antiprocreationism. And it became clear that he was mistaken in invoking Buddhism and Hinduism as modern vehicles of his teachings in favour of non-procreation. Despite this Kurnig could well have appe-aled to another religion as a paragon that was at once nihilistic and antinatalistic: the Gnostic systems. According to the Gnostics the creator of this world is evil and the world is bad. In the teachings of the Gnostics, the creator of this world, the biblical God, is a mere demiurge. In Gnostic thinking the demiurge appears as a degraded *"symbol of cosmic oppression."*[439] The real and good God who is not responsible for this world resides outer worldly. He is the native land of the souls which, having been lured away from him, precipitated into this world and who will one day return to him – unless man continues the evil of procreation.

Schopenhauer – who is Kurnig's most important source with regard to the history of ideas – deals with Gnosticism in his presentation of church father Clement of Alexand-ria's (150–215) critique of the Gnostic religion. Schopenhauer is familiar with Clement's judgement of Marcion (~90–160), one of the main exponents of the Gnostic religion and gives the following account:

"(...) He [Clement] objects to the Marcionites that they find fault with the creation, after the example of Plato and Pythagoras; for Marcion teaches that nature is bad, made out of bad materials; therefore one ought not to people this world, but to abstain from mar-riage."[440]

Schopenhauer continues his account of Clement's critique against the Marcionites with a presentation of what Clement says about the Gnostics' handling of the ancient prin-ciple of *enkrateia* (*self-restraint*) which entails antinatalism:

"The same thing then takes place with regard to the second point, the εγκρατεια [en-krateia], through which, according to his view, the Marcionites show their ingratitude to-wards the demiurgus and the perversity with which they put from them all his gifts. Here now the tragic poets have preceded the Encratites (to the prejudice of their originality) and have said the same things. For since they also lament the infinite misery of existence,

---

[438] Kurnig (1903, p. 110).
[439] Jonas (1963, p. 93).
[440] Schopenhauer (1909b, p. 431).

they have added that it is better to bring no children into such a world; which he now once again supports with the most beautiful passages, while at the same time, accusing the Pythagoreans of having renounced sexual pleasure on these grounds. But all this does not touch him; he sticks to his principle that all of them sin against the demiurgus, in that they teach that one ought not to marry, ought not to beget children, ought not to bring new miserable beings into the world, ought not to provide new food for death..."[441]

It is difficult to say why Schopenhauer did not elaborate on the concept of a depopulation of the world that he had come across in Gnosticism. It might be due to the above mentioned systemic reasons of his metaphysics of the will: abstention from procreation requires will-power and would thus confirm the will rather than negating it. Regardless, this interpretation is not too convincing and the riddle remains unsolved offering itself to further research.

While Kurnig seems to have received Schopenhauer's most important works, he curiously remains silent on Schopenhauer's remarks on the Gnostics such as Marcion, who – in Schopenhauer's representation – are very much in favour of an abstention from procreation. This constitutes a further riddle in the history of antinatalism. Schopenhauer's account of Gnostic thought would have been an excellent point of reference for Kurnig's own neo-nihilism. Why he did not do so remains left to speculation, at least for the time being. Perhaps Kurnig never read what Schopenhauer wrote about Gnosticism.

As indicated above, Kurnig is somewhat misguided in his self-assessment. He puts himself in the tradition of Brahmanism and Buddhism, mistakenly perceiving them as religions that pray abstention from procreation to the present day. In himself Kurnig sees the executer of the supposed antinatalism of these religions. Rather, however, his neonihilism continues the protohistoric antinatalism of the Gnostics. With greater justification it could be said that Kurnig is a Neo-Gnostic than a Neo-Nihilist. Probably in no other religious teaching was antinatalism more pronounced and explicit than in Gnostic thinking. To emphasize this I cite from Clement of Alexandria (150–215) as quoted by Hans Jonas in his book *The Gnostic Religion*:

"Not wishing to help replenish the world made by the demiurge, the Marcionites decreed abstention from matrimony, defying their creator and hastening to the Good One who has called them and who, they say, is God in a different sense: wherefore, wishing to leave nothing of their own here, they turn abstemious not from a moral principle but from hostility to their maker and unwillingness to use his creation."[442]

---

[441] Schopenhauer (1909b, p. 432).
[442] Clement of Alexandria (1963, pp. 144n.).

What is valid for the Marcionites does also apply to Manichaeism: *"(...) One should abstain from all ensouled things and eat only vegetables and whatever else is non-sentient, and abstain from marriage, the delights of love and the begetting of children, so that the divine Power may not through the succession of generations remain longer in the Hyle. However, one must not, in order to help effect the purification of things, commit suicide."*[443]

In view of the aforesaid and put in a nutshell Kurnig's thinking appears to be a combination of Gnosticism freed from the idea of a malevolent demiurge and of Schopenhauer's philosophy freed from his metaphysics of the will. Unfortunately, Kurnig did not make wise use of the Gnostic religion even though its antinatalism was at the tip of his fingers in the form of Schopenhauers writings. What Kurnig does, however, is to inadvertently equip the Gnostic religion with a moral principle, the lack of which Hans Jonas emphasizes in his book *The Gnostic Religion*, namely the minimization of suffering.

Education

Kurnig conceives of the abolition of suffering as a complete depopulation of the world, which has to be initiated and accompanied by antinatalistic enlightenment and education. In this respect, he considers his writings to be both a basic theoretical foundation and propaganda against procreation.

In the word *depopulation*, as used by Kurnig, connotations of war or illness may resonate. However, Kurnig is an outspoken antimilitarist, who regards war as an almost always unpunished crime, for which people are prepared by a wrong education: *"The ground in which the war between the peoples is rooted and thrives is the education of the children."*[444] In Kurnig's diagnosis the educational system prefers to morph the child *"into a warrior, a criminal, and to prepare it from the outset for the wars it will have to participate in once it is grown up."*[445] Opposed to this, Kurnig resumes, we have to *sissify* the educational system in the spirit of antimilitarism and to reform it in order to make people refrain from having descendants.

The supreme goal of Kurnig's neo-nihilism is our *exodus* from being, mankind's dying out. To achieve this, we have to start early on with the right pedagogical principles. Kurnig seems optimistic that education will be able to form an antinatalistic attitude towards life and he claims: *"An order of things aiming at extinguishing soon, obviously entails different laws, a different education than one aiming at an unpredictable continuation."*[446]

---

[443] Alexander of Lycopolis (1963, p. 231).
[444] Kurnig (1903, p. 25).
[445] Ibid. (p. 25).
[446] Ibid. (p. 52 and 64).

Kurnig's pedagogical principles are well-suited for clearing up a common misunderstanding, namely the idea that those who oppose the creation of new people must dislike children. Contrary to this, Kurnig says: *"Always treat children very respectfully, keep in mind their immaturity. Educate the children in a spirit of fraternity, of peaceful international rapprochement, of harmony: nurture in them a taste for studying abstract sciences and especially the fine arts – the only means to perhaps... make them forget – at least intermittently – this miserable world into which the error or misdeed of their creators has put them."*[447]

Perhaps one can sum up Kurnig's pedagogical principle as follows: It is right to provide all existing children with an anti-militaristic and anti-procreationistic education. It is wrong to act in such a way that new children begin to exist and then to rejoice in the way in which they thrive under the educational measures taken. Kurnig paraphrases: *"I beget you (says such a nurturer) to have the pleasure of seeing what is within you and what is not. Doing this I am forcing upon you a lot of suffering and, at last, the nasty catastrophe of dying..."*[448] In order to make people abstain from procreation Kurnig points to the *desideratum* of a comprehensive depiction of how people die: *"The unwritten annals of the death hour would make a very strong contribution to pessimism."*[449]

Special Role of the Doctor

Surprisingly, Kurnig recognises antinatalism's natural ally in doctors: *"The doctor may (...) work more and more towards gentle depopulation."*[450] *"I believe to hear the following exclamation from a doctor after reading my writings: 'I cannot go to see people and, as it were, adjure them not to bring a child into the world!' And why shouldn't he? (I'd like to know.) If he doesn't, who should do it? The priest? Once the doctor has reached the highest pessimism, he will have to be counted among the highest benefactors of mankind in the exercise of his profession."*[451] Why did Kurnig ascribe a special role to doctors when it comes to antinatalism? Probably being a doctor himself and judging from himself he obviously conceded to physicians a high degree of insight into the misery of the world. At the same time, doctors are at the forefront when it comes to questions of the beginning and the end of a life.

---

[447] Kurnig (1903, p. 92).

[448] Ibid. (p. 125).

[449] Ibid. (p. 149). In our days it is Sherwin Nuland with his book *How We Die: Reflections on Life's Final Chapter* in which he shows that we rarely die *with dignity*. With his *Letzte Worte* (*Last Words*) Karl S. Guthke presents a history of last utterances in which he also makes reference to earlier such collections. Typical for these utterances, however, is that they are mostly strongly stylised.

[450] Ibid. (p. 80).

[451] Ibid. (pp. 159n.).

The Death Catastrophe

Philosophically, the history of mankind is sometimes presented as a cosmic adventure. In literature, the existence of an individual is oftentimes depicted as an adventurous journey. For Kurnig, however, *"the death of a human being is such a nasty adventure (...) that nothing is able to make it beautiful or less ugly."*[452] He continues: *"(...) The horrors of this one hour would be enough to make you condemn the whole of life."*[453] Here, Kurnig is understating the case since the process of dying is frequently not over after one or a few hours but may take days or even weeks. And, regrettably, Kurnig does not explain more in detail why the *nasty death catastrophe* that ends every existence cannot be compensated for by a fulfilled life. In order to parry this whitewashing of life, it should be pointed out that dying persons are so overwhelmed and absorbed by the imperatives of their failing organism that they have little psychological or physical strength to reminisce.

What Kurnig does explicitly fend off is an argumentative move that draws the conclusion from the *"desire to endure the final catastrophe as late as possible"*[454] that life must be beautiful after all. No, rather it is true that the final chord is anticipated to be so dissonant that we do not want to hear any of it for ourselves, and we therefore continually want to reject it and postpone it. Even people struggling to live on at the very end of their lives are no proof of the prevailing affirmation of life: *"At this moment, you are almost numb with pain and fear of death, your senses almost swoon – you are ready to confess that you have always been wrong when you only live, live on (...)."*[455] The desire to continue living at all costs sets in where reason gives way to fear of death, where what constitutes man is overwhelmed by the biological radicals of the organism. Such desires for survival are blackmailed bionomically – not autonomously, but inhumanly.

Suicide Cynicism

Kurnig has no problems in parrying those who would fling at him the well-known anti-antinatalistic argument of *"If you do not like life, why not commit suicide?"*[456] The reader learns that some people indeed recommended to him *"to take his own life – one of them even had such words printed."*[457] Kurnig retorts to this objection: *"Once alive, you want to see the sinister catastrophe of death postponed as long as possible; but never to*

---

[452] Kurnig (1903, p. 84).
[453] Ibid. (p. 148).
[454] Ibid. (p. 145).
[455] Ibid. (p. 147).
[456] For the topic of suicide-cynicism and related topics cf. Akerma (2017, p. 592).
[457] Kurnig (1903, p. 116).

have been you would have deemed a thousand times better."[458] Demanding that a person who finds their continued existence unpleasant should commit suicide; or that a person who finds themselves severely ill – but nonetheless at the mercy of their organism's claim for continued existence – should take their own life is a cynicism that can hardly be surpassed. Moreover, according to Kurnig, there is something important that is to be done until the unavoidable decay and death, which will occur anyway, comes: namely to spread propaganda directed against procreation.[459] Rather than committing suicide, we are to spread pessimistic propaganda, which according to Kurnig, is morally and philosophically superior to committing suicide.[460]

Never to Have Been

Kurnig perhaps exaggerates, when he says that, with regard to life, *"no unborn would ask for it."*[461] Everyone would have preferred to never have been. Did he ever carry out a survey among a substantial number of people, though? Kurnig knows very well how difficult it is to think of oneself as never having been, without thinking at the same time that one would have missed out on something. He labels this the *main point: "(...) The consideration to never have existed, the idea of one's own self as never having been! The absence of one's very self, of one's highly important personality on the world stage; the chair one sits on, the bed one sleeps in: empty (...)."*[462] All in all, Kurnig's conception of how people would react to the idea of never having been remains somewhat contradictory: no unborn would have asked for existence – the idea to never have existed is scary to everyone.

Those Who Put Us in Danger of Life and of Death – The Parent Taboo

With what one can label the parent-taboo,[463] Kurnig addresses a powerful psychological impediment which constitutes an obstacle to his ethics of depopulation: *"(...) The love, the reverence for our parents mandates to us that we don't criticize our life, which we received from them as a gift.... let alone to try to shake it off as an ugly gift (...)."*[464] How does Kurnig argue in view of the mighty parent taboo? He registers the conflict between children (who see the gift of life as a burden) and their progenitors once the taboo has been breached, *"as a major part of the suffering fallen to us."*[465] In an immense and perhaps desperate overestimation of his future influence Kurnig even gives out

---

[458] Kurnig (1903, p. 146).
[459] Cf. Ibid. (p. 116).
[460] Cf. ibid. (p. 146).
[461] Ibid. (p. 51). For the topic of the unborn cf. Akerma (2017, pp. 625nn.).
[462] Ibid. (p. 105).
[463] Cf. Akerma (2017, pp. 199n.).
[464] Kurnig (1903, p. 107).
[465] Ibid.

the recommendation to parents to arm themselves against the natalistic rebellion ema-
nating from him (Kurnig): *"'If you play with fire, you must expect to get your fingers bur-
ned,' the proverb says. And why should someone who creates a child – thereby, among
other things, putting it in danger of life and of death – be gay and in cheerful spirits?"*[466]

KURNIG - ZAPFFE

Let us now demonstrate an astonishing similarity between some of Kurnig's and Zapffe's formulations. In his *Neo-Nihilism* Kurnig describes how, with human beings, a gap
has opened up between nature and the realm of living beings:

*"Now, however, humanity has the power to say to nature: 'You, nature, you persist us
poor people; we suffer infinitely more here on earth than we enjoy; and, moreover, this
pleasure itself is largely ephemeral, even deceptive. We are therefore withdrawing from
your vicious circle as if from bad company. You yourself have shown to us the way out
through our intellect, e.g. by the means of facultative sterility.'"*[467]

Decades later it was Zapffe who formulated this insight in more poetic words in his *Om
det tragiske*:

*"You got me. But my son you will not get. You were committing a fateful mistake when
assigning even procreation to my will. And you did not do this out of love (...), but rather
to burden me with the heaviest of all responsibilities (...): Am I to perpetuate this species
or not? And from now on I will ask no longer what you want; rather you shall ask what
I want. And I will no longer offer further sacrifices to the God of life. I will punish you with
the ability you bequeathed to me in order to torment me; I will turn my clairvoyance
against you and thus bereaving you of your victims. And the abused millions will stand
behind me like a plough (...). And evermore will two people create one human being (...).
Thus you will feel your powerlessness begging me on thy bloody knees."*[468]

For Kurnig, antinatalism – more precisely, neo-nihilism – belongs fully to the category
of *corrections to nature*.[469] This assessment echoes in the following formulation that
Zapffe made: *"I will have to desist from the creation of new holders of interest. This decision would initialise a terminal epoch in the development of humankind; (...) This renoun-*

---

[466] Kurnig (1903, p. 150).
[467] Ibid. (p. 103).
[468] Zapffe (1996, pp. 239n.).
[469] Kurnig (1903, last part, p. 8).

cement, this refusal of a continuation represents the utmost cultural possibility of mankind."[470]

Both Kurnig and Zapffe bring to bear the guiding principle of philosophical anthropology (cf. the works of such authors as Helmuth Plessner and Arnold Gehlen),[471] according to which man is a cultural being by nature. It is only in antinatalism that man – to use an expression of Karl Marx – fully severs himself from the umbilical cord of the natural nexus of the species.

KURNIG'S REPLICA TO COUNTERARGUMENTS

As is customary for a circumspect thinker, Kurnig confronts himself with a remarkable series of objections against our *exodus from being* via abstention from procreation:

1. Consider: no one has seen behind the curtain hiding the essence of the development of the world as a whole.[472] Therefore, the depopulation of the planet would have to be postponed until further insights are gained: First of all, we are to understand the world as a whole in much more detail. Now, as Kurnig explains, science has already lifted the curtain and found nothing worthy of perpetuation.[473]

2. One must not tamper with God. This presupposes a faith in which Kurnig is not rooted. – As opposed to the arch-pronatalist Hans Jonas, who as a philosophical theologian would later formulate that we must not abandon God even if we wanted to abandon ourselves.[474]

3. One aspect of what was later to become known as *deep ecology* is anticipated in the following hypothesis: "*Nature needs mankind as an integral part of its essence (...).*"[475] Kurnig labels the perpetuation of suffering for the sake of an imaginary

---

[470] Zapffe (1996, p. 402). For more translations from Zapffe see my blog for the propagation of non-propagation (Akerma, 2018).

[471] See *Philosophische Anthropologie* (Akerma, 2000, chap. 14, pp. 153–167).

[472] Interestingly I raised the very same question in Akerma (1995) where I pointed to parapsychological phenomena as an indicator for the possibility of man's being imbedded into something and being an integral part of something we do not yet understand. Cf. *Motive der Parapsychologie als Argument gegen das Verebben* [*Motives of Parapsychology as an Argument against Mankind's Ebbing away*] (Akerma, 1995, chap. 11, pp. 84nn.).

[473] See Kurnig (1903, last part, p. 7).

[474] See *Der Mensch als Hüter des Seins* [*Man as Guardian of Being*] (Akerma, 2000, chap. 19, pp. 250–292).

[475] Kurnig (1903, p. 102).

system of nature (which is an integral component in which man would have to persist) as immoral and sinful.

4   In one of Kurnig's numerous replicas to reviews of his *Neo-Nihilism* we read: *"Referent is of the opinion that I bring in nothing as proof of the sentence that suffering outweighs pleasure in life. He overlooks the fact that I had (and am still having) the experience personally – isn't that proof enough to him?"*[476]

Here Kurnig for his part overlooks the fact that he cannot extrapolate from his own experience of existence to that of others, and that one cannot force anyone – to put it bluntly – to realise their own objective misfortune. Today, cognitive psychology confirms that cognitive distortions are oftentimes the parents of our beliefs. An example of such a cognitive distortion is a systematic misinterpretation, which Eduard von Hartmann in his day called *memory glasses.*[477] It is a psychological mechanism that causes the remembering memory to shed a better light on negative events of the past. The existence of Hartmann's memory glasses is confirmed by modern cognitive psychology,[478] and they are capable of unmasking rampant optimism as involuntary self-deception from our psychological constitution. This is of utmost importance for the evaluation of Kurnig's anti-procreationism, since he claims: The real driving force that keeps human life going on everywhere is optimism.

CONCLUSION

As an author, Kurnig described his experiences by saying: whoever tries to expand the Christian and Buddhistic basic teachings and whoever is *"constantly working towards rapid depopulation,"* will be *"hushed up at all costs."*[479] This prophecy has come true. It may have been facilitated by the fact that *Kurnig* is a pseudonym. While in his time his writings were discussed in numerous reviews, his memory seems to be erased from the cultural tradition except perhaps for one reference in Jean-Claude Wolf's book *Eduard von Hartmann: A Philosopher of the Gründerzeit.*[480] Kurnig deserves better, as we can see in him a progenitor of a secular antinatalism that, unlike Schopenhauer's proto-

---

[476] Kurnig (1903, last part, p. 15).
[477] Cf. Akerma (2017, pp. 210n.).
[478] Cf. Kahnemann (2011).
[479] Kurnig (1903, p. 157).
[480] Cf. Wolf (2006, pp. 24n.). In the three sentences which Wolf dedicates to Kurnig, he presents it as a fact that Kurnig was a medical doctor. Wolf continues: *"Perhaps Kurnig saw the meaning and his mission life in pleading for pessimism and its practical consequence of contraception and the prevention of birth."* Kurnig makes it clear, though, on almost every page of his writings that this is definitely the case.

antinatalism, manages without will metaphysics appealing only to man's commiseration.

Concessions to Schopenhauer's doctrine of will in Kurnig's text can only be found inasmuch as Kurnig has a gutted concept of *blind will* which corresponds to the reproductive instinct, the desire for survival and the mechanically unconscious origin of the world as a whole. While it is widely assumed that modern antinatalism first took shape during the second half of the 20th century, Kurnig is its early herald at the turn of the 20th century. After Kurnig, modern antinatalism was formulated, especially towards the end of the 20th century, by a series of thinkers who worked independently from one another, almost like intellectual islands. And it is only now that they are becoming aware of one another. Here, Zapffe is an early exponent followed by Martin Neuffer[481] (1924–2004) e.g. with his book *Nein zum Leben* [*No to Life*] which was published in 1992.

In Kurnig we will have to honour a thinker who – animated by Schopenhauer's writings – left behind Schopenhauer's metaphysics early on. It is a metaphysics of the will under the spell of which the anthropofugal Eduard von Hartmann explicitly rejected antinatalism since the primal ground (the persisting unconscious) by means of evolution would again produce a human type. This does not hold for Kurnig, who achieved a breakthrough to a new secular antinatalism: *"The only possible progress of the whole is to stop procreation – as I said before, the gentle depopulation of our globe. Anything that benefits a gentle, and the fastest possible definitive depopulation must be supported. This will be the moral of the future."*[482]

---

481 See Akerma (2017, p. 476).
482 Kurnig (1903, p. 51).

CONTEMPORARY ANTINATALISM

AUTHORS:

Jan Koumar
ANTINATALISM AND SEXUAL ETHICS
(pp. 149–165)

Julio Cabrera
ANTINTALISM AND NEGATIVE ETHICS
(pp. 167–188)

ANTINATALISM AND SEXUAL ETHICS

INTRODUCTION

Antinatalism is a philosophical position which may sound quite weird when one hears it for the first time.[483] Its weirdness probably steams from the fact that antinatalism opposes our everyday intuition as same as our deeply rooted feeling we should be grateful for being alive. Though, once we connect it with the ethics of sexuality this weirdness even grows. The ethics of sex is a discipline viewed with scorn, distrust and doubts in general because it reminds us too much of moralism and hypocrisy,[484] thus antinatalistic ethics of sexuality sounds like an explosive mixture unadvisable to use.

Although such popular notion might have taken some roots even in professional circles such distrust and scorn are not necessary. It is true that the ethics of sexuality was viewed through the optics of Roman-Catholic variation of Christianity for too long and led to the two-faced Victorian society: monogamous on the one hand, but with 80,000 prostitutes in London alone[485] on the other. But it is not less true that in relation to our sexual behaviour each of us happens to get in moral dilemmas which cannot be solved by law or by obeying simple rules and those are moments when we start asking what is good or bad in sex – there comes the need for sexual ethics.

Due to the abovementioned discomfort connected not only with antinatalism but also with sexual ethics, it is first necessary to clear out what ethics of sexuality does *not* consist of. First of all, its aim is not to create a conspiracy silence around sexuality or to control and limit its public manifestations. This all belongs to manners, one layer of the whole ethical area, which deals with the socially shared and enforced custom. Man-

---

[483] Throughout this chapter I try not to assess the quality of the Benatar's asymmetry argument (see below), as same as I do not argue for or against it. The discussion on this topic is wide and sometimes confusing (see e.g. Weinberg, 2012; Belshaw, 2012, and others).

[484] Hawthorne's *Scarlet Letter* can be mentioned here as quite an illustrative example of a sexual hypocrisy in classic fiction, and it does not stand alone: Tolstoy's *Anna Karenina* or Flaubert's *Madame Bovary* are other ones.

[485] Schopenhauer (1970).

ners[486] (like all customs) change in time and place and they effectively summarize cultural models of action and behaviour, which should be done.[487] Their simplicity and effectiveness makes the social life and contacts possible, however, they completely fail when one tries to act individually. It means silence or subtle hints in which sexuality is often spoken may have an important role in society, but the individual action sometimes needs to step over them and to oppose what the social majority requires. It means to enter the second layer of the ethical area – morality, which is not disconnected from manners, though it goes beyond them.

While manners control manifestations of sexuality in public, or speaking about it and especially in the past, they lead to the abovementioned hypocritical double life (one sexual, the other social), morality is what leads an individual to act or not to act in certain way.[488] However, customs are not only about limiting and silencing sexuality, they are changeable and right now their rules about sexuality seem to be remarkably weakening. At least for the sake of this chapter, sexual ethics deals much more with morality than with customs, though a complete autonomy of an individual is often more desired than achieved and so morality itself is based on manners.

Secondly, the ethics of sexuality is not to sublimate all sexual incentives into a romantic love. As Giddens notices,[489] romantic love is an invention of the 18th and 19th century and its expectations and requirements are very often illusive since they only tend to hide the sexual needs by a sublime and exalted theory. According to Giddens, intimate relationships were deeply transformed by the development of plastic sexuality – that is *"decentred sexuality, freed from reproduction"*[490] – whose boom was caused both by the development of contraceptive methods and of a conception of an individual Self. Giddens claims, that thanks to the plastic sexuality the ideals of romantic love disintegrate and are substituted by a simultaneous love, an active form of untied love having a wide field of choices. Simultaneous love is linked to the development of pure relationships, which are not formed to satisfy desires or society anymore, but due to both partners' free choices, such a relationship lasts as long as it is beneficial and satisfying.

Last but not least, the ethics of sexuality is not to moralise, that is to overvalue ethical judgements or to make moral judgement without deeper understanding. As Craig Taylor observed, moralism is a vice that involves a distortion of moral thoughts, reflections

---

[486] In *Elements of the Philosophy of Right* Hegel called manners *Sittlichkeit* and distinguished them from the subjective life of the individual – *Moralität* (Hegel, 1991).
[487] Sokol (2016).
[488] In order to be neat the third level of the ethical area must be mentioned: Sokol divides the whole ethics into: 1) social custom, 2) individual morality and 3) ethics as a search for what is best. Even though practical philosophy as the whole can be called ethics, ethics as the third layer means going beyond all the rules and longing for something that heroes found: the best (pp. 62–69).
[489] Giddens (1992).
[490] Ibid. (p. 10).

and judgements and does not belong to a moralist – a person who evaluates morally relevant features of some situation – but to a moralizer – a person who morally judges in a wrong and usually offensive way.[491] A moralizer universalizes his own moral level and expects everybody to observe his ethical standards. But because morality – opposed to the collectively shared social custom – is always individual, a moralizer is wrong when they expect that their individual principles ought to be kept generally hence they resort to unfounded condemnations.

The differentiation between a moralist and moralizer also establishes a certain borderline. Even though ethics of sexuality is not about the abovementioned matters, to a certain degree they always play a part in it. However, the fact that somebody expects their moral principles to rule the whole society does not mean we must renounce ethics *en bloc*, and likewise the fact that ethics of sexuality reminds people of the Victorian double standards, hypocrisy or moralism does not mean sex ought to have no ethical dimension at all. Sex is not only a blind animal urge which cannot be opposed,[492] it is a social activity and as such it follows some rules.

Therefore, one may ask now what sexual ethics *is* about? From the broadest view, it tells us how to have good sex, where the goodness does not mean the biggest satisfaction or emotional strength but its general goodness. Since our sexual identities contribute a lot to our well-being and since our social roles of parents, lovers, partners, spouses etc. influence a lot of people around us, our sexuality affects our world more profoundly than we tend to think. Sex that is considered satisfying by one partner may be seen as a rape by the other. Where one spouse feels comfortable with non-binding sexual encounters, the other's heart is broken. And finally, sex can result in calling somebody into existence.

THE ANTINATALISTIC ETHICS OF SEXUALITY

For the antinatalistic philosophy, the last example is crucial. The fact that we are born without explicitly wanting to, is a truism which hardly anybody thinks of. Nevertheless, there are instances in which this truism is suddenly in focus. A pregnant woman having been told her fetus has a serious genetic disease can be taken as an example. Suppose,

---

[491] Taylor (2012).

[492] Such an immature view of sexuality is more than common, though. However, sexuality seen as a simple animal urge would be a solitary activity (such as solitary masturbation), but sexuality mostly occurs between at least two people, hence it is a social activity. It is remarkable that while people act according to rules of manners in more explicit body needs like urination of defecation, sexuality is more and more taken as a rule-free activity. This leads to more frequent speaking of marginal sexual behaviour and to a recession from ordinary sex to its extraordinary, yet favoured sex (see e.g. Jackson, 2008).

for the matter of this case, she refuses abortion and gives birth to such a seriously impaired child. She can surely rely on the developed social and medical care, which is able to make the life of such a child more pleasant, but her action may pose simple questions: Did she have any right to bring such an impaired child knowingly into existence? Is not that an act of selfishness? She can get a lot of pleasure from having a baby,[493] but will the child really enjoy such a life? And finally: Would such a child like to be born if they knew what life consists of?

Due to the famous David Benatar's asymmetry of pleasure and pain,[494] more or less justifiably, the same questions may be posed about anybody else, just in the everyday life we tend to instantly reject them as non-beneficial or fruitless. However, such a rejection is a result of the unreliable assessment of one's own life. Its unreliability comes from Pollyannism,[495] adaptation and accommodation.[496] Owing to the asymmetry of pleasure and pain hidden by these three psychological processes, to come into existence means always a serious harm. There is no wonder that sexual ethics is deeply influenced by such a presumption, there is also no surprise that in antinatalism, the sexual ethics is central. If each life consists of more suffering than pleasure it is a duty not to create new life, for by creating it we would cast another person into suffering.

Therefore, the antinatalistic sexual ethics is clear: only a non-procreative sex is morally correct and if sex leads to procreation in spite of all contraception methods, abortive option is (or ought to be) a matter of second choice for everybody. Such verdict definitely seems to go against the innate intuition and the most people would call it pessimistic. Truth be told, from the viewpoint of a believer, who is used to listening to affirmation about God's goodness and world's perfection, the antinatalistic sexual ethics sounds depressive.[497] But despite its darkness, it probably does not go against the real practise. Sexual behaviour – especially when we do not reduce it to a mere coitus[498]

---

[493] To simplify the case I am not paying attention to the child's life quality after his mother dies. Such child is likely to be as same unable to take care of themselves as at the moment of birth.

[494] Which, in short, says that: 1) the presence of pain is bad and 2) the presence of pleasure is good. 3) The absence of pain is good, even if that good is not enjoyed by anybody, but 4) the absence of pleasure is not bad, unless there is somebody for whom this absence is a deprivation (Benatar, 2006, p. 30).

[495] A tendency towards optimism named after Pollyanna, a girl character of the book by Eleanor Porter, who knows how to be happy even in the most tragic situation (ibid., pp. 64n.).

[496] See ibid. (pp. 64–69).

[497] Schopenhauer foresaw such objections with his typical sarcasm: *"I suppose I shall have to be told again that my philosophy is cheerless and comfortless simply because I tell the truth, whereas people want to hear that the Lord has made all things very well. Go to your churches and leave us philosophers at peace!"* (1974, p. 300).

[498] Contrary to the view of many teenagers, sexuality does not consist only of coitus and the ways of achieving orgasm, it also consists of seducing, ritual hesitation and seemingly useless ado and these activities take up much more time.

– definitely does not always aim to procreation: the consumption of the contraceptive pills and condoms can be taken as evidence.[499]

Yet, the everyday practise is not identical to the antinatalistic view, whose aim is not just a headless enjoyment of pleasure with procreation as an unwanted but not forbidden side effect. An antinatalist sees sexual pleasure as an incentive which lures us to the activity, while without it everybody would *"feel so much sympathy for the coming generation that he would prefer to spare it the burden of existence."*[500] Only the fact that the act of procreation is accompanied by the intense pleasure is to blame for the existence of the human beings whom it makes *"tortured souls on the one hand and the devils on the other."*[501]

The most important modern expression of the antinatalistic sexual ethics is the above-mentioned David Benatar's book *Better Never to Have Been*. It presents us three possible views of sexual ethics: reproductive view – where only reproductive sex is morally acceptable; neutral view – in which there is no moral difference between reproductive and non-reproductive sex; and anti-reproductive view, in which only non-reproductive sex is moral.[502]

Nevertheless, such a division suits only as long as we see reproduction as the focal point of sexual morality, though in practise, it does not seem to be what matters the most. On top of that, if moral goodness is to be the incentive which makes people engage in the certain activity, to engage in sex in order not to procreate does not make much sense (it would be smarter and for achieving its moral target easier not to engage in it at all); as the ethics of sexuality with only three options: reproductive, non-reproductive, neutral is very reductive and leads to misunderstandings,[503] I would like to have a closer look at other possible approaches so as to clear out what their central point, which makes sexuality moral or immoral, is and also to create a context in which the antinatalistic morality stands.

---

[499] *"Indeed many people are brought into existence not because their parents sought to satisfy their own procreative interests, but because their parents were satisfying their own coital interests"* (Benatar, 2006, p. 96).

[500] Schopenhauer (1974, p. 300).

[501] Ibid.

[502] Benatar (2006, p. 127).

[503] For example, when Benatar wonders why the reproductive view *"is not thought to rule out coitus within a marriage in which one of the partners is infertile"* (p. 126), the unitive end of marriage is omitted (for more see below).

THE TRADITIONALISTIC AND KANTIAN VIEW

Probably up to now the most frequently spoken ethics of sexuality has been traditionalistic, conventional or, in Benatar's view, reproductive morality.[504] This frequency does not come from its perfection but much more from the influence it was given throughout the history mainly by the Catholic Church. No matter how strange it may sound today, this ethical view has been prominent in the Western society for centuries. In a nutshell it states the complete opposite of the antinatalistic view: only sex leading to procreation is moral; such sex must be carried out within the bounds of marriage.

The starting point of such ethical position is firstly the Old Testament, in which the newly created mankind is encouraged to multiply and fill the Earth,[505] but secondly philosophical traditions arising from dualism of body and mind such as Platonism or the Pythagorean tradition. In the Christian view it is connected with Saint Augustine, who had sex in scorn due to its deep connection with irrational, unruly lust, existing as a result of the original sin;[506] and with Thomas Aquinas who thought only procreation to be the natural end of sexual activity.[507]

Such a view creates an unreasoned dualism of natural/unnatural sex and reveals one deep problem of the traditionalistic view. Procreation is the *natural* end of sexuality only when it was given by God, all other meanings of the label *unnatural* are false and hide just the visceral distaste of an individual.[508] A God given purpose is undoubtedly a strong argument and a famous papal encyclical *Humanae Vitae*, with its view of birth control as a violation of natural law, is based on it, however, it is completely invalid for a non-believer.

That may be why the more liberal conventionalists do not insist on procreation as a core of the sexual ethics but admit that unlike the other procreating animals, for humans, sexuality also has a unitive end.[509] Such a move is important also for non-believers, because a view of solely marital sexuality as moral is based on considerations of social unity: procreation can take place only in a stable unit – in a family consisting of a wife

---

[504] While Primoratz (1999) calls it traditionalistic, Mappes and Zembaty (1992) calls it conventional. Benatar (2006) calls it reproductive.

[505] Gen. (1:28).

[506] Augustine did not limit this lust by binds of marriage, according to him, even within a marriage sexuality does not stop being bad and despicable, as he famously wrote: every thinking human living in a marriage *"would prefer to beget children without lust of this kind, if such thing were possible"* (1998, p. 614), which is the complete opposite of what Schopenhauer thought (see above).

[507] Aquinas account on sexuality is a base of a prominent theory defending conventional morality: New Natural Law.

[508] Koumar (2017). A good philosophical analysis of unnatural sexuality was also given by John Corvino (2013, pp. 77–97).

[509] See e.g. Feser (2003).

and a husband – which is maintained and reinforced by the fact sex is (or should be) available exclusively in it, which in turn leads people to get and stay married.

I believe there is no need to say such a consideration is doubtful. Firstly, because it claims marriage is a bond in which people must be forced to stay by unavailability of extramarital sex. Secondly, because it turns marriage into a kind of a breeding section in a cowshed. Thirdly, because it somehow says the deeper purpose of our existence is unfounded reproduction. Moreover, the two statements of conventional view do not follow from each other: a procreative sex can be carried out even outside marriage and marriage can exist even without sex (much less without procreative sex) thus their connection does not seem necessary. The traditionalistic view is also largely negated by practice: that is why Georg Denzler thinks that sexual morality, which ignores or trivializes the problem of today people, deserves to be marked as immoral.[510]

Despite all these problems, the traditionalistic ethics has been revived many times. A strong reason for these revivals may be philosophically more influential and better elaborated view resulting in similar ethical position provided by the Kantian ethics. Even though Kant did not base his sexual ethics on God and necessity to procreate, he recognised that in sexuality *"human being is designed by nature as the Object of another's enjoyment,"*[511] which means that a desired sexual object is nothing but a thing for a desiring human. But as Kant famously argues in his *Groundwork of the Metaphysics of Morals*, we must never treat anybody merely as a means to an end, like we treat a tool. People have dignity and so we must respect them as ends in themselves.[512] Since by desiring the other as the object of enjoyment, each partner dishonours the humanity of the other and even the desiring people feel ashamed for their lust because they feel that by presenting themselves to the other as an object they degrade their humanity and make themselves similar to a beast,[513] sexuality is immoral in itself.

Nevertheless, without sexuality, there would be no people and our sexual appetite is also deeply rooted in our natures, Kant therefore thinks a person without sexual desires would be an imperfect individual.[514] Kant shows a great deal of intellectual gymnastics in order to connect these contrary views. He claims that the only space in which sexual desires can take place in accordance with law is provided by marriage because only in marriage the partners give themselves fully (not only sexual organs) and in return each of them takes the other one completely (including themselves). In fact, one partner owns themselves within the possession of their spouse. All non-marital ways of sexuality are just cannibalistic.[515]

---

[510] Denzler (1991).
[511] Kant (1963, p. 163).
[512] Id. (2002, pp. 44–46).
[513] Id. (1963).
[514] Ibid.
[515] Kant is quite serious about cannibalism and does not mean it as a metaphor. In *Metaphysic of Morals*

I hope it is visible from this very short summary of Kant's sexual ethics[516] that even though the aim of sexuality is to preserve the species,[517] Kant obviously does not declare only the procreative sex moral.[518] However, the non-cannibalistic sexuality can take place only within the marriage, i.e. in the legal protection of spouses with respect to the sexual objectification. It inevitably means the outcome of the Kantian sexual ethics is very similar to the conventional one, yet, Kantian ethics does not necessarily have to be called reproductive.[519]

THE ROMANTIC VIEW

The conventional view is correct in one important point: sexuality is definitely a tool of procreation. However, it is a big mistake to see it only from that point of view; it is also connected with one important human feeling: love. Even though love does not necessarily mean sex and sex does not necessarily involve love, the romantic view assumes that sex and love are deeply connected. Romantics do not see sex as the animal urge we have to satisfy, but according to them, sexual desire is directed at an object and its aim is the union with the other.

Such an assumption sounds like a good starting point for the sexual ethics, but it has some weak points. There is a fact that romantic love definitely is not hidden behind every sexual incentive, no matter how many people claim so. Furthermore, as Gabriel Bianchi noticed, our culture provides a wide acceptance to the serial monogamy, but people still feel much more secure in their short-term relationships when they start with at least a short period of amorousness.[520] From this point of view, the existence of love is what makes sex moral.

However, love is a vague conception which is not always easy to recognize and a lot of people tend to disguise anything complying with their needs by love, and so it must be put at solid bases. Such bases were built by Roger Scruton, a British philosopher

he claims that intercourse can really consume the given person, also pregnancy demands a lot on woman's body and can result in death, and man's body can be exhausted by frequent sex (1996). It is also necessary to note that Kant condemned masturbation and same-sex activity as *crimina carnis contra naturam* (carnal crime against nature). There were made numerous more or less successful attempts to reconcile the Kantian ethics and same-sex debate, see for example Arroyo (2017) or Altman (2010).

[516] For more see Kant (1963), for more about the Kantian ethics as the whole see id. (2002).
[517] Id. (1996).
[518] See Arroyo (2017, pp. 166–168).
[519] Benatar deals with Kantian requirement not to treat people merely as means from the non-sexual point of view when he discusses the amount of narcissism in having children (see Benatar, 2006, pp. 128–131).
[520] Bianchi (2011).

and the soundest advocate of the romantic view. In his book *Sexual Desire* Scruton defines sex as a need directed at object, but according to him this object is an irreplaceable individual. The aim of sexual desire is, thus, a spiritual union with the one and only human, such a union is realized through the deep erotic love and leads to the embodiment of another human being, who is the body. Such embodiment can happen solely within the institution of marriage, which is in turn protected by a conservative society with a state religion.[521] As visible, Scruton's aim is progressive in one important regard. It is not to free sexual morality from proscriptions but to base them on different foundations. Where the conventional sexual ethics holds good mainly for religious people, Scruton wanted to place its rules on different, but more widely accepted grounds. Therefore, instead of accented procreation there is a special theory of sexual desire, however, the results are practically the same. All prohibitions that make up traditional sexual morality: *"masturbation, adultery, promiscuity, prostitution, pornography, and homosexuality – are explicitly or implicitly endorsed."*[522]

As same as every restrictive moral teaching, Scruton's vision of sexual morality has been criticized. Martha Nussbaum condemned Scruton as a Thatcherite conservative and a Wagnerian romantic and provided a deep philosophical analysis of his vision of sexual desire;[523] Igor Primoratz quite aptly objected that Scruton identified love with something that was oddly out of touch for many preliterate cultures and even for the present bar-hangers or prostitute-seekers. These people may be at the edge of society but their sexuality seems to be quite strong yet not at all desiring embodiment of the irreplaceable other.[524] Vannoy on the similar base argued that erotic love is full of limits and inner tensions and that sex is enjoyed the best *as sex*, that means unburdened with love.[525]

THE HEDONISTIC VIEW

Vannoy's opinion leads to the sharp opposite of Scruton's romantic morality – hedonism.[526] In this view, sexual morality is based purely on one's own pleasure, which is

---

[521] Scruton (1986).

[522] Primoratz (1999, p. 25).

[523] See Nussbaum (2012, chap. 2).

[524] Primoratz (1999, pp. 26n.).

[525] Vannoy (1980).

[526] It must be mentioned, though, that Vannoy's account on sex definitely is not hedonistic. He argues that a really humanistic and satisfying sex exists only when it is enjoyed for its own sake and it is separated from all traditional forms of love (1980). For that reason his view should be ranked to the liberal one (see below).

the highest good. It makes sense at the first sight: sexuality is an appetite satisfied with a lot of emotional and physical pleasure, hence a lot of people would agree, its main ethical measure should be the pleasure it brings. However, at the second sight, such a view brings a lot of problems. Firstly, the hedonistic view is very self-centred thus it may apply to masturbation or other individually pursued sexual activities, but hardly to sexuality seen as a social activity in which the self-centredness disqualifies a given individual from any future contacts of the same kind. Secondly, owing to the fact sexuality is hardly ever straightforward but it is burdened with a lot of games[527] and hidden meaning, it is hard to judge how much pleasure sexual intercourse really brings to the other side and it is easy to make a lot of harm in the false hope of making pleasure. Eventually, hedonism may lead even to sociopathic and socially irresponsible behaviour. For all these reasons Kelly claims that a purely hedonistic lifestyle is led by very few people because complications of interpersonal relationships get in its way.[528]

For the sake of this book, though, it is necessary to distinguish hedonism from antinatalism, because despite their frequent confusion, each of them is based on a different presumption. While for a hedonist, pleasure is the main moral satisfaction for sexual activity and procreation is its unwanted or even feared consequence, for antinatalists only non-reproductive sex is moral, although they may engage in sexual activity for various reasons. From Benatar's point of view, a hedonist (as same as a follower of Scruton's vision of the romantic approach to sexual ethics) belongs to the neutral view of sexual ethics, that is the one in which it makes no moral difference whether sex is reproductive or not. An antinatalist by contrast, follows a strictly anti-reproductive sexual ethics, because for them only non-reproductive sex can be moral for it does not bring more people into the generally evil world.[529]

THE ASCETIC VIEW

The complete opposite of the hedonistic approach is the approach of ascetic traditions. Broadly seen, the ascetic view is ethics of no-sex, however, it is still a kind of ethics of

---

[527] To speak about games people play one does not necessarily have to refer to Eric Bernie (though his account of psychology of the human relationships is applicable, see Bernie, 1964) or to Goffman's theatrical model of society (1959). Kelly for instance, mentions *Power Games*, in which power is expressed and struggled for; *Relationship Games*, in which certain patterns of behaviour appear and are brought into relationships; and most of all *Communication Games* in which people *"fool themselves into thinking that some rough spots have been logically resolved, but in actuality, their differences are still simmering under the surface"* (1996, p. 199).

[528] Kelly (1996).

[529] Benatar (2006, p. 127).

sexuality because such an approach draws a clear line between the moral action (no-sex) and the immoral action (any sex). The goal of this view is to climb above basic physical pleasures to the life of mind or spirit. Sexual asceticism is usually a part of religious or spiritual traditions and its core is celibacy. In the European context asceticism is typically expected of the Roman-Catholic priests, nuns and monks, though, it is not limited to them. For instance, the ascetic tradition has strong roots in Buddhism. In general, the denial of sexual pleasure helps a human to get closer to the spiritual needs and to God.[530]

It must be obvious that the denial of sexual activity does not mean their complete cease; the nature of sexual desire would shortly prove such claim guilty. The purpose of this denial – spiritual closeness to God or higher wisdom – ought to be much more than their sufficient substitution: the body needs are to undergo a kind of sublimation. Whether we agree with this sublimation or not, it is important to note antinatalism does not incline to asceticism because its purpose is not to resign completely from sexual activity, but just from the reproduction connected with it. Thus, while in asceticism any sexual activity is immoral because it violates the ability of an individual to a spiritual rise, in antinatalism only the one regard of sex, that is reproduction, is immoral because it makes harm to the potentially newly born people.

THE VISION OF SEXUALITY IN SARTRE'S BEING AND NOTHINGNESS

Proceeding from the conventional ethical view to probably the most contemporary one – liberal ethics, I cannot miss the often mentioned, yet probably not widely followed view of sexuality described by Sartre. Even though he is famous mainly for his uttered apophthegms such as: life is meaningless; there is no moral law; a man is a useless passion; the world is a nauseating viscous mess etc.,[531] in his principal ontological work *Being and Nothingness* Sartre expressed a famous view of sexuality. Explained in brief, Sartre distinguishes Being-in-themselves (*en-soi*), which is dark, massive and the book pays only superficial attention to it from Being-for-themselves (*pour-soi*), which is Nothingness i.e. consciousness and its modifications.[532] One of the modifications, presen-

---

[530] Kelly (1996).

[531] Cranston (1962, p. 11).

[532] Sartre's ontology is much more complicated. For Sartre, cogito yields two kinds of being, which exist in different ways. Consciousness has Being-for-themselves (*pour-soi*), while the objects of consciousness have Being-in-themselves (*en-soi*), they have objective being, so they are. But the consciousness is an entity that cannot be perceived as an object in fact, it is not, so we can speak about it only as about no-

ted in part 3, is Being-for-others a desire to be seen as an object through the eyes of the other subjects, and in that way to create a subject-object unity. Nevertheless, such a unity is radically impossible in love, because love means giving up one's own freedom for the sake of the Other:

"(...) But if the Other loves me, he radically deceives me by his very love. I demand on him that he should find my being as a privileged object by maintaining himself as a pure subjectivity confronting me; and as soon as he loves me he experiences me as subject and is swallowed up in his objectivity confronting my subjectivity."[533]

The Other is, therefore, a dangerous Thing among things, even though one always desires them as a subject, one of them must be an object, which makes the real connection impossible. Love is therefore always unsatisfied, and the subject is forever left desiring and endlessly desolated. Love together with masochism, hate and sadism is just an attempt to effectuate the desire, but it remains without solution, they are all doomed to fail.

Similarly, sexuality is not a desire to be easily satisfied by pleasant feelings; these were attributed to it for external reasons, of which Sartre names procreation, strength of pleasure provoked by ejaculation or symbolic value attached to sex.[534] Sexual desire, therefore, is not an instinct, which is for example on the male side caused by erection and satisfied by ejaculation, it is a desire for a transcendent object, in particular for a living body as an organic totality with consciousness at the horizon. I want to have the body of the Other, but not for the body, according to Sartre *"I want his transcendence as pure transcendence and at the same time as body, to reduce the Other to his simple facticity."*[535] The pleasure is the end of desire but it shows the impossibility to get what I desired. *"I try to utilize the Other-as-object in order to call her to account for her transcendence, and precisely because she is all object she escapes me with all her transcendence."*[536] As same as in case of love, in sexuality we are constantly referred from Other-as-object to Other-as-subject and this circle is endless, yet we never give up, *"we pursue the impossible ideal of the simultaneous apprehension of his freedom and of his objectivity."*[537]

---

thingness (*le néant*). Though, this nothingness i.e. consciousness has an objective existence as a human reality. Hence as Being-for-themselves I am nothing, but for other people I have an outside and nature. For more see Sartre (2007, mainly parts 1n.).
[533] Sartre (2007, p. 398).
[534] Ibid. (p. 407).
[535] Ibid. (p. 416).
[536] Ibid. (p. 420).
[537] Ibid. (p. 430).

This view even darkness when Sartre points out that *"sexual behaviour is a primary behaviour towards the Other,"*[538] his view of sexuality is deeply connected with his view of absolute freedom. We are condemned to be free and responsible for everything we do and we can never curse the fact we were born, *"I am condemned to be fully responsible for myself."*[539] However, sexual encounters in Sartre's view are based on rivalry for freedom. The lover wants to be given love by a free person but at the same time they strive for the very same freedom of their beloved person. The resulting relationship reminds us of Hegel's master-slave dialectic, but in addiction one seeks themselves in the Other and can never get to their goal, because the Other is unattainable.

It is necessary now to sum up Sartre's view of sexuality in *Being and Nothingness* and in short it claims: we can never achieve mutual recognition of each other's freedom, Kantian principle according to which no person can be treated as a mere object is dead, since we meet the Others only as objects and the essence of relationships (including sexual ones) is a conflict, therefore sexuality tends to fall into masochism or sadism. Moreover, our inability to meet the other differently than as an object makes any ethics impossible, there is no morally right sex, because ontologically, sexuality is a conflict and so it only exercises power struggles and a need that can never be satisfied. It may be the main reason why Sartre never wrote his work about ethics promised at the end of *Being and Nothingness.*[540]

Although, in his play *Les Mouches* [*The Flies*] he clearly expresses that morality is based on man-made decisions and his well-known novel *Nausea* expressed a clearly antinatalistic rejection of existence and having children,[541] nothing of those can be found in his principal philosophical work. Nevertheless, there is one important point connecting this non-ethical view with antinatalism: sex in Sartre's view is deeply flawed and its very core – subject-object unity – leads us to pain of sadism, masochism or hate. Sex also is not a tool of procreation; it is primarily a never-satisfied desire for a transcendent object in which reproduction is not morally significant, it has just been attributed to it.[542] If there were not for Sartre's own busy sexual life, one could almost finish by saying that in Sartre's view, sex is not worth doing.[543]

---

[538] Sartre (2007, p. 428).

[539] Ibid. (p. 576).

[540] But it is also necessary to know Sartre created different ethical opinions elsewhere. For example his lecture *L'existentialisme est un humanisme* claims we must respect the freedom of the others equally as our own. It should be noted, though, Sartre himself was dissatisfied with this lecture of his.

[541] For more see Coates (2014, pp. 149–163).

[542] Sartre's non-reproductive stance can be derived from his own life, his stance to sexuality can be derived from his numerous sexual activities or from his unconventional relationship with Simone de Beauvoir (see e.g. Cranston, 1962).

[543] A bit different conclusion can be found in Pearce (2011).

THE MARXIST-FEMINIST VIEW

Sartre's uneasy ontology of love and sex was criticised many times[544] and it can hardly be taken as a base for moral reasoning. However, when he cleansed sex of procreation and drew attention to power manipulations hidden in its background, he followed the trends of Marxist and feminist criticism of meanings hidden behind sex.

Marxism concentrates on the class inequality and oppression which affects women's sexuality: they are forced to trade sex for money, hence their success and even their marriage often has a form of trade. Marxism also expects a radical change: as soon as the present class system is replaced by classless society, sex will no longer be this kind of traded service but it will finally be cleaned of all these external tools of power and will become a matter of mutual attraction of free and equal people. There will be a society in which men will never learn what it is like to buy a woman's surrender by their power and in which women will give themselves to a man only for erotic love.[545] The feminists adopted a lot of the Marxist critique, but emphasised gender inequality and oppression instead of the class ones. Radical feminists claim that present sexuality is *"a social construct of male power: defined by men, forced on women, and constitutive of the meaning of gender,"*[546] sexual interactions in general are in their point of view even the base of existence of rape.[547]

Therefore, the Marxist-feminist view of sexual ethics is easy to derive: it is based on the presumption that only sex freed of all the power manipulations – whether class or gender ones – is moral. It also notices the fact that conventional morality is deeply connected with the idea of a traditional patriarchal marriage and creates a generally accepted demand for compulsory heterosexuality, despite the fact, sexual orientation in the real society is much more complicated and there is no reason why marriage should be patriarchal.

Such a view is more than attractive. It does not emphasise procreation and it invites us to enjoy sex for itself, without being necessarily hedonist. Unfortunately, the main presumption is also the main point of criticism. It seems, Marxists and feminists were absolutely right in their criticism, but the requirement we ought to engage in sex only for sex itself is problematic. Even though in the present society sex seems to be more and more adored, the requirement to purge it of all meanings and functions seem exaggerated. We do not usually take the tram just for the delight of the tram ride – we nor-

---

[544] Though, a lot of this criticism came from religious authors (e.g. Miceli, 1975; De Marco and Wiker, 2004) and a lot of other authors built their philosophy on Sartre's account on sexuality (e.g. Nagel, 1979).
[545] Engels (1985).
[546] MacKinnon (1989, p. 113).
[547] Foa (1977, p. 347).

mally expect a tram to take us to some destination – and so we also do not engage in sex just for sex itself, but for its many meanings a lot of which are unconscious. Such separation of sex from all other activities makes sexual ethics different from other kinds of ethics without reasoning why. It suggests we should enjoy complete freedom in all sexual actions but consequently, it suggests we are not free in all other activities. Since only such an activity we do for its own sake is free hence moral, we would act immorally in all our doings except for sex.[548]

THE LIBERAL VIEW

Where the most of abovementioned approaches, except for hedonism, took sexual ethics as a special ethics, the last one, liberal view, does the contrary. It does not create a special ethics for sexual behaviour, but instead, it claims sexual actions are nothing different from all other activities we engage in. As Igor Primoratz noticed, many socially shared ideals of good sex are not in fact moral but only prudential. Thus, he claims that whatever our moral duties are, they are as same in sexuality as in other areas of our lives. Sex itself is morally neutral and it can become immoral only when it violates some general moral concept, not when it does the same to manners and their customary moral codex.[549]

Together with hedonism, this is the only approach that does not make sexual ethics distinct, however, while hedonism can easily fall into mere selfishness and the followers of hedonistic-sexual-ethic are not probably in crowds, there is no wonder that liberal view has found its followers among sexologists. It deprives people of many neurotic incentives and does not cast a shadow of a sin on frequent kinds of behaviour such as masturbation, lustful fantasies or even one-night stands. Unlike Marxists and feminists, the followers of the liberal view do not want us to engage in morally neutral (i.e. unburdened by power and class manipulations) sex. They claim sex is as same morally neutral as any other activity. It does not mean it cannot be connected with romantic love or procreation, though. All these things can be contained but they are not elevated to its supreme justification. It also does not mean every sex is moral: non-consensual sex, rape, harm caused to somebody, this all and more can constitute morally wrong acts as same as any other non-consensual activity or harm.

Such a view has two main weak points. Firstly, it relies a lot on the general values shared by a society. If the whole society were antinatalistic, all liberals would be antinatalists,

---

[548] Primoratz (2013).
[549] Id. (1999).

because morality of sex does not differ from morality of any other action. The second problem is the fact that sexual misdemeanours may sometimes be distinctively differrent from the other ones. An act of rape is not just a non-consensual activity; it is an activity violating a very intimate and private human physical and mental sphere.

CONCLUSION

In this chapter, I offered seven possible views of sexual ethics supplemented with one non-ethical, yet from the position of antinatalistic ethics interesting ontological view of Jean-Paul Sartre. I hope the fact, that the presence or absence of reproduction is not what always makes sex im/moral was made visible enough: sex is the activity with many meanings hence with many possible opinions on which of these meanings is morally the most significant one.[550] Even though the traditionalistic view may be the most often discussed one and (wrongly) equated with sexual ethics as the whole, it is arguable how widely it is followed in real. Procreation is a possible, not inevitable and, in Western society, not necessarily logical consequence of sex. Therefore, it is expectable that under the influence of Hollywood production and remarkably economical way of solving the bodily needs presented in current literature,[551] love, pleasure and no-harm approach will probably be the most frequently followed ones.

Moreover, it can be said that reproduction matters only for the conventional and the antinatalistic view, the other approaches concentrate on different values: love, pleasure, pure sex itself, or a rejection of sexuality as the whole. Traditionalism and antinatalism therefore stay in the opposite sides of the boxing ring, each with a complete antithesis of what the other claims. Here, I disagree with a possible objection that the traditionalistic view is apparently more apt. Its alleged aptness comes from the everyday intuition, but due to the century-long influence of religion and of Pollyannism, our intuition is exactly what should not be trusted.

Except for two cases it seems that in all the ethical views presented, sexuality is an ethically important action: in the most of abovementioned cases so important that it needs to be singled out of all other human activities. No matter whether we base ethics on procreation, non-procreation, marriage, love, or whether we require sexuality to be free

---

[550] The existing double moral standards around male and female sexuality must be also mentioned. The research conducted in the Australian National Rugby League in 2004 is an interesting account on this topic (Albury, Carmody, Evers et al., 2011), though, there may be named numerous similar accounts.

[551] All works of Japanese writer Haruki Murakami can be taken as examples – even though they depict the Japanese way of thinking, their presence and success in Western societies makes them quite influential. Currently very successful saga *A Song of Ice and Fire* by George Martin, which was turned into a form *of Game of Thrones* HBO series, can be taken as another one.

of any external influences at all, this basic conception creates a special ethics, applicable only on sex. Antinatalism is no exception. Only the liberal and the hedonistic approaches, which do not distinguish sex from writing letters or shopping – only these two views talk about their main principle, ethics as the whole stands on, and not about ethics of sexuality only.

Additionally, in some views, sex has a meaning and it is engaged in, so as to do something. This *something* is optimally the same reason, which makes sexuality moral. If only procreative sex is moral, then procreation ought to be a reason why we engage in sex, similarly if only sex with a beloved single person is moral, then it is love for which we ought to engage in sex. This does not hold true in antinatalism though because its moral reasoning does not make sense as an incentive. Since it is hardly improbable that anybody would engage in sex so as not to have children, an individual may engage in it for other reasons and the moral assessment of the action itself reminds us of the liberal view. If only non-reproductive sex is moral then all non-reproductive sexual activities are further guided by the general moral principles in a society (such as consent, causing no harm, mutual regards etc.).

Finally, if we accept Sartre's ontology of love and interpersonal relationships, sexuality is suffering. Such a conclusion must sound very odd considering the amount of pleasure it brings. However, supported by Sartre's ontology, sexuality is a painful paradoxical effort to reach the Other, who is out of reach and to find ourselves within the Other, where ourselves are inaccessible. Even from behind the veil of Pollyannism, accommodation and adaptation, the antinatalistic view of the world looks much less controversial in the light of such ontology.

ANTINATALISM AND NEGATIVE ETHICS

INTRODUCTION

Two questionable features of antinatalism are pointed out in this chapter. These criticisms are addressed from an antinatalistic perspective in order to strengthen the antinatalistic stance. First, it can be perceived some rather *non-systematic* character, a lack of a more solid philosophical background on which antinatalistic theses should be grounded. The issue of procreation is embedded in a complex network of questions about life, death, and the situation of human beings in the world. The main elements of a negative ethics (such as formulated in Cabrera 1989, 1996 and 2009) will be presented with the objective of providing a theoretical basis – certainly not the only possible one – for antinatalism.

Secondly, antinatalism presents some indecision in relation to assuming or not a radical pessimistic attitude on the human life to the last consequences. This is noteworthy in the idea of a human life being not worth-starting *in general* but, nonetheless, worth-continuing *in general* (until facing special and exceptional situations). This chapter tries to show that if ethical requirements are accentuated and not only the sensible ones, human life should be regarded as ethically not worth-continuing *in general* even when sensibly tolerable. It will be shown how the posture that considers human life as worth-continuing *in general* may unintentionally weaken the antinatalistic stance.

AN ETHICAL-NEGATIVE BACKGROUND FOR ANTINATALISM (NEGATIVE ANTINATALISM)

The current and more usual pronatalistic position spread out in the world, from which to be born and giving life are ethically good and even naturally admirable facts, arises within a general affirmative conception of human life, which philosophy traditionally admitted without much discussion. Affirmative ethics are sustained upon many ideas, but the basic ones and more relevant to our purposes here are the following:

A   Human life has an obvious positive value that does not need proofs; it is the supreme or basic value and the fundamental presupposition of ethics.

B   What is ethically relevant are not the poles of human life (birth and death), but what is in the middle; morality of birth is excluded from ethical considerations, and morality of death is studied just as a moral preparation for a rather remote event in life.

C   On this level of analysis, morality is conceived as perfectly viable for humans, considered *free* and *responsible* for their actions; moral *dignity* can be arduous and difficult to attain, but not impossible for those who strive.

D   What is investigated is just *how* to define, implement and reach the moral ideals (how to live well, how to be happy, how to be worth of respect, how to be a good father and so on).

At the affirmative context of thinking, natalism is not even a thesis but an obvious fact. Affirmativism is the last theoretical and practical background for natalism (and also of anti-suicide stance and many other questions regarding human life). That is the reason why the first part of negative ethics should be destructive, consisting of a critique of affirmative morality.[552] In a second step, in opposition to affirmative ethics, a negative ethics is outlined along the following lines:

1   The positive value of human life is neither obvious nor evident and should be proved by arguments; usually these arguments are of the *in-spite-of* form (in spite of pain, in spite of suffering, in spite of moral corruption and so on), suggesting a negative way open to a real evaluation of life, after the fall of religious categories of thinking.

2   On this way, it is perfectly possible to prove, by contrast, that human life as imposed at birth constitutes a situation that causes a sensible and moral discomfort to beings like humans. This lack of sensible and moral value is not merely empirical but structural, based on the phenomenon of *terminality of being*, the crude fact that all things – stones, water, non-human animals, humans, human relations, stars and galaxies – are terminal, in the sense of things that begin to end at its very starting point, not calmly but painfully, affected by all kinds of frictions.

---

[552] This is precisely the title of my second book on these subjects; first published in Barcelona in 1996.

3   In the case of humans, they are compelled to react by trying to generate positive values (cultural, affective, artistic, sportive, erotic etc.) in order to support the frictions of terminality; no positive value arise from the terminality itself, but all positive values are products of this persistent and arduous human opposition against the constant advance of terminality, which will win the battle at the end.

4   But precisely in trying to escape from terminality, humans do damage to other humans; they become terminal to each other. The main impact of terminality in human animals is the phenomenon of moral *impediment,* the impossibility of being ethical (in the minimal sense of not manipulating and not harming others) with all humans and all not humans in all our multiple scenarios of action and reaction.

5   This panorama – the sensible and moral devaluation of human life by terminality, the oppressive presence of structural moral impediment and compelling reactive positive values – would seem to lead directly to the radical *denial of morality* in general and this is a perfectly possible step. However, *negative ethics* is the attempt to *negativize* morality rather than deny it. This can be seen as the last chance to still sustain a morality – based on the minimal requirements of non-manipulating and non-damaging – before taking the step of simply denying morality.

6   In a more constructive vein, *negative ethics* recommends a minimalistic form of living (or a survival) characterized by the following four primary negative imperatives:

6.1   Never put the others as the structural causes of our sensible and moral discomfort; all of us are terminal for each other without being structurally responsible for this, being just immediate agents acting in specific circumstances. The others are not the primary cause of our moral misfortune and sensible pain, and their annihilation will not turn our own life better.

6.2   Do not kill any other human, not even those who do not have representation or conditions to formulate their rights in the first person. We are all negatively inviolable to each other, because we all have the same structural value, that is, none.[553]

6.3   Do not procreate; do not put anyone else in the structural discomfort of terminality via unavoidable manipulation. It is more advisable to create works instead of children, preferably negative works, such as dark poems,

---

[553] It is not difficult to extend this imperative to protect also non-human animals, but this step needs an argument that I cannot develop here.

tragic romances, shocking movies or works of pessimistic philosophy, which critically portray the terrors of existence and the morally problematic character of human life.

6.4   Be permanently disposed or available to death at any time (tonight if necessary) when moral demands require so, given the constant and oppressive presence of terminality and of moral impediment, not maintaining any kind of indefinite preservation of life. However, such *disposition towards death* must be *ethically guided*; a negative ethics assumes the terminality received at birth putting our own life at risk when ethical demands so require; these risks cannot be merely sportive, playful or frivolous (Russian roulette); to continue living for helping others in supporting their hard lives, trying to convince people not to have children, or engaging in cultural creations or political militancy *until death becomes ethically preferable or even advisable*.

Ultimately, negative ethics is an ethics of borderlines, not a new ethics of *how to live*, but of how to die ethically, since, in any case, we have to die (this issue is discussed in the second part of the penultimate sub-chapter).[554] As can be seen, just as natalism emerged historically within the context of an affirmative view on human life, negative antinatalism emerges within the complex context of a critique of the affirmative morality and the construction of a negative minimalistic ethics. As we see, not procreating is only one of the four main negative imperatives of negative ethics and presupposes more primitive categories, such as terminality of being, moral impediment, lack of value of human life and a minimal idea of morality as non-manipulation and not causing damage to others.

The first observation given within a critique of antinatalistic reason is that, in general, the antinatalistic thesis appears in a loose or isolated way, without a solid theoretical basis, specifically without an ethical theory, within which antinatalism finds its place and meaning. In most of the antinatalistic positions we do not know what philosophical assumptions we have to accept or reject in order to accept or reject the antinatalism supposedly based on them (for instance, what conception of human being or of human condition is being assumed). Negative ethics aims to provide antinatalism – and a certain kind of pro-mortalism, as we shall see – a theoretical basis of this kind, without pretending to be the only one to be offered. We shall see now that negative ethics can also provide relevant elements for questioning one of the most important asymmetries of many antinatalistic positions, questioning their non-radical character.

---

[554] This kind of ethics is *negative* only in explicit opposition to the current and hegemonic affirmative ethics. If human morality is ever *negativized,* radically changing its relationship to birth and death, it will no longer be *negative* or *affirmative* but simply ethics.

THE ASYMMETRY BETWEEN
NOT WORTH-STARTING AND WORTH-CONTINUING

Many antinatalists have sustained that a human life is not worth-starting, strongly recommending abstention from procreation. In the chapter *How Bad Is Coming into Existence?* of his famous book, Benatar states that the order, intensity and position of sufferings within life are relevant to assess its value in a not simplistic way. He points to hunger, thirst, bowel, bladder distension, tiredness, stress, thermal discomfort, itch, chronic for billions of people.[555] He observes that people experience these negative states every day at some extent. Of course, chronic ailments and advanced age make matters still worse. We have aches, pains, lethargy, allergies, headaches, frustration, irritation, colds, menstrual pains, hot flushes, nausea, hypoglycaemia, seizures, guilt, shame, boredom, sadness, depression, loneliness, body-image dissatisfaction, AIDS or cancer.[556]

The so-called *normal* human lives are affected by the dissatisfaction in the fulfillment of desires, long periods of frustration and expectations never totally or very ephemerally fulfilled. Health and youth are quickly lost (and life itself at the end) and we all loose also our dear ones. Finally, Benatar accepts Schopenhauer's thesis that "(...) *suffering is endemic to and pervasive in life.*"[557] In the book *Debating Procreation*, Benatar discusses with Wasserman and he further increases the list of misfortunes of human life: waiting in traffic or in queues, inefficiency, stupidity, evil, Byzantine bureaucracies, unemployment, dissatisfaction with jobs, professional aspirations unfulfilled.[558] Pleasures are short-lived whereas pains are enduring.[559] Any of us can be injured in seconds, but the path to recovery is slow and uncertain or even impossible.[560]

This gloomy picture seems more than sufficient to establish the thesis of a life not-worth starting and subsequent antinatalism. In Benatar's terms, why bringing someone to suffer chronically all the endemic empirical obstacles that can be easily described? In the negative ethics' terms, why bringing more people to a situation of having a decaying structure, against which they will have to fight arduously, creating reactive positive values until the inevitable moment of being defeated by the terminality given at birth? From an ethical perspective, if understood minimally as a demand of not to manipulate and not to harm others, it seems clear that we do both when we procreate: we give the unborn child a life of very poor quality and in doing so we manipulate it for our own benefit or by an act of irresponsible carelessness. We do not just create a suf-

---

[555] Benatar (2006, p. 71).
[556] Ibid. (p. 72).
[557] Ibid. (p. 77).
[558] Id. (2012, p. 46).
[559] Ibid. (pp. 48n.).
[560] Ibid. (p. 49).

fering being, but also an immoral one, submitted to moral impediment, not only some-body who suffers but also a being who will provoke suffering on others. (I will insist on this point later). Life, therefore, may be seen as clearly not worth-starting, and an ab-stention from procreation as strongly recommended *from an ethical point of view*.

Life Normally Worth-Continuing

Why cannot we, from the premise of the bad quality of human life, make the inference that life is also not worth-continuing? If everyday illnesses, injustices and annoyances are terrible things for merely possible beings – grounding the thesis of the not worth-starting character of a human life – they are even more calamitous for real human be-ings. It would seem that liberating living, present, and sentient beings from these suf-ferings is even more urgent than saving possible beings from them. But this is precisely the step that many antinatalists refuse to make. Just from the beginning, in the same chapter where Benatar relates the many calamities of life, he adverts: *"To clarify, I shall not be arguing that all lives are so bad that they are not worth continuing."*[561]

According to Benatar's version of antinatalism, one needs more arguments for ending the life of an existing person than for starting a not existing life, because the thresholds to be considered for future and for present lives are rather different.[562] Present lives are compared with death, whereas possible or future lives are compared with a mere possibility of coming to existence: *"(...) The view that coming into existence is always a harm does not imply that death is better than continuing to exist, and a fortiori that suicide is (always) desirable. Life may be sufficiently bad that is better not to come into existence, but not so bad that it is better to cease existing."*[563]

Benatar's line of argument passes essentially through the notion of *interest.* He claims that, between a possible life and a real life, there is the mediation of interests that peo-ple have created throughout life, and that now make it *worth continuing.*[564] He deve-lops his argument by distinguishing among different kinds of *interests*, trying to unravel those which have (what he calls) minimal *moral relevance*, namely the *conscious inte-rests*, and taking particular care with the *interests in existing*: *"Those who exist (in the moral relevant sense) have interests in existing. These interests, once fully developed, are typically very strong (...);"*[565] and they are primarily *"interests of continuing to exist."*[566] These *interests* make for him the difference between a life declared to be not worth-

---

[561] Benatar (2006, p. 61).
[562] Ibid. (p. 23).
[563] Ibid. (p. 212).
[564] Ibid. (pp. 25n.).
[565] Ibid. (p. 25).
[566] Ibid. (p. 149).

starting and a life which, at present, we consider to be generally worth-continuing, at least until it becomes really unbearable.

THE NOTION OF WORTH-CONTINUING ON THE ETHICAL TRIAL: THE ISSUE OF INTERESTS

At this point it must be remembered that it was assumed from the beginning *the ethical point of view* concerning the value of starting life, understanding ethics in the minimal sense of not manipulating and not harming others. Life cannot be judged just in sensible or hedonistic terms, or by the physical and psychological impact of life on humans, but also and especially *in moral terms*. In this trend, we immediately see that the very expression *worth continuing* is ambiguous. It can mean *sensibly* worth-continuing or *morally* worth-continuing. Certainly, Al Capone and his partners considered their lives of crimes and criminal gains as *worth-continuing,* but this cannot be the sense of *worth-continuing* used by the defenders of the asymmetry between a life not worth-starting and nevertheless worth-continuing. A *moral* element seems to be relevant here.

Therefore, when it is said that for the humans already born a life may be worth-continuing because they have *interests in continuing to exist, we must ask whether these interests in continuing are ethical* and not merely a product of instinctive or volitional impulse. Since the not-worth starting character of human life was scrutinized and judged *from the moral point of view*, we must do the same in the case of the presumed worth-continuing character of human life. *Ab initio*, from the ethical-negative view, the terminal structure of a human life is the same for the possible beings and for the present beings; the *interests* only change the perspective, which we see the same structure from. If we assume the moral point of view to judge human life, we have to evaluate not just whether life is sensibly tolerable in terms of pleasures and pains, but whether life is worth-living from a moral view.

From the internal perspective of each human being, as Benatar profusely showed, most people think their lives are good and want to continue living. Not even very bad health or extreme poverty interferes with the good opinion that people have of their lives.[567] Human beings have an incredible ability to adapt, and, after a period of discomfort, they adjust to the new circumstances, however painful. They use countless psychological mechanisms for that.[568] In general, from the internal point of view, people have

---

[567] Benatar (2006, p. 66).
[568] Ibid. (pp. 66–69).

the tendency to consider their lives as worth-continuing even when, if seen from an external perspective, they could be considered of a very poor quality.

Some may contest this difference between internal and external views alleging that a life not viewed as bad by the person in question cannot be established externally as bad. But this is highly problematic. It seems important to maintain the distinction between the internal point of view (almost systematically optimistic and positive) about our own lives, and the external view that can question our self-image. If we do not distinguish clearly the external bad quality of life and the internal positive reactions to it, we would be driven to the absurdity of admitting that long prison terms, painful impairment or awful social injustice (like being interned in a concentration camp) are positive things because people were able to endure them and even to take some benefits from them for their lives. We still consider all these experiences as *bad* even when people can adapt almost perfectly to them or find some momentary contentment or even take moral lessons from these terrible experiences.

Nevertheless, if we see *interest* as a category generated by the internal point of view, alleging that life is *worth-continuing* merely because we have *interests in continuing,* these *interests* may be seen as products of the usual optimistic and delusional psychological and biological mechanisms pointed out by Benatar, that lead people to think that their lives are better than they really are. What prevents considering the *interests* that people create throughout their lives, even the interests of continuing living, as permeated by these same optimistic and misleading mechanisms? To say that a real life is *worth continuing* because one has *interests* in it is perfectly equivalent to saying that a real life is worth continuing because one remembers more positive experiences than negative ones, or because one has good expectations for the future, or one adapted well to adverse conditions, or that a life is better than the life of most people, and all the other statements usually affected by the psychological mechanisms.[569] It has been clearly shown how these statements are unreliable, therefore, why would be reliable the statements about *interests in continuing?* And particularly, why would they be reliable from an *ethical* perspective? Bad, corrupt and cruel people can have supreme *interests in continuing living,* but we should be concerned with the ethical conditions for continuing, after having evaluated life-starting from a moral view.

The crucial point here is that wanting to continue a life considered, from the moral point of view, as not worth-starting (in order to spare the offspring the misfortunes of life) does not show that it is *morally* good to continue living without some additional ethical condition; it merely provides an explanation of why, in fact, people tend sensibly, instinctively or inertly to continue living following the stimuli of their self-deceitful *interests.* This can suggest, in a Schopenhauerean vein, that the main motivation to

---

[569] Benatar (2006, pp. 64–69).

continue living is a powerful and almost irresistible impulse of nature. One fundamental fact of life is *that human beings are ready to desire intensely and unconditionally something that lacks sensible and moral value.*

In this sense, Benatar seems to employ a very weak notion of *moral* when he claims that already existing people, at some point of gestation, have interests *deserving of moral consideration*: "*Those who exist (in the morally relevant sense) have interests in existing. These interests, once fully developed, are typically very strong (...).*"[570] But *strong* is not *per se* a moral category; not all strong interests are moral interests. To say that we are pushed by nature to continue living does not provide any *moral* justification for this continuing. On the contrary, some moral motive (in a stronger sense than Benatar's) may oblige us to opt for *not* continuing to live, going against the natural will for surviving. We could say more: maybe morality begins precisely at the moment when the powerful impulse to survive is challenged in benefit of some moral value created *in* life and maybe *against* life.

In fact, from the purely internal viewpoint, we do everything to continue, and in doing so, we can be transgressing moral demands, precisely the rules that could give life some *worth* or *dignity*. This is very clear in extreme cases, for example in the moral corruption of prisoners in a camp, who want to survive at any cost.[571] This conflict between morality and *continuing to live* is present in daily life, but it is clearer in extreme situations, where even honest people can be driven to tell great lies, or to steal, or even to kill in order to survive. This means that for continuing to live we may have to assume a very flexible sort of morality, or even immorality. If giving life morally harms the newborn, continuing to live may morally harm the others and me.

High Moral Price of Life-Continuing

According to the structural account of negative ethics, *any* human life, regardless its eventual contents and balance of pleasures and pains, is an anxious creation of defensive and protective values against the quick and irreversible advance and consummation of the terminality of being given at birth. The onus of living is also *moral* because, in the attempt to escape the consummation of a decaying being that elapses quickly, we have to fight against other people trying to open a way for our own life projects. Strong conflicts between humans are unavoidable. Therefore, existence is always a serious sensible and moral harm not just because of the empirical calculation between

---

[570] Benatar (2006, p. 25).

[571] The case of the Jewish counsels during Nazism can provide a terrible illustration for that (Bauman, 1996, chapter 5: *Asking for the collaboration of the victims*). Cinema also presents life experiments useful for philosophical reflection; in the British film *Bent* (1997), by Sean Mathias, Max complies with the order of a Nazi officer to beat his best friend to death in exchange for survival. At the end of the film, Max recovers his moral condition precisely when he puts some value above survival, and he is able to see his life as not worth-continuing in moral terms.

pains and pleasures is always unfavorable, but because our lives are terminal at birth, from the very beginning, and its terminality is consummated day after day, inexorably and painfully, with all its moral consequences. Both initiating and continuing a human life implies manipulating, causing discomfort and harming other's lives and my own. Negative ethics invites us in the first place to think carefully on three strictly moral prices of continuing to live:

1   The risk of procreation,
2   the risk of manipulating and harming others and
3   the risk of not being able to end one's life with dignity.

First of all, if for antinatalists procreation is the capital sin, the longer we continue to live the more we will be at risk of procreation, unless we accept to lead a life of monastic sexual abstinence, a high price to pay (such as stopping driving to avoid accidents). For heterosexual people, who are still majority in the world (and even homosexuals and perverts also sometimes engage in heterosexual practices with risk of procreation), preventive procedures are now rather safe but none of them 100 percent reliable. After the permanent risk of procreation, we live a life of permanent risk of harming and manipulating others in at least one of the many scenarios (family, work, clubs, travels, traffic, meetings) where we act, and it is very difficult to be morally correct with everyone in all circumstances; we live in a very complex network of actions in which we cannot foresee all the consequences of our actions, which can be more serious than we expected. The world is a dangerous and arduous place, and *living a life* includes maneuvers, strategies and methods not always orthodox, so as not to lose opportunities (because *life is short, opportunities do not come back* etc.).

Many do not accept that in order to live we have to harm others; they think that this refers to primitive lifestyles, in which humans had to kill for surviving. But even if we do not have to kill we have to defend ourselves, to respond offenses and aggressions with energy and try to maintain our self-esteem, without which our personality falls. Our daily lives are much more violent and aggressive than we suppose. But of course, to realize this, one must have an adequate sensitivity; those who adapt perfectly well and accept to be as immoral and aggressive as life demands, will not feel affected by the violence of continuing to live; the more ignorant, insensitive and immoral a human being is, the better they will accept life *as it is* and the more likely they will be *happy* and indifferent to the sufferings of others, especially of the more distant ones. Just as Benatar showed that people usually do not realize how painful their lives are, so they do not realize how immoral and disrespectful their lives are as well. People have of themselves the best of moral images and think that immorality is always of others.

Finally, at any moment in our life-continuing we may be suddenly affected by some of the tragic circumstances described by Benatar, which happen in a minute and can end our life possibilities: terrible diseases, traffic accidents, medical errors, assaults etc. At one point we may be unable to terminate our lives with moral dignity, and the more we wait and let time pass and we get older, the more that situation becomes plausible. Apart from the ethical risk of procreating and harming others, we may run out of even the ethical possibilities of dying, being in the hands of other people that we harm with our state and that we cannot ask to end our life without compromising them ethically and legally. To end one's life in a pessimistic approach is a task for each one of us; we cannot delegate it to others.

On the other hand, the antinatalistic literature has been rather insensitive about political issues, but to continue living also pays high social prices. In the first place, we are born into societies that are systematically unequal; from time immemorial there have always been rich and poor, and it seems that human societies are sustained by the poverty of the majority. Between 70 or 80 percent of humanity has always been in subaltern situations, of slavery or of proletarianization; any child born has a high probability of falling within that margin, with all the moral problems of a very cruel need for survival; and if we are lucky enough to fall into the privileged 20 or 30 percent, to accommodate ourselves in that situation without doing anything to resolve the inequalities, just taking profit from our privileges, puts us in an initial situation of immorality, manipulation and harm.

In the antinatalistic literature the emphasis is placed on the sensible sufferings, physical and psychological,[572] but assuming the ethical point of view, we have many reasons to defend a very strong *moral pessimism*. For even if we succeed in being *happy* and *intellectually successful,* reducing our sufferings and increasing our pleasures, we do not realize how this happiness and professional fulfillment is obtained at the expense of the unhappiness of others, maybe of the greatest number of them. *Great civilizations* arose in the midst of the most cruel slavery, and modern societies were built upon the proletarian system of exploitation of the greater part of the planet's population.

On Three Alleged Moral Motives for Life-Continuing

In order to strengthen the asymmetry between a life *in general* not worth-starting but *in general* worth-continuing, at least three moral motives to continue living (supposing minimal or tolerable suffering) are usually put:

A   The possibility of helping others to endure such an arduous life.

---

[572] Antinatalists speak of *good* or *bad* lives accentuating the issue of pleasure and suffering, not the moral motive. Cf.: "*We can, and often do, have good lives. And those good lives remain good even if they have periods of pain within them*" (Belshaw, 2012, p. 123). This type of statement is common in the literature. Here it is not considered that a life can be sensibly good and deeply immoral; and that there may be a connection between both things: as long as I am more indifferent to the sufferings of others, I have more chances to lead a *good life* or *happy life* (for me).

B   To create beautiful works that can delight and make life more bearable.

C   Do not hurt our beloved ones with our death.

It will be shown how, in a pessimistic view of human life and using theoretical elements from negative ethics, these three reasons for life-continuing are highly controversial. Regarding the motive of *helping others*, we have three remarks to make:

1   We may see attitudes of care and benevolence concerning others as attempts to lighten the weight of our own existence when it becomes unbearable. Caring for others can be a way of manipulating them for our own benefit; in the same way that it is not the progenitors who give their children a help, but the children who help their parents (saving empty lives or failed marriages), in a similar way those who we help (and that we use as presumed motives for continue living) sustain us and help us to continue. We do not continue living for helping them, but helping them helps us to continue.

2   Since we always act in a very complex network of actions, we are never sure that we are helping the right people (we may be getting a good job for someone who later exploits thousands of employees), or that our assistance will not have disastrous consequences even for the person we intend to help (Vilém Flusser's wife who drove the car to protect her short-sighted husband and caused his death in a traffic accident);

3   Trying to help other people we can be struck by ingratitude and ungratefulness of those we intend to help (the case of the Argentine liberator San Martin, who freed three countries with enormous sacrifice of his life and health, and then was considered a traitor and forced to go into exile). The discomfort and moral impediment in which we were placed at birth makes that the help we give to others is always conditional, risky, and perhaps inglorious and counterproductive.[573]

As far as the works that we can make is concerned, whether literary, cinematographic or philosophical, they are without any doubt a good substitute for procreation: better to create works than to generate people; and to the extent that our works are beautiful, they can help a lot of people improve their lives. Nevertheless, it is not clear how pessimistic and antinatalistic works can do this job, how can works called *All Cradle Is a Grave* or *Procreation Is Murder* improve or animate the life of a reader. Of course, these works can be illuminating for many, but nothing guarantees that they cannot be devastating. The books and films that can help are precisely the affirmative ones, which

---

[573] Here we are talking only about minimal help, trying to reduce other people's suffering (the goal of negative utilitarianism); any maximum help, of altruistic intention, still proves to be much more improbable.

preach everything that pessimists criticize and reject; on the contrary, negative literature (such as my own negative ethics books) can cause traumatic impressions. Books, even if well intentioned, can lead to insanity or suicide. Again, creating such works may be something that helps their authors to continue living, not necessarily something that helps others.

At last we come to the most important reason alleged to continue living, and specifically for not committing suicide: the damage impinged on others. Benatar puts this very popular and accepted point very clearly: *"Suicide, like death from other causes, makes the lives of those who are bereaved much worse. Rushing into one's own suicide can have profound negative impact on the lives of those close to one. (...) This places an important obstacle in the way of suicide. One's life is bad, but one must consider what affect ending it would have on one's family and friends."*[574] But at this point of the argumentation, we should properly place intentional life-ending within the scope of the pessimistic approach on human life, where we can find many significant difficulties in claiming that suicide harms memorably other people.

When thinking on the supposed great impact that a suicide could provoke in others, it may be convenient to reflect more carefully on what kind of *others* we are talking about. The immense majority of humanity does not know us and will not be affected by our death; and if we are very famous, we can be well-known but not at the point of devastating our admirers or readers with our death; to the contrary, many admirers prefer their idols to be dead (and sometimes they kill them, as in the case of John Lennon and many others). But letting aside the multitudes, we could distinguish, to elucidate this point seriously at least three kinds of close survivors:

A   Our progenitors;

B   Our friends, colleagues and dear ones;

C   Our enemies.

It is understandable that our parents will be affected by our suicide (even when this is not always the case). Nevertheless, their reactions must be inserted in the pessimistic and antinatalistic environment. When somebody does not abstain from procreating, they risk a gamble about the *good life* of the offspring, gamble that can perfectly be lost. Since it is a one-sided and perfectly avoidable gamble, the genitors seem to be morally imputable in manipulating and harming their children independently of the results of the gamble, favorable or not to the newborn. Moral imputation refers to the mere possibility of harming, not to its effective accomplishment. And manipulation is sure. Therefore, progenitors are morally imputable even when the procreated is succes-

---

[574] Benatar (2006, p. 220). See also Hwang (2017, p. 13).

sful in attaining some equilibrium in between, in ethical-negative terms, the terminality given at birth and the creation of reactive positive values.

In the specific case of the son's or daughter's suicide, the progenitors lost the gamble, at least from their own perspective. They initially put their child in a very difficult situation that they did not know the offspring would be able to confront with success, and they procreated in their own benefit all the same. Within the pessimistic approach, we cannot as children accept not critically any commitment of retaining a structurally valueless life just in order of not harming precisely those who imposed this painful structure to us. The harm provoked in the parents by the children's suicide mirrors the harm impinged in the offspring by bringing them into a painful and dangerous world through a risky gamble and manipulation. The terrible violence of voluntary death reflects the terrible violence of involuntary birth. The most of the newborns might succeed in enduring the hardships of life, to the extent that their mechanisms of defense work well turning their lives worth-continuing, and this may be their merit; yet we cannot morally charge those who do not succeed.

I will invert the order of the list and let the impact caused in friends and the dear ones to the end. Let us see case (C). If we are not hypocrite or self-benevolent and assume the pessimistic point of view, we know perfectly well that along our lives we make many enemies, from jealous colleagues of work to envy relatives and even mortal enemies, who wish to see us dead. Newspapers report cases of businessmen commending colleagues' murders, and during totalitarian states many were sent to concentration camps or prisons denounced by their neighbors and enemies. We do not need to be particularly mean or hideous to have many enemies, but just having the personality we have and the ideas we sustain; the mere exposition of our convictions in politics, religion or even sport in some environments or groups, or the way we make gestures or use our voice can irritate and make others be very angry with us. We can be hated just for being shy or cautious. We are frequently victims of gossips and libels just for talking and thinking as we talk and think. So, in the case of our enemies our suicide will give them a great benefit and a great joy. If we think that it is a great obstacle to suicide the damage done to our friends, with the same logic we can say that our suicide is a great gift done to our enemies, that, in the pessimistic approach, can be in much greater number than our friends. Assuming pessimism we must sadly admit that it is much easier in life to have many real enemies than just one real friend.

But let us pass to the more important case, the impact of suicide on our friends and dear ones. I have five main objections to this frequently repeated and generally accepted point:

1   Dear ones, if they are really our friends and love us, are going (and are at some extent morally obliged) to accept our will to end our life, and make special efforts to overcome as soon as possible the fact of our disappearance.

2   Even pessimists admit that deaths and suicides do not prevent the most of people from considering their lives as worth-continuing even after the loss. Precisely, the same powerful psychological and biological mechanisms pointed by Benatar that people use to evaluate their lives will do their job also in the case of losses.

3   In fact, as showed by empirical observation, many few people kill themselves or remain totally blocked by the death of a loved one, even when by suicide; the most *push the boat forward* and continue living as they can.

4   Nature and society insistently impel people to oblivion of their dead ones.

5   Of course, we all vehemently want to be remembered and not to be forgotten; this is a part of our strong desire not to die totally, but this desire is not rationally justified on facts.

I will say something very briefly about each one of these five points. First, under the hypothesis that we are committing suicide by reasons we consider sensibly and morally relevant (not only in extreme cases, like a serious illness or a risk of persecution and torture, but by moral reasons we can justify), we can rationally suppose that our real friends are going to understand our motives and approve them, even when they feel comprehensibly anguished with our disappearance. If they do not understand this way and repudiate our act, we can rationally doubt whether they are *really* our friends. They must understand that – recovering a Kantian distinction – we can inflict on them some evident *sensible* pain or anguish without damaging them *morally*.

Second, one of the motives claimed by those sustaining that life is generally worth-continuing even when not worth-starting, is that we are provided with powerful psychological and biological mechanisms to withstand the pain of loss of our loved ones; it is generally admitted that these losses, even when terrible, do not cause most people to consider that their lives are not worth-continuing. So there seems to be some incongruity in the pessimistic approach in stating that our death, especially by suicide, affects our loved ones in a terrible way to the extent that it is a reason to not kill us, but, on the other hand, admitting that, in general, people continue to regard their lives worth-continuing despite sufferings. It is at least reasonable to assume that the same powerful mechanisms that lead people to continue living, even in very bad conditions, and to consider their lives worth-continuing and much better than they really are (as Benatar pointed out), the same mechanism will also lead our friends to forget about our death and to continue living after the loss, however painful.

Third, this is precisely what we see happening all the time in real life. What we see is that people mourn their dead at first, grieve for a while, and then they *rebuild their lives* after the loss. We empirically observe that very few persons kill themselves or remain definitively paralyzed or blocked because of the suicide of a beloved one.[575] How many of them get crazy or seriously ill? How many people stop completely and definitively working and developing the sexual and affective dimensions of their lives after the suicide of a beloved one? Usually people get affected for a few weeks or months, but rarely for years and years or forever.[576] Of course, internal suffering can continue and be terrible and last forever, but it does not prevent human beings from considering their lives as worth-continuing, despite everything, and continue working and loving. In the long run, suicides and deaths in general will be absorbed by the flow of living and subjected to the same protective mechanisms of oblivion.

Fourth, not only nature but also society keeps pushing people who have suffered losses to gather new forces and take other opportunities of life, forgetting the past. Far from stimulating and reinforcing our sadness or leaving us weeping and wailing for a long time, our friends and family will insist at all times that we must forget and continue to live our life; many people marry again, have children with another person, continue to work, earn money and create works after the losses, without forgetting internally the beloved ones but without annulling their lives for many long periods or forever. Relatives, friends and close people in general get impatient when we cannot forget, and if after a year we continue to mourn a loss, they will send us to a good psychologist.

Finally, we all strongly want to be remembered and not to be forgotten; this is part of our narcissistic desire of not disappearing completely. However, this is only a wish not supported by empirical facts; our lives are insignificant from the external point of view.[577] Our lives gained value while we were alive, by force of our efforts and other's in creating reactive positive values. Once we died, we recovered the same lack of value that we had at birth. The great Portuguese poet Fernando Pessoa has expressed very well in his famous poem *Se te queres matar* [*If you want to kill yourself*] the contrast between the great importance that we give ourselves and the brutal indifference of the world.[578]

---

[575] The French actor Charles Boyer committed suicide three days after his wife's death, but this is a completely exceptional case and many see this type of action as pathological or excessively romantic.

[576] In jobs, bosses and administrators give employees who have lost their mother or father exactly one week to cry, mourn and make the necessary arrangements; after that period, it is considered that they are ready to resume their usual tasks.

[577] *"From a position sufficiently external, my birth seems accidental, my life meaningless and my death insignificant; but from an inner perspective, it seems almost impossible to imagine that I was never born, my life is of monstrous importance, and my death is a catastrophe"* (Nagel, 1986, chap. 11, p. 349).

[578] *"Does anyone miss you? Nobody misses you. You are not needed for anyone. (...) Without you everything will run without you. Maybe for many it is worse that you exist than you kill yourself (...) Maybe you hurt more lasting than stop lasting (...). Relax; very few will weep you (...). The vital impulse wipes the tears little*

On the other hand, it seems morally wrong to put the others as obstacles to assume personal responsibilities; this can be seen as a kind of manipulation. We could even feel offended and aggressed if someone says to us that they are very unhappy, that they cannot support life any more, but that they do not commit suicide for not provoking to us a great damage.[579] This is a point always heavily rejected in discussions and the only way to settle it is by serious empirical research. I am not stating that this way of seeing things is absolutely true, but it is a psychologically plausible hypothesis, especially within the pessimistic approach, which admits the regular functioning of these powerful mechanisms of self-protection and delusion. Perhaps the ethically correct attitude would be to die along with those we love, but we see that life works differently;[580] that being so, the argument that we cannot morally commit suicide so as not to injure the dear ones loses much of their apparently obvious force.

BREAKING THE ASYMMETRY: MAKING ROOM FOR INMINENT DISPOSITION TO DEATH

A human life is regularly afflicted by constant and unpredictable illnesses, nuisances, attacks and dangers, sensible and moral, natural and social. We are regularly put into a situation of sensible and moral suffering where we must do everything in order to survive and to *live well*, imposing our interests in spite of others'. When life seems to be pleasant or *good* it pays high moral prices, because our happiness may be built on the basis of the unhappiness of most other human beings. If all this is seriously assumed, *human life should be regarded as ethically not worth-continuing in general;* continuing to live in a human society is, in general, ethically questionable, even when not too much unpleasant or harmful. All this makes one suspect that the real motives for which humans consider life worth-continuing and in fact continue to live are not of

---

by little (...). There is first in all a relief from the boring tragedy of you having died (...). Then the conversation lightened daily, and everyday life resumed its day (...). Then, slowly, you are forgotten. You are only reminded on two dates: when you were born and how many years passed from your death (...). If you want to kill yourself, kill yourself (...). Do not have moral scruples or fears of intelligence! Do not you see that you have no importance at all?" (Pessoa, 1993, p. 22). Translation from Portuguese by the author.

[579] In a vein of *dark humor* an adequate answer to this would be: *"Don't worry about that, sir/lady. Nature and society provided me with strong mechanisms to assimilate losses and psychological shocks however devastating. I will be very sorry for your death at the beginning but, in the long run, I will accept your disappearance. Go ahead!"* This line of thought is not only humoristic but also ethical, because it intends to restore the suicidal a serious ethical commitment unfairly assigned to others.

[580] Perhaps only in cinema human deaths have all the impact they should have. For dramatic reasons, in movies humans actually kill, kill themselves, and perform extreme actions in complete mortal coherence. The philosopher Slavoj Žižek frequently pointed out, in books and videos, how people today have their desires not only satisfied but shaped and organized by the images of cinema.

a moral nature.[581] On the philosophical level, philosophers have tried to provide ethical reasons for continuing to live, but we saw that all these supposedly moral motives are controversial. If so, we could rationally suspect that they may be a subterfuge in order to conceal lack of courage to involve in risky militancy or commit the terrible act of suicide.

From the viewpoint of negative ethics, we can say that people continue living because they succeed in maintaining a rather unstable and delicate balance between the structural components of life (terminality, suffering, aging, decadence), and the amount and force of reactive positive values that humans are able to create, when they succeed in living a number of sufficiently intense or pleasant experiences such that they help them to cope successfully with the bitterness of the inexorable passage of time, the daily sufferings, the painful losses of those we love and so on. When the structural terminality given at birth closes all the possibilities of creation of reactive positive values, as in the case of terminal illness, people, in a natural way, ask to die.[582] We do not think of people in this situation as cowardly suicidal (we do not think so about people who jumped from the burning World Trade Center towers on this horrible day). We see them as people placed in a narrow or null existential space of choices, where the creation of reactive values is no longer possible, and where the terminal structure of life occupied the totality of the space of decisions, a situation in which any of us can be placed in any moment of our lives (not, as in the optimistic view, in some distant day).

Can Life be Ethically Worth-Ending?

If life is, according to negative ethics, *ethically not-worth continuing in general*, does this mean immediate voluntary dying, suicide now? Not necessarily. If to continue living without qualifications could be, as we saw before, immoral, ending life without qualifications is not immune to immorality as well. In this sub-chapter it will be shown a possible way of visualizing a life-continuing guided by negative moral categories. It is, as we shall see, a dramatic and risky continuing, not a peaceful one. There is *ab initio* something that already speaks in favor of voluntary death in ethical terms; ethics always required us to fight against purely instinctive impulses and to impose reason on them; voluntary death succeeds in challenging the powerful impulse to survive even in moral indignity or extreme suffering. But of course, this alone is not enough: although we can accept that all morality, or much of it, is based on the capacity to challenge survival

---

[581] In the recent article *Better No Longer to Be*, Rafe McGregor and Ema Sullivan-Bissett have tried to show, following Benatar, that "(...) *while interests are sufficient to show that continued existence is not immoral, they are insufficient to show that it is not irrational (...)*" (2012, p. 66). In this article I try to take a step forward and show that if the interests in continuing to live are not ethically sustainable, continuing to live may be also immoral.

[582] See Singer (1994, chap. 7).

impulses, this does not mean that any challenging of these impulses will be moral for that alone; we need more elements.

In the first place, voluntary death is something broader than suicide. We have seen before that the first immoral situation, which we are placed in from the beginning, is our insertion into a deeply unjust society whose successful functioning is possible thanks to the immense effort of the majority of the planet's population. Faced with this situation, many attitudes are possible, from simply accommodating in the situation of inequality or adopting total indifference or else to involve into political revolt and social struggle. Negative ethics is extremely concerned with negative militancy as a form of life and death, with involvement in fights for liberation that put one's life at serious risk; either in protest fasts or unarmed war experiences, or in the care of very sick people at risk of contagion etc. All these situations can lead to voluntary deaths, species of *indirect suicides. A life guided by negative ethics is not only non-procreative but also a way of life in which we put our lives at risk much more than usual.* In these negative lives, living is not worth-continuing gratuitously and indefinitely, but always within a tension where we may have to die anytime – tonight if necessary – if ethics demands so.

If we accept, in the lines of the arguments above, that life is *in general* ethically not worth-continuing, that the catastrophes, sensible and moral, described by the pessimists are constant, endemic and inevitable and invade our daily lives, *a much greater space for what we can call availability for death should be open in the pessimistic point of view on human life.* Life-ending, in this view, cannot be postponed *indefinitely*, but be subjected to more frequent ethical scrutiny, to see whether to continue living is more ethically worth than ending life. We have a tension here, ethically relevant, between life-continuing and life-ending regarding the question of ethical *dignity.* Nothing guarantees that to continue living or to stop living are, in absolute terms, more ethical than the opposite in some point of life. Here, therefore, one must take distance from two extremes: immediate suicide and indefinite continuation of life. Neither one nor the other is *a priori* excluded but the choice has to arise from an ethical consideration of each case.

Assuming, from the beginning, the ethical point of view – at least minimally defined by the demands of not manipulating and not harming others.[583] – we must speak here of a *morally guided life-ending.* That is the reason why negative ethics cannot simply recommend immediate suicide because this may be motivated just by fear or weakness; dying is ethically advisable when the conditions for generating positive values have been exhausted for natural reasons – terrible diseases – or social – persecution or risk of torture, or in any circumstance in which to continue living means the breaking of

---

[583] It is important to insist on the minimalistic character of this moral requirement, because the antinatalists and pessimists are often accused of subjecting human life to ethical standards that are too high or unattainable. Not manipulating and not harming others is the least we can ethically require.

moral demands of non-manipulating and not harming. We are always in a situation of moral impediment, but it is possible that our continued existence is more ethically relevant than dying (for example, if someone occupies an important place in a struggle for emancipation); but we have to be willing, at any moment, to die by what we are fighting for.[584]

Of course, throughout our lives we have been creating affective and cognitive ties with other humans, and we cannot simply put an end to our lives in any moment without all sorts of considerations affecting these other people. (In this sense, the famous *right to die* has yet to be ethically weighed; one cannot simply exercise one right without *any* consideration for others). It is clear that the dear ones and colleagues will be taken into account in the decision, but without using them to escape from responsibilities. We must respect their suffering for our death not killing ourselves for spurious reasons; but when the time comes to kill us to save our ethical dignity, the harm we can do to them cannot be a pretext for us not to fulfill our moral obligations.

What was exposed in this sub-chapter can be considered a form of pro-mortalism within the background of a negative ethics, or *negative pro-mortalism*. This position rejects both *suicide now* and indefinite continuing of life, and relies on the category of ethical availability for death.[585] The fact that people in general prefer to continue living indefinitely does not refute this. We should not confuse the weakness of our bodies and souls with the soundness of our philosophical theses. The fact that we are not able to assume the not worth-continuing character of our present lives should not lead us to reject this idea.

CONCLUSION

In this chapter, I have attempted to show that antinatalistic theses can be more clearly and precisely exposed when put into a more systematic theoretical framework. The issue of procreation is not an isolated item, but theoretically articulated with a view of a human being and their situation in the world. I have tried to offer this framework outlining the fundamental lines of a negative ethics. From this theoretical framework, it is possible to treat with rigor crucial questions like the asymmetry between a life not

---

[584] This provides an additional political argument against procreation: it is very difficult to engage in a dangerous militancy having children to take care of. Great political activists were in general bad parents.

[585] Among the two kinds of pro-mortalism indicated in the post-script of McGregor and Sullivan-Bissett (2012, p. 66), negative pro-mortalism chooses to commit suicide later, not when one's life becomes sufficiently bad, but when one's life becomes ethically unsustainable, even if not too bad.

worth-starting and worth-continuing, emphasizing the ethical point of view and radicalizing the pessimism, in such a way as not to give spaces for natalism.

Pessimists will certainly accept that *in some extreme cases*, life becomes not worth-continuing; but they consider these situations *exceptional*, accepting that, *in general* a not-worth starting life is normally worth-continuing, even when, as we saw before, they seem to accentuate the sensible aspect of this worth-continuing more than the moral one. They think that, in general and normally, life is worth-continuing, perfectly tolerable and sometimes even pleasant.[586] This view is, of course, perfectly tenable, but I just want to point out that this can weaken the thesis that life is never worth-starting and give some force to natalism; because if life is *in general* reasonably worth-continuing, why not to procreate in order to give the offspring this perfectly bearable (and sometimes pleasant) life, currently worth-continuing, even when never – conceding the pessimistic thesis – entirely happy? The pronatalist could argue that people procreate in the rational expectation that, in spite of the difficulties of life, the offspring will be able to create *interests* to turn their life *worth-continuing*, as most people do.

In the ethical-negative view, by contrast, procreation is immoral, among other things, because it puts us in a situation where voluntary death becomes an inminent possibility, and sometimes the only open door; not as something remote and exceptional. Suicide is always a terrible act, but we can be morally committed to it because we were put at birth in this complex situation of deciding between continuing or stopping, given the sensible and moral sufferings of life and our will to guide our lives ethically. Nevertheless, if the pessimist thinks that the suicidal situations are rather exceptional and life is, in general, worth-continuing, then procreation does not seem so immoral, because it makes sense to procreate a life that has many chances to be a life *worth-continuing* and where suicide is a very remote possibility. The pessimist can reply that procreation is still immoral because there remains the manipulation that is made on the other; but if a human life is not unbearable but regularly worth-continuing, manipulation can be tempered by saying that it was an inevitable step in order to give the unborn a life that they have very high chances of considering worth-continuing. Pessimists are here situated between advisable suicide and reasonable natalism.

In face of this situation, the pessimist may perhaps prefer to abandon the moral frame of reference accepting that continuing to live may rely on non-moral motives, such as

---

[586] Benatar does not usually talk in *liking life*, but in *creating interests in life*, because *liking* is a rather embarrassing term for a pessimist to employ. However I do not see any problem in expressing Benatar's insights on a life worth-continuing in terms of pleasure: those who exist like existing. Mere *having interests* seems to be a very dry rational expression for describing our curious daily involvement in a life that we recognize rationally and morally as not worth-continuing; an affective element seems to be relevant here.

the sensible discomfort that naturally causes the idea of dying; we remain in life for non-moral reasons. However, this move faces at least two problems:

A   When we judged human life as not-worth starting, we did it *from the moral point of view*; we cannot abandon this frame of reference in the middle of the road, but we must also apply ethical criteria to judge the continuation of living.

B   Just as there may be non-moral reasons for continuing to live, the natalist may say that there may be non-moral reasons for procreation. If we are going to accept that continuing is immoral but we will continue to live anyway, we can procreate even knowing that procreation is immoral.

My idea as a convinced pessimist and antinatalist is not to give all this room so easily to the natalist – not even to the pessimistic natalist! – and accept the idea that a human life is sensibly painful and morally impeded, endemically and not eventually, in the majority of the everyday situations of life. This posture saves us from the objections of the natalist and greatly strengthens the antinatalistic stance: if the life that is going to be given to the unborn will be *certainly* ethically not worth-continuing, besides being also sensibly painful, with greater reason this life should be considered not worth-starting.

BIBLIOGRAPHY

ABAELARD, Peter. 1922. *Historia calamitatum* [online]. Fordham University. Internet Medieval Source Book. Corrected 1999 [accessed 5.3. 2018]. Available at: https://sourcebooks.fordham.edu/halsall/basis/abelard-histcal.asp

AKERMA, Karim. 1995. *Soll eine Menschheit sein? Eine fundamentalethische Frage*. Cuxhaven-Dartford: Traude Junghans Verlag. ISBN 3926848367.

AKERMA, Karim. 2000. *Verebben der Menschheit?: Neganthropie und Anthropodizee*. Freiburg/Munich: Verlag Karl Alber. ISBN 3495479120.

AKERMA, Karim. 2014. Ist der Vegetarismus ein Antinatalismus? [online]. *Pro iure animalis*. 24.3.2014 [accessed 4.2.2018]. Available at: http://pro-iure-animalis.de/index.php/antinatalismus/articles/ist-der-vegetarismus-ein-antinatalismus.html

AKERMA, Karim. 2015. Exodus aus dem Sein. Kurnigs Neo-Nihilismus als buddhistisch säkularisierter Geist des frühen Christentums [online]. *Tabularasa: Zeitung für Gesselschaft & Kultur*. 1.6.2015 [accessed 26.3.2018]. Available at: http://www.tabularasamagazin.de/exodus-aus-dem-sein-kurnigs-neo-nihilismus-als-buddhistisch-saekularisierter-geist-des-fruehen-christentums/

AKERMA, Karim. 2017. *Antinatalismus: Ein Handbuch*. Berlin: Epubli. ISBN 9783741892752.

AKERMA, Karim. 2018. *Antinatalismblog: For the Propagation of Non-propagation* [online]. [Accessed 26.3.2018]. Available at: www.antinatalismblog.wordpress.com

ALBURY, Kath, Moira CARMODY, Clinton EVERS et al. 2011. Playing by the Rules: Researching, Teaching and Learning Sexual Ethics with Young Men in the Australian National Rugby League. *Sex Education: Sexuality, Society and Learning*, vol. 11, no. 3, pp. 339–351. ISSN 1468-1811.

ALEXANDER OF LYCOPOLIS. 1963. Quoted from: JONAS, Hans. *The Gnostic Religion: The Message of the Alien God & The Beginnings of Christianity*. 2nd edition. Boston: Beacon Press, p. 231. ISBN 0807057991.

ALTMAN, Matthew. 2010. Kant on Sex and Marriage: The Implications for the Same-Sex Marriage Debate. *Kant-Studien*, vol. 101, no. 3, pp. 309–330. ISSN 0022-8877.

ANNABA, Philippe. 2008. *Proférations gnostiques*. Toulon: Les presses du Midi. ISBN 9782878679472.

ARENDT, Hannah. 1998. *The Human Condition.* 2nd edition. Chicago: The University of Chicago Press. ISBN 0226025993.

ARISTOTLE. 1984. *The Complete Works of Aristotle: The Revised Oxford Translation.* Princeton: Princeton University Press. ISBN 0691099502.

ARISTOTLE. 1888. Eudemos. In: PLUTARCHOS. *Moralia: Consolatio ad Apollonium.* Lipsko: Teubner. Available at: http://penelope.uchicago.edu/Thayer/E/Roman /Texts/Plutarch/Moralia/Consolatio_ad_Apollonium.html.

ARISTOTLE. 1993b. *Der Protreptikos der Aristoteles.* Frankfurt am Main: Klostermann. ISBN 3465025997.

ARISTOTLE. 2003. *De Partibus Animalium 1, De Generatione Animalium 1.* Oxford: Clarendon Press. ISBN 0198751281.

ARROYO, Christopher. 2017. *Kant's Ethics and the Same-Sex Marriage Debate: An Introduction.* Providence: Springer. ISBN 9783319557311.

AUGUSTINE. 1887. On the Good of Marriage. In: SCHAFF, Philip (ed.). *Selected Library of the Nicene and Post-Nicene Fathers: First series: St. Augustine: On the Holy Trinity, Doctrinal Treatises, Moral Treatises.* Vol. 3. Buffalo: The Christian Literature Company, pp. 397–413.

AUGUSTINE. 1998. *The City of God against the Pagans.* Cambridge: Cambridge University Press. ISBN 9780521468435.

AUGUSTINE. 2001. *De Bono Coniugali – De Sancta Virginitate.* Oxford: Clarendon Press. ISBN 0198269951.

BASTEN, Stuart. 2009. *Voluntary Childlessness and Being Childfree: The Future of Human Reproduction* [online]. 2009 [accessed 5.3.2018]. Available at: http://citese-erx.ist.psu.edu/viewdoc/download?doi=10.1.1.701.9495&rep=rep1&type=pdf

BAUMAN, Zygmund. 1996. *Modernity and the Holocaust.* Oxford: Polity Press. ISBN 9788571104839.

BAWULSKI, Shawn. 2013. Do Hell and Exclusivism Make Procreation Morally Impermissible?: A Reply to Kenneth Himma. *Faith and Philosophy: Journal of the Society of Christian Philosophers*, vol. 30, no. 3, pp. 330–344. ISSN: 2153-3393.

BEISER, Frederick. 2016. *Weltschmerz: Pessimism in German Philosophy, 1860–1900.* New York: Oxford University Press. ISBN 9780198768715.

BELSHAW, Christopher. 2012. A New Argument for Anti-Natalism. *South-African Journal of Philosophy*, vol. 31, no. 1, pp. 117–127. ISSN 0258-0136.

BENATAR, David. 1997. Why It Is Better Never to Come into Existence. *American Philosophical Quarterly*, vol. 34, no. 4, pp. 345–355. ISSN 0003-0481.

BENATAR, David. 2006. *Better Never to Have Been: The Harm of Coming into Existence*. Oxford: Clarendon Press. ISBN 0199296421.

BENATAR, David. 2010. Introduction. In: BENATAR, David (ed.). *Life, Death & Meaning: Key Philosophical Readings on the Big Questions*. 2nd edition. Lanham Md.: Rowman & Littlefield Publishers, pp. 1–16. ISBN 9781442201699.

BENATAR, David. 2012. Every Conceivable Harm: A Further Defence of Anti-Natalism. *South African Journal of Philosophy,* vol. 31, no. 1. pp. 128–164. ISSN 2137-74402.

BENATAR, David. 2013. Still Better Never to Have Been: A Reply to (More of) My Critics. *Journal of Ethics*, vol. 17, no. 1, pp. 121–151. ISSN 1382-4554.

BENATAR, David. 2015. Anti-Natalism. In: BENATAR, David and David WASSERMAN. *Debating Procreation: Is it Wrong to Reproduce?* New York: Oxford University Press, pp. 10–132. ISBN 9780199333554.

BENJAMIN, Walter. 1991. *Gesammelte Schriften*. Vol. 2. Frankfurt am Main: Suhrkamp. ISBN 3518098322.

BERNIE, Eric. 1964. *Games People Play: The Psychology of Human Relationships*. London: Penguin Books. ISBN 0140027688.

BIANCHI, Gabriel. 2011. Subjektivnost sexuality. In: ŠULOVÁ, Lenka, Tomáš FAIT, Petr WEISS et al. *Výchova k sexuálně reprodukčnímu zdraví*. Prague: Maxdorf. ISBN 9788073452384.

[*Bible*]. 1992. *Bible de Jérusalem*: La Sainte Bible traduite en français sous la direction de l'école biblique de Jérusalem. Paris: Editions du Cerf. ISBN 2204014915.

[*Bible*]. 2018. *English Standard Version* [online]. [Accessed 21.1.2018]. Available at: https://www.biblegateway.com/

[*Bible*]. 2018. *New Revised Standard Version: Catholic Edition* [online]. [Accessed 21.1.2018]. Available at: https://www.biblegateway.com/

BLUMENBERG, Hans. 1975. *Die Genesis der kopernikanischen Welt: Die Zweideutigkeit des Himmels. Eröffnung der Möglichkeit eines Kopernikus*. Vol. 1. Frankfurt am Main: Suhrkamp. ISBN 3518079522.

BOCK, Gisela. 1994. Antinatalism, Maternity and Paternity in National Socialist Racism. In: CREW, David (ed.). *Nazism and German Society 1933–1945*. London, New York: Routledge, pp. 110–140. ISBN 0415082404.

BOËTHIUS, Anicius Manlius Severinus. 1918. *De Consolatione philosophiae.* In: BOËTHIUS, Anicius Manlius Severinus. *Tractates, De Consolatione philosophiae.* Cambridge: Harvard University Press. ISBN 8071980218.

BOURETZ, Pierre. 2010. *Witnesses for the Future: Philosophy and Messianism.* Baltimore: John Hopkins University Press. ISBN 9780801894503.

BROWN, Peter. 1995. *Le renoncement à la chair: Virginité, célibat et continence dans le christianisme primitif.* Paris: Gallimard. ISBN 2070730506.

BURKE, Edmund. 1823. *A Philosophical Inquiry into the Origin of Our Ideas of the Sublime and Beautiful.* London: Thomas M'Lean.

BURTT, Edwin Arthur. 1951. *The Metaphysical Foundations of Modern Physical Science.* London: Routledge.

CABRERA, Julio. 1989. *A ética e suas negações: Não nascer, suicídio e pequenos assassinatos.* Rio de Janeiro: Rocco. ISBN 9788581221052.

CABRERA, Julio. 1996. *Crítica de la Moral Afirmativa: Una reflexión sobre nacimiento, muerte y valor de la vida.* Barcelona: Gedisa. ISBN 8474325862.

CABRERA, Julio, Di SANTIS and Thiago LENHARO. 2009. *Porque te amo não nascerás!: Nascituri te salutant.* Brasil: LGE Editora. ISBN 9788572384087.

CASSIN, Barbara at al. 2014. *Dictionary of Untranslatables: A Philosophical Lexicon.* Princeton: Princeton University Press. ISBN 1400849918.

CICERO, Marcus Tullius. 2017. *De finibus bonorum et malorum.* Oxford: Oxford University Press. ISBN 0191838071.

CLEMENT OF ALEXANDRIA. 1963. Quoted from: JONAS, Hans. *The Gnostic Religion: The Message of the Alien God & The Beginnings of Christianity.* 2nd edition. Boston: Beacon Press, pp. 144n. ISBN 0807057991.

CLEMENT OF ALEXANDRIA. 2005. *Stromateis: Books One to Three.* Washington, D.C.: Catholic University of America Press. ISBN 0813214335.

COATES, Ken. 2014. *Anti-Natalism: Rejectionist Philosophy from Buddhism to Benatar.* Sarasota: First Edition Design Publishing. ISBN 9781622875702.

COLES, Andrew. 1997. Animal and Childhood Cognition in Aristotle's Biology and the Scala Naturae. In: KULLMANN, Wolfgang and Sabine FÖLLINGER (eds.). *Aristotelische Biologie: Intentionen, Methoden, Ergebnisse: Akten des Symposions über Aristoteles' Biologie vom 24.–28. Juli 1995 in der Werner-Reimers-Stiftung in Bad Homburg.* Stuttgart: F. Steiner Verlag. ISBN 3515070478.

COMENIUS, Jan Amos. 2014. *De rerum humanarum emendatione consultatio catholica Europae lumina, Panegersia, Panaugia*. Prague: Academia. ISBN 8020024484.

CORVINO, John. 2013. *What's Wrong with Homosexuality?* Oxford: Oxford University Press. ISBN 9780199856312.

CRANSTON, Maurice. 1962. *Jean-Paul Sartre*. New York: Grove Press.

DAVIDSON, Herbert. 1992. *Alfarabi, Avicenna, and Averroes on Intellect: Their Cosmologies, Theories of the Active Intellect, and Theories of Human Intellect*. New York: Oxford University Press. ISBN 0195074238.

DENZLER, Georg. 1991. *Die verbotene Lust: 2000 Jahre christliche Sexualmoral*. Munich: Zürich: R. Pipper. ISBN 9783492025348.

DESCARTES, René. 1996. *Œuvres de Descartes*. Vol. 4. Paris: J. Vrin. ISBN 2711612678.

DIELS, Hermann and Walther KRANZ. 1952. *Die Fragmente der Vorsokratiker: Griechisch und Deutsch*. Berlin: Wiedmann.

DOSTOEVSKY, Fyodor Mikhailovich. 1981. *Bratya Karamazovy*. Moscov: Sovremennik.

EHRMAN, Bart. 2003. *Lost Scriptures: Books That Did Not Make It into the New Testament*. New York: Oxford University Press. ISBN 0195141822.

ENGELS, Friedrich. 1985. *The Origin of the Family, Private Property and the State*. Harmondsworth: Penguin. ISBN 9781500133894.

EPICURUS. 1926. *To Menoeceus*. In: BAILEY, Cyril. *Epicurus: The Extant Remains: With Short Critical Apparatus, Translation and Notes*. Oxford: Clarendon Press, pp. 82–93.

FARKAŠOVÁ, Etela. 2006. *Na ceste k 'vlastnej izbe': Postavy/podoby/problémy feministickej filozofie*. Bratislava: Iris. ISBN 8089256007.

FARRINGTON, Benjamin. 1953. *Greek Science*. Melbourne: Penguin Books.

FEBER, Jaromír and Jelena PETRUCIJOVÁ. 2015. K otázce vymezení ruské filozofie. In: FEBER, Jaromír and Jelena PETRUCIJOVÁ (eds.). Ruská filozofie a její reflexe v Česku a na Slovensku. Ostrava: Vysoká škola báňská – Technická univerzita Ostrava, pp. 5–16. ISBN 8024837471.

FEHIGE, Christoph. 1998. A Pareto Principle for Possible People. In: FEHIGE, Christoph and Ulla WESSELS (eds.). *Preferences*. Berlin: Walter de Gruyter, pp. 508–543. ISBN 3110150077.

FESER, Edward. 2003. The Role of Nature in Sexual Ethics. *National Catholic Bioethics Quarterly*, vol. 13, no. 1, pp. 169–176. ISSN 1532-5490.

FOA, Pamela. 1977. What's Wrong with Rape. In: VETTERLING-BRAGGIN, Mary et al. (eds.). *Feminism and Philosophy*. Totowa, NJ: Littlefield, Adams & Co., pp. 347–359.

FRIEDELL, Egon. 2009. *Kulturgeschichte der Neuzeit: Kulturgeschichte Ägyptens.* Frankfurt am Main: Wunderkammer Verlag. ISBN 9783861508939.

GHYKA, Matila Costiescu. 2016. *The Golden Number: Pythagoreans Rites and Rithms in the Development of Western Civilization.* Canada: Inner Traditions International. ISBN 9781594771002.

GIDDENS, Anthony. 1992. *The Transformation of Intimacy: Sexuality, Love and Erioticism in Modern Societies.* Polity Press: Cambridge. ISBN 9780804722148.

GIRAUD, Théophile de. 2006. *L'art de guillotiner les procréateurs: Manifeste anti-nataliste.* Nancy: Le Mort-Qui-Trompe. ISBN 2916502009.

GOFFMAN, Erving. 1959. *The Presentation of Self in Everyday Life.* London: Penguin Books. ISBN 9780140135718.

De GONCOURT, Edmond and Jules de GONCOURT. 1868. *Journal: Mémoires de la vie littéraires.* Vol. 3 [online]. Wikisource: La bibliothèque libre. 18.3.2016 [accessed 26.3.2018]. Available at: https://fr.wikisource.org/wiki/Journal_des_Goncourt

GRAEBER, David. 2011. *Debt: The First 5,000 Years.* New York: Melville House. ISBN 9781933633862.

GRAY, John. 2003. *Straw Dogs: Thoughts on Humans and Other Animals.* London: Granta Books. ISBN 1862075964.

GREGORIĆ, Pavel. 2007. *Aristotle on the Common Sense.* Oxford: Oxford University Press. ISBN 0199277370.

GREGORY OF NYSSA. 1999. *On Virginity.* In: GREGORY OF NYSSA. *Ascetical Works.* Washington: Catholic University of America Press. ISBN 0813209692.

GRUA, Gaston. 1953. *Jurisprudence universelle et théodicée selon Leibniz.* Paříž: Presses Universitaires de France.

GUTHKE, Karl. 1990. *Letzte Worte.* Munich: Verlag C. H. Beck. ISBN 3406344437.

HACKING, Ian. 1975. *The Emergence of Probability: A Philosophical Study of Early Ideas about Probability, Induction and Statistical Inference.* London: Cambridge University Press. ISBN 0521204607.

HANNAM, James. 2010. Lost Pioneers of Science. *History Today,* vol. 60, no. 1, pp. 5n. ISSN 0018-2753.

HANOCK, John. 1776. *Declaration of Independence* [online]. Inru. Actualisation 12.6.2012 [accessed 11.7.2017]. Available at: http://www.inuru.com/index.php/spolecnost/dokumenty/490-deklarace-nezavislosti-usa-1776

HAYRY, Matti. 2004. A Rational Cure for Prereproductive Stress Syndrome. *Journal of Medical Ethics*, vol. 30, no. 4, pp. 377n. ISSN 0306-6800.

HEGEL, Georg Wilhelm Friedrich. 1991. *Elements of the Philosophy of Right*. New York: Cambridge University Press. ISBN 0521344387.

HELOISA. 2007. Third Letter: Heloise to Abelard. In: ABAELARD, Peter and HELOISE. *The Letters and Other Writings. Cambridge:* Hackett Publishing Company, pp. 71–84. ISBN 9781603840514.

HIMMA, Kenneth Einar. 2004. Harm, Sharm, and One Extremely Creepy Argument. *Faith and Philosophy: Journal of the Society of Christian Philosophers*, vol. 21, no. 2, pp. 250–255. ISSN 0739-7046.

HIMMA, Kenneth Einar. 2010. Birth as a Grave Misfortune: The Traditional Doctrine of Hell and Christian Salvific Exclusivism. In: JOHNSON, Mark and Joel BUENTING. *The Problem of Hell: A Philosophical Anthology*. Canada: Ashgate. ISBN 9780754667636.

Von HUMBOLDT, Alexander. 1894. Quoted from: MAINLÄNDER, Philipp. *Die Philosophie der Erlösung*. Vol. 1. 3rd edition. Frankfurt am Main: Jaeger'sche Verlags- Buch- und Landkartenhandlung.

HUTCHINSON, Douglas and Monte Ransome JOHNSON. 2015. *Protrepticus or Exhortation to Philosophy: Citations, Fragments, Paraphrases, and Other Evidence.* Notre Dame: Workshop in Ancient Philosophy.

HWANG, Jiwoon. 2018. *On Pro-Mortalism* [online]. 2018 [accessed 18.02.2018]. Available at: http://jiwoonhwang.org/pro-mortalism/

CHALUPECKÝ, Jindřich. 2005. *Evropa a umění*. Prague: Torst. ISBN 8072152645.

CHESTERTON, Gilbert Keith. 2004. *Saint Thomas Aquinas* [online]. The Catholic Primer. 2004 [accessed 18.02.2018]. Available at: https://www.basilica.ca/documents/2016/10/G.K.Chesterton-Saint%20Thomas%20Aquinas.pdf

CHRYSOSTOM, John. 1966. *La virginité: Traduction de Bernard Grillet*. Paris: Editions du Cerf, Sources chrétiennes. ISBN 9782204039178.

JACKSON, Stevi. 2008. Ordinary Sex. *Sexualities*, vol. 11, no. 1–2, pp. 33–37. ISSN 1363-4607.

JAEGER, Werner. 1968. *Aristotle: Fundamentals of the History of His Development.* Oxford: Clarendon Press.

JANAVAY, Christopher. 1999. Introduction. In: JANAWAY, Christopher (ed.). *The Cambridge Companion to Schopenhauer*. Cambridge: Cambridge University Press, pp. 1–17. ISBN 0521621062.

JEROME. 1893. *Against Jovinianus*. In: SCHAFF, Philip. *A Select Library of Nicene and Post-Nicene Fathers of the Christian Church*, Second Series. Vol. 6. New York: The Christian Literature Company.

JOHNSON, Paul. 1984. *A History of a Modern World: From 1917 to the 1980s*. London: Weidenfeld & Nicolson. ISBN 0297784757.

JOLLEY, Nicholas. 1995. *The Cambridge Compation to Leibniz*. Cambridge: Cambridge University Press. ISBN 9780521367691.

JONAS, Hans. 1963. *The Gnostic Religion: The Message of the Alien God & The Beginnings of Christianity*. 2nd edition. Boston: Beacon Press. ISBN 0807057991.

JONAS, Hans. 1979. Toward a Philosophy of Technology. *Hastings Center Report*, vol. 9, no. 1, pp. 34–43. ISSN 0093-0334.

JONAS, Hans. 1997. *Das Prinzip Leben: Ansätze zu einer philosophischen Biologie*. Frankfurt am Main: Suhrkamp. ISBN 3518391984.

JONAS, Hans. 1992. *Das Prinzip Verantwortung: Versuch einer Ethik für die technologische Zivilization*. 2nd edition. Frankfurt am Mein: Suhrkamp Verlag. ISBN 3518375857.

JONAS, Hans. 2001. Is God a Mathematican?: The Meaning of Metabolism. In: JONAS, Hans. *The Phenomenon of Life: Toward a Philosophical Biology*. Evanston: Northwestern University Press, pp. 64–95. ISBN 0810117495.

KAHNEMANN, Daniel. 2011. *Thinking, Fast and Slow*. London: Penguin Books. ISBN 9780141033570.

KANT, Immanuel. 1963. *Lectures on Ethics*. New York: Harper and Row.

KANT, Immanuel. 1996. The Metaphysics of Morals. In: KANT, Immanuel. *Practical Philosophy*. Cambridge: Cambridge University Press, pp. 353–603. ISBN 9780521654081.

KANT, Immanuel. 2002. *Groundwork for the Metaphysics of Morals*. New Heaven, London: Yale University. ISBN 0300094876.

KELLER, Jan. 1995. *Přemýšlení s Josefem Vavrouškem*. Prague: G plus G. ISBN 809018961X.

KELLER, Jan. 2008a. *Abeceda prosperity*. 3rd edition. Brno: Doplněk. ISBN 9788072392278.

KELLER, Jan. 2008b. *Nedomyšlená společnost*. 4th edition. Brno: Doplněk. ISBN 8072390910.

KELLY, Gary. 1996. *Sexuality Today: The Human Perspective.* 5th edition. Madison, WI: Brown & Benchmark. ISBN 0697265870.

KIERKEGAARD, Soren. 1946. *Kierkegaard's Attack upon Christendom 1854–1855.* Princeton: Princeton University Press.

KIERKEGAARD, Soren. 1961. *Journal (Extraits): 1854–1855.* Vol. 5. Paris: Gallimard.

KIERKEGAARD, Soren. 1968. *The Last Years: The Kierkegaard Journals 1853–1855.* London: Collins.

KIERKEGAARD, Soren. 2017. *Kierkegaard's Journals and Notebooks.* Vol. 9: Journals NB26–NB30. Princeton: Princeton University Press. ISBN 9780691172415.

KLÍMA, Ladislav. 1993. *O Solovjevově etice.* Prague: Lege artis. ISBN 8071101257.

KLÍMA, Ladislav. 2000. *The Sufferings of Prince Sternenhoch: A Grotesque Tale of Horror.* Prague: Twisted Spoon Press. ISBN 8086264335.

KOLDINSKÁ, Marie Šedivá. 2013. Dějiny raného novověku jako badatelský problém. In: ŠEDIVÁ KOLDINSKÁ, Marie, Ivo CERMAN et al. (eds.). *Základní problémy studia raného novověku.* Prague: Lidové noviny, pp. 9–21. ISBN 9788073084851.

KOSTALEVSKY, Marina. 1997. *Dostoevsky and Soloviev: The Art of Integral Vision.* New Haven: Yale University. ISBN 0300060963.

KOUMAR, Jan. 2017. Unnatural as a Category in Sexual Ethics. *Individual and Society,* vol. 20, no. 3, pp. 60–69. ISSN 1335-3608.

KRATOCHVÍL, Zdeněk. 2016. *The Philosophy of Living Nature.* Prague: Charles University. ISBN 9788024631318.

KRECAR, Antonín. 1926. Předmluva. In: ROUSSEAU, Jean Jacques. *Emil: Čili O vychování.* 3rd edition. Olomouc: R. Promberger, pp. 5–42.

KURNIG. 1903. *Der Neo-Nihilismus: Anti-Militarismus – Sexualleben (Ende der Menschheit).* 2nd edition. Leipzig: Verlag von Max Sängewald.

KÜNG, Hans. 2005. *Spurensuche: Die Weltreligionen auf dem Weg: Stammesreligionen, Hinduismus, Chinesische Religion, Buddhismus.* Vol. 1. Munich: Piper. ISBN 3492242928.

LAERTIUS, Diogenes. 2012. *The lives and opinions of eminent philosophers.* Memphis, USA: General Books. ISBN 1458928160.

LAKOFF, George. 1987: *Woman, Fire, and Dangerous Things.* Chicago: University of Chicago Press. ISBN 0226468046.

LEIBNIZ, Gottfried Wilhelm. 1849–1863. *G. W. Leibniz: Mathematische Schriften.* Berlin: A. Asher.

LEIBNIZ, Gottfried Wilhelm. 1875–1890. *Die philosophischen Schriften von G.W. Leibniz.* Vol. 4. Berlin: Weidmannsche Buchhandlung.

LEIBNIZ, Gottfried Wilhelm. 1923. *Sämtliche Schriften und Briefe.* Berlin: Berlin Academy.

LEIBNIZ, Gottfried Wilhelm. 1969. *Philosophical Papers and Letters.* 2nd edition. Chicago: University of Chicago Press.

LEROI, Armand. 2012a. *BBC: Aristotle's Lagoon* [online]. Youtube. 2.4.2012 [accessed 14.11.2017]. Available at: https://www.youtube.com/watch?v=e12pbSHrzAs

LEROI, Armand. 2012b. *BBC: Aristotle's Lagoon.* [online]. Youtube. 2.4.2012 [accessed 14.11.2017]. Available at: https://www.youtube.com/watch?v=8Oa5CZGNHD4&t=8s

LEROI, Armand. 2012c. *BBC: Aristotle's Lagoon* [online]. Youtube. 2.4.2012 [accessed 14.11.2017]. Available at: https://www.youtube.com/watch?v=Fhu4tiwcwr4&t=88s

LIVINGSTON, Gretchen and D'Vera COHN. 2010. *Childlessness up Among All Women; Down Among Women with Advanced Degrees* [online]. 25.6.2010 [accessed 5.3. 2018]. Available at: http://www.pewsocialtrends.org/2010/06/25/childlessness-up-among-all-women-down-among-women-with-advanced-degrees/

LOCKE, John. 1999. *An Essay Concerning Human Understanding.* Book 2. Hazleton: The Pennsylvania State University.

LUCAS, Peter. 1956. *The Leibniz-Clarke Correspondence: Together with Extracts from Newton's Principia and Opticks.* Manchester: Manchester University Press.

MACKINNON, Catharine. 1989. *Towards a Feminist Theory of the State.* Cambridge: Harvard University Press. ISBN 9780674896468.

MACLEAN, Ian. 2017. Pascal, Blaise (1623–62). In: *Routledge Encyclopedia of Philosophy* [online]. [Accessed 11.7.2017]. Available at: https://www.rep.routledge.com/articles/biographical/pascal-blaise-1623-62/v-1

MAGEE, Bryan. 1978. *Men of Ideas.* London: B.B.C. ISBN 9780670468881.

MAPPES, Thomas and Jane ZEMBATY. 1992. *Social Ethics: Morality and Social Policy.* 5th edition. New York: McGraw-Hill. ISBN 0070401438.

De MARCO, Donald and Benjamin WIKER. 2004. *Architects of the Culture of Death.* San Francisco: Ignatius Press. ISBN 9781586170165

MASARYK, Tomáš Garrigue. 1996. *Rusko a Evropa: Studie o duchovních proudech v Rusku.* Prague: Ústav T. G. Masaryka. ISBN 8090197175.

MCGRATH, Alister. 1999. *Christian Spirituality: An Introduction.* Oxford: Blackwell Publishing. ISBN 0631212809.

MCGREGOR, Rafe and Ema SULLIVAN-BISSETT. 2012. Better No Longer to Be: The Harm of Continued Existence. *South-African Journal of Philosophy,* vol. 31, no. 1, pp. 55–68. ISSN 0258-0136.

MENSINGA, Wilhelm. 1882. *Über die facultative Sterilität vom prophylaktischen und hygienischen Standpunkt.* Berlin: Verlag Louis Heuser.

La METTRIE, Julien Offray. 1970. *Euvres philosohiques de Monsieur de La Mettrie.* Vol. 1. Berlin: G. Reimer.

MEYNS, Chris. 2017. Leibniz and Probability in the Moral Domain. In: STRICKLAND, Lloyd, Erik VYNCKIER and Julia WECKEND (eds.). *Tercentenary Essays on the Philosophy and Science of Leibniz.* Cham: Springer, pp. 229–253. ISBN 3319388290.

MICELI, Vincent. 1975. *The Gods of Atheism.* New Rochelle, NY: Arlington House. ISBN 9780870000997.

MIKEŠ, Vladimír. 2008. Scala naturae u starých stoiků. In: CHVÁTAL, Ladislav and Vít HUŠEK (eds.). *Přirozenost ve filosofii minulosti a současnosti: Sborník z konference Centra pro práci s patristickými, středověkými a renesančními texty.* Brno: Centrum pro studium demokracie a kultury, pp. 44–53. ISBN 9788073251437.

De MONTESQUIEU, Charles Louis. 1950. *Œuvres complètes.* Vol. 1. Paris: A Masson.

MOREAU, Joseph. 1956. *L' univers leibnizien.* Paris: Emmanuel Vitte.

MÜLLER, Philippe. 1990. *Cicéron: Un philosophe pour notre temps.* Lausanne: L' Âge d'homme. ISBN 2825100331.

NAGEL, Thomas. 1979. *Mortal Questions.* Cambridge: Cambridge University Press. ISBN 9780521406765.

NAGEL, Thomas. 1986. *The View from Nowhere.* Oxford: Oxford University Press. ISBN 8533619685.

NARVESON, John. 1967. Utilitarianism and New Generations. *Mind,* vol. 76, no. 301, pp. 62–72. ISSN 0026-4423.

NEUFFER, Martin. 1992. *Nein zum Leben: Ein Essay.* Frankfurt am Main: Fischer Taschenbuch. ISBN 3596113423.

NULAND, Sherwin. 1994. *How We Die: Reflections on Life's Final Chapter.* New York: Knopf. ISBN 0679414614.

NUSSBAUM, Martha Craven. 2012. *Philosophical Interventions: Book Reviews, 1986–2011.* New York: Oxford University Press. ISBN 9780199777853.

OPATRNÝ, Dominik. 2015. K etickým aspektům tzv. autoplagiátů: Aneb technologie zpracování vědeckého recyklátu. *Caritas et Veritas,* no. 5, pp. 42–50. ISSN 1805-0948.

OTISK, Marek. 2005. *Středověké myšlení*. Ostrava: University of Ostrava. ISBN 8073681145.

OTISK, Marek. 2009. Dějiny filosofie jako zdroj útěchy. *Αἰθήρ: Časopis pro studium řecké a latinské filosofické tradice*, vol. 1, no. 1, pp. 89–92. ISSN 1803-7860.

PAPE, Wilhelm (ed.). 1914. *Handwörterbuch der griechischen Sprache Λ – Ω*. Vol. 2. Braunschweig: Vieweg.

PASCAL, Blaise. 1923. *Œuvres complètes: Depuis son arrivée à Paris (1647) jusqu'à l'entrée de Jacqueline à Port-Royal (1652)*. Vol. 2. 2nd edition. Paris: Hachette.

PATOČKA, Jan. 1996. *Nejstarší řecká filosofie*. Prague: Vyšehrad. ISBN 8070211954.

PEARCE, Richard. 2011. Escaping into the Other: An Existential View of Sex and Sexuality. *Existential Analysis*, vol. 22, no. 2, pp. 229–243. ISSN 1752-5616.

PELCOVÁ, Naďa et al. 2004. *Základy společenských věd: Vztah ke světu jako celku*. Vol. 4. Prague: Eurolex Bohemaia.

PESSOA, Fernando. 1993. *Obras completas de Álvaro de Campos*. São Paulo: Companhia de bolso.

PETRŮ, Marek. 2016. Tapu a maska smrti. In: DOLÁK, Antonín et al. *Subjekt v moderním prostředí, jazyce a komunikaci*. Ostrava: University of Ostrava. ISBN 9788074648472.

PLATO. 1966–1979. *Plato in Twelve Volumes*. Vol. 1. Cambridge, MA: Harvard University Press.

PLUMACHER, Olga. 1879. Pessimism. *Mind*, vol. 4, no. 13, pp. 68–89. ISSN 0026-4423.

PLUTARCH. 1962. *Plutarch's Moralia: In Fifteen Volumes*. Vol. 2: 86B-171F. London: W. Heinemann.

POINCARÉ, Henri. 1907. *The Value of Science*. New York: The Science Press.

POLÁCH, Rudolf. 2007. *O pojmu vesmír: Společník na cestách staletími se známými mysliteli*. Pelhřimov: Nová tiskárna Pelhřimov. ISBN 8086559661.

PRIMORATZ, Igor. 1999. *Ethics and Sex*. London, New York: Routledge. ISBN 0415093341.

PRIMORATZ, Igor. 2013. Sexual Morality. In: LAFOLLETTE, Hugh (ed.). *The International Encyclopaedia of Ethics*. Chichester: Blackwel Publishing, pp. 4855–4867. ISBN 9781405186414.

RAGON, Jan. 1938. *Smysl antických mysterií*. Vol. 1. Prague: Heřman Kempfer.

RAWLS, John. 1999. *Theory of Justice*. 2nd edition. Cambridge: The Belknap Press of Harvard University Press. ISBN 0674000773.

RÁDL, Emanuel. 2000. *Útěcha z filosofie*. 7th edition. Olomouc: Votobia. ISBN 8071983993.

REYNOLDS, Vernon and Ralph TANNER. 1983. *The Biology of Religion*. London, New York: Longmann. ISBN 0582300215.

ROLDANUS, Johannes. 1977. *Le Christ et l'homme dans la théologie d'Athanase d'Alexandrie*. Leiden: Brill. ISBN 9004049053.

RONSIN, Francis. 1980. *La grève des ventres: Propagande néo-malthusienne et baisse de la natalité en France (XIXe–XXe siècles)*. [Ebook]: Aubier. ISBN 2403000604.

RORTY, Richard. 1995. *Rorty & Pragmatism: The Philosopher Responds to His Critics*. Nashville: Vanderbilt University Press. ISBN 0826512631.

ROSS, William David. 1952. *The Works: Selected Fragments*. Vol. 12. Oxford: Clarendon Press.

ROUSSEAU, Jean-Jacques. 1964. *Œuvres complètes: Du contrat social; Ecrits politiques*. Vol. 3. Paříž: Gallimard.

ROUSSEAU, Jean Jacques. 1979. *Emil: Or On Education*. USA: Basic Books. ISBN 0465019307

RÖD, Wolfgang. 2001. *Novověká filosofie: Od Francise Bacona po Spinozu*. Vol. 1. Prague: Oikoymenh. ISBN 8072980394.

RÖD, Wolfgang. 2004. *Novověká filosofie: Od Newtona po Rousseaua*. Vol. 2. Prague: Oikoymenh. ISBN 8072981099.

RUBY, Jane. 1986. The Origins of Scientific 'Law'. *Journal of the History of Ideas,* vol. 47, no. 3, pp. 341–359. ISSN 0022-5037.

SALMIERI, Gregory. 2008. *Aristotle and the Problem of Concepts*. Doctoral Thesis. University of Pittsburgh. The College of Arts and Sciences.

SAMUELSON, Hava Tirosh. 2008. Understanding Jonas: An Interdisciplinary Project. In: SAMUELSON, Hava Tirosh and Christian WIESE. *The Legacy of Hans Jonas: Judaism and the Phenomenon of Life*. Leiden: Brill Academic Publishers. ISBN 9789004167223.

SARTRE, Jean-Paul. 2007. *Being and Nothingness: An Essay on Phenomenological Ontology*. London, New York: Routledge. ISBN 9780418278485.

SCRUTON, Roger. 1986. *Sexual Desire: A Philosophical Investigation*. London: Weidenfled and Nicolson. ISBN 9780297784791.

SENECA, Lucius Annaeus. 1889. Of consolation: To Marcia. In: SENECA, Lucius Annaeus. *Minor dialogues: Together with the Dialogue on Clemency.* London: George Bell and Sons, pp. 162–203.

SHEA, Donal. 2007. *The Pincaré Conjecture: In Search of the Shape of the Universe.* New York: Walker Publishing Company. ISBN 080271532X.

SCHOPENHAUER, Arthur. 1909a. *The World as Will and Idea.* Vol. 1. London: Kegan Paul, Trench, Trübner & Co.

SCHOPENHAUER, Arthur. 1909b. *The World as Will and Idea.* Vol. 3. London: Kegan Paul, Trench, Trübner & Co.

SCHOPENHAUER, Arthur. 1926. *Selected Essays of Schopenhauer.* London: G. Bell and Sons.

SCHOPENHAUER, Arthur. 1970. *Essays and Aphorisms.* Harmondsworth: Penguin Books. ISBN 9780141921754.

SCHOPENHAUER, Arthur. 1974. *Parega and Paralipomena: Short Philosophical Essays.* Vol. 2. Oxford: Oxford University Press.

SCHOPENHAUER, Arthur. 2004. *On the Suffering of the World.* London: Penguin Books. ISBN 9780141964911.

SCHOPENHAUER, Arthur. 2005. *Studies in Pessimism: The Essays.* Pennsylvania: PSU.

SCHOPENHAUER, Arthur. 2007. *Parerga and Paralipomena: A Collection of Philosophical Essays.* New York: Cosimo. ISBN 9781602063440.

SINGER, Peter. 1994. *Rethinking Life and Death: The Collapse of Our Traditional Ethics.* Melbourne: The Text Publishing Company. ISBN 1875847049.

SINGER, Peter. 2010. *'Last Generation?': A Response* [online]. 16.6.2010 [accessed 5.3. 2018]. Available at: https://opinionator.blogs.nytimes.com/2010/06/16/last-genera-tion-a-response/

SLOTERDIJK, Peter. 2001. *Critique of Cynical Reason.* 5th edition. London: University of Minesota Press. ISBN 0816615853.

SMITH, Martin. 2013. *No Baby no Cry: Christian Antinatalism.* [Ebook]: CreateSpace Independent Publishing Platform. ISBN 1482676656.

SOKOL, Jan. 2016. *Ethics, Life and Institutions: An Attempt at Practical Philosophy.* Prague: Carolinum Press. ISBN 9788024634296.

SOLOVYOV, Vladimir Sergeyevich. 1918. *The Justification of the Good: An Essay on Moral Philosophy.* London: Constable and Company LTD.

SOLOVYOV, Vladimir Sergeyevich. [1902]. *Sobranie sochineni Vladimira Sergeevicha Solovyova.* Vol. 3. In: SOLOVYOV, Vladimir Sergeyevich. *Sobranie sochineni Vladimira Sergeevicha Solovyova.* Vol. 3–4. Sankt-Peterburg: Obshestvennaya polza, pp. 1–168.

SOLOVYOV, Vladimir Sergeyevich. 1903. *Sobranie sochineni Vladimira Sergeevicha Solovyova.* Vol. 8. Sankt-Peterburg: Obshestvennaya polza.

SOLOVYOV, Vladimir Sergeyevich. 2010. *Opravdanie dobra: Nravstvennaya filosofia.* Moscow: Akademicheskiy proekt. ISBN 5829111608.

SOLOVYOV, Vladimir Sergeyevich. 1926. Pismo k L. Tolstomu o voskresenii Christa. Put': Organ russkoj religioznoy mysli. *The Paris Review,* no. 5, pp. 97–99. ISSN 0031-2037.

SOPHOCLES. 1889. *The Oedipus Coloneus.* Cambridge: Cambridge University Press.

STRAUSS, David Friedrich. 1872. *The Old Faith and the New.* Quoted from: KURNIG. 1903. *Der Neo-Nihilismus: Anti-Militarismus – Sexualleben (Ende der Menschheit).* 2nd edition. Leipzig: Verlag von Max Sängewald, p. 130.

STRICKLAND, Lloyd. 2006. *Leibniz Reinterpreted.* London: Continuum International Publishing Group. ISBN 082649028X.

SUITS, David. 2010. Why Death Is Not Bad for the One Who Died. In: BENATAR, David (ed.). *Life, Death & Meaning: Key Philosophical Readings on the Big Questions.* 2nd edition. Lanham Md.: Rowman & Littlefield Publishers, pp. 265–284. ISBN 9781442201699.

SULLY, James. 1877. *Pessimism: A History and Criticism.* London: Henry S. King.

SVOBODA, Filip. 2015. Možné vlivy Θεωρία na φιλοσοφία v Aristotelově Protreptiku a knize A, s přihlédnutím k jeho předchůdcům i následovníkům. *Aithér: Časopis pro studium řecké a latinské filosofické tradice,* vol. 7, no. 13, pp. 96–115. ISSN 103-7860.

SVOBODA, Karel. 1980. *Řečtí atomisté.* 2nd edition. Prague: Svoboda.

SVOBODA, Ludvík (ed.). 1973. *Encyklopedie antiky.* Prague: Academia.

ŠILER, Vladimír. 2005. *Etika.* Ostrava: University of Ostrava. ISBN 9788073683238.

ŠIMEK, Vojtěch. 2014. Etika techniky podle Hanse Jonase. *Filosofie dnes,* vol. 6, no. 1, pp. 50–83. ISSN: 1804-0969. Available at: http://filosofiednes.ff.uhk.cz

ŠÍMA, Antonín. 2013. Radim Kočandrle: Apeiron Anaximandra z Mílétu. *Reflexe,* no. 45, pp. 160–165. ISSN 0862-6901.

TAYLOR, Craig. 2012. *Moralism: A Study of a Vice.* Durham: Acumen. ISBN 9781844654949.

TENACE, Michelina. 1993. *La beauté unité spirituelle dans les écrits esthétiques de Vladimir Soloviev*. Troyes: Editions fates. ISBN 2909452042.

The Family Planning Association. 2010. *Contraception: Past, Present and Future Factsheet* [online]. Updated 2010 [accessed 7.1.2018]. Available at: https://www.fpa.org.uk/factsheets/contraception-past-present-future#Ro1J

THEILER, Willy. 1983. *Über die Seele*. Darmstadt: Wiss Buchges.

THIERCELIN, Alexandre. 2008. On Two Argumentative Uses of the Notion of Uncertainty in Law in Leibniz's *Juridical Dissertations about Conditions*. In: DASCAL, Marcelo (ed.). *Leibniz: What Kind of Rationalist?* Dodrecht: Springer, pp. 251–266. ISBN 9781402086670.

TOMKINS, Stephen. 2006. *A Short History of Christianity*. Grand Rapids, Mich.: William B. Eardmans Publisher. ISBN 9780802833822.

VANNOY, Russell. 1980. *Sex without Love: A Philosophical Exploration*. Bufalo, New York: Prometheus Books. ISBN 9780879751289.

VETTER, Hermann. 1971. Utilitarianism and New Generations. *Mind*, vol. 80, no. 318, pp. 301n. ISSN 0026-4423.

VOHÁNKA, Vlastimil. 2015. Nebýt či být?: O zmatcích, které přináší asymetrický argument. *Studia Theologica*, vol. 17, no. 3, pp. 50–74. ISSN 1212-8570.

VOHÁNKA, Vlastimil. 2019. Dismantling the Asymmetry Argument. *The Journal of Value Inquire*, vol. 53, no. 1, pp. 75–90. ISSN 0022-5363.

VOLTAIRE. 1997. *Candide*. London: Penguin Books. ISBN 0140622632.

VRIES, Katja. 2010. *On Probable Ground: Probabilistic Thought and the Principle of Reason in Law and Data Science*. Disertation thesis. Leiden University. Department of Philosophy. Supervisors: Theodorus Christiaan Wouter Oudemans and Thomas Mertens.

VŘEŠŤÁL, Antonín. 1909. *Katolická mravouka*. Vol 1, n. 49. Prague: Cyrillo-methodějská knihtiskárna V. Kotrby.

WAGNER, Hans. 1956. Die Schichtentheoreme bei Platon, Aristoteles und Plotin. In: *Studium Generale*. Vol. 9, Band 6, pp. 283–291. Berlín: Springer.

WEINBERG, Rivka. 2012. Is Having Children Always Wrong? *South African Journal of Philosophy*, vol. 31, no. 1, pp. 26–37. ISSN 0258-0136.

WHITEHEAD, Alfred North. 1967. *Adventures of Ideas*. New York: The Free Press. ISBN 0029351707.

WIENER, Philip. 1951. Introduction. In: WIENER, Philip (ed.). *Leibniz: Selections.* New York: Charles Scribner's Sons, pp. XI–LI.

WIESE, Christian. 2007. *The Life and Though of Hans Jonas: Jewish Dimensions.* Waltham: Brandeis University Press. ISBN 1584656387.

WITTGENSTEIN, Ludwig. 2009: *Philosophical Investigations.* Oxford: Basil Blackwell. ISBN 9781405159296.

WOLF, Jean-Claude. 2006. *Eduard von Hartmann: Ein Philosoph der Gründerzeit.* Würzburg: Verlag Königshausen & Neumann. ISBN 3826032276.

ZAPFFE, Peter Wesell. 1959. 'Fragments of an Interview'. Quoted from: LIGOTTI, Thomas. 2011. *The Conspiracy against the Human Race: The Contrivance of Horror.* New York: Hippocampus Press, pp. 20–37. ISBN 0984480277.

ZAPFFE, Peter Wessel. 1996. *Om det tragiske.* Oslo: Pax Forlag A/S. ISBN 9788253018423.

ABREVIATIONS

A	Leibniz: *Sämtliche Schriften und Briefe*	Jn.	John
Apo.	Aristotle: *Analytica posteriora*	1 Jn.	First Epistle of John
Apoc	Apocalypse	Jr.	Jeremiah
AT	Descartes: *Œuvres de Descartes*	Leg.	Plato: *Laws*
CF	Boëthius: *De Consolatione philosophiae*	L	Leibniz: *Philosophical Papers and Letters*
1 Cor.	1 Corinthians	LC	Leibniz: *The Leibniz-Clarke Correspondence*
DFBM	Cicero: *De finibus bonorum et malorum*	Lk.	Luke
DK	Diels & Kranz: *Die Fragmente der Vorsokratiker*	MD	Seneca: *Minor dialogues*
DL	Diogenes Laertius: *Lives of Eminent Philosophers*	Men.	Epicurus: *To Menoeceus*
DM	Leibniz: *Discours de Métaphysique*	Mk.	Mark
Dt.	Deuteronomy	Mt.	Matthew
EC	Pascal: *Euvres Complètes*	Müller	Müller: *Cicéron: Un philosophe pour notre temps*
Ecc.	Ecclesiastes	OC	Rousseau: *Oeuvres complétes*
Euthyd.	Plato: *Euthydemus*	PA	Aristotle: *De partium animalium*
EE	Aristotle: *Ethica Eudemia*	Paneg.	Comenius: *Panegersia*
EN	Aristotle: *Nicomachean Ethics*	PEP	Aristotle: *Protrepticus*
EU	Aristotle: *Eudemus*	Phys.	Aristotle: *Physics*
Ex.	Exodus	Pol.	Aristotle: *Politics*
Gal.	Galatians	Prv.	Proverbs
Gen.	Genesis	Rom.	Romans
Gorg.	Plato: *Gorgias.*	Sir	Sirach
GC	Aristotle: *De generatione et corruptione*	Strom.	Clement of Alexandria: *Stromata.*
GM	Leibniz: *Die Mathematische Schriften*	Tim.	Plato: *Timaius*
GP	Leibniz: *Die Philosophischen Schriften*	Wis	Wisdom
HA	Aristotle: *Historia animalium*		
Iz.	Isiah		
Jb.	Job		

LIST OF AUTHORS

Mgr. Kateřina Lochmanová, the editor, author of the chapters *Protohistory of Antinatalism: Antiquity and the Middle Ages* (pp. 37–52) and *History of Antinatalism: From Modern Age to Present* (pp. 91–109), is currently finishing her postgraduate studies of philosophy at the University of Ostrava, where she graduated with a diploma thesis entitled *Iracionality of a Wager on Life in the Context of Benatar's Antinatalism* (in Czech). She is one of the coorganisators of conferences on antinatalism in Ostrava as well as in Prague (with Vlastimil Vohánka, Filip Svoboda, David Černý and Tomáš Hříbek). At present, she is primarily concerned with geometry and metaphysics of space by a German philosopher Gottfried Wilhelm Leibniz (doctoral thesis: *Analysis Situs within Leibniz's Correspondence with Clarke* – in Czech), but peripherally she is still interested in the subject of antinatalism too, especially in (the history of) Benatar's asymmetry argument. Apart from the paper *Hermeneutical Aspects of the Asymmetry between Good and Evil* (in Czech) she devoted a few of other articles to selected ethical topics as well.

Mgr. Vlastimil Vohánka, Ph.D., the author of the *Preface* (pp. 5–8), is an assistant professor in the Department of Philosophy and Patrology, Sts Cyril and Methodius Faculty of Theology, Palacký University Olomouc. He was also an assistant professor in the Department of Philosophy, Faculty of Arts, University of Ostrava, where he lectured in epistemology, applied ethics, applied metaphysics, and philosophy of religion. He graduated at Palacký University Olomouc, Czech Republic. Vohánka is the author of *Modality, Logical Probability, and the Trinity* (2014), a co-author of *Selected Issues in Epistemology* (2015, with Lukáš Novák, in Czech) and of *The Moral Philosophy of Dietrich von Hildebrand* (with Martin Cajthaml). He published his articles in *Studia Neo-aristotelica*, *Ethical Perspectives*, and *International Philosophical Quarterly*. Besides antinatalism, he is interested in effective altruism, phenomenological ethics, and probabilistic philosophy of religion.

Mgr. Ing. Michal Kutáš, Ph.D., the author of the chapter *To Be or Not to Be: Is Analytical Approach Suitable?* (pp. 9–34), is a researcher at the Department of Philosophy, Faculty of Philosophy and Arts, Trnava University, Slovakia (from 2012 till present), where he teaches courses on logic (both classical and non-classical), cognitive science, cognitive linguistics, philosophy of Peter Singer, Daniel Dennett and others. He is also a member of the Center for Cognitive Studies at the Department of Philosophy. He defended his dissertation thesis in systematic philosophy in 2012 at Trnava University in Trnava, Faculty of philosophy and Arts, and his diploma thesis in philosophy at the same institution in 2009. His professional interests lie mainly in logic, philosophy of Peter

Singer and in spirituality and spiritual traditions of the world, in particular in Buddhism and Buddhistic philosophy and spirituality. His interest in antinatalism is connected to the fact that Buddhism offers its answer to the fundamental question of *To be or not to be?*, which is partly similar, but not identical to the answer antinatalists defend.

Mgr. Filip Svoboda, the author of the chapter *Aristotle and His Eudemus* (pp. 53–67), is a postgraduate student of philosophy at the University of Ostrava, where he graduated with a diploma thesis entitled *Love to Wisdom or Cataclysmic Obsession?*. His current doctoral thesis is focused on the question concerning the nature of philosophy in works of Aristotle. The thesis is entitled *The question 'What is Philosophy?' in the context of Aristotle's Metaphysics 980a21–993b31*. His interest covers mainly ancient philosophy (especially Aristotle) and the philosophy itself – its meaning and usefulness. He was a researcher at the Department of Library studies, Faculty of Natural sciences and Philosophy, Silesian University, where he taught courses on philosophy, religion, logic, sociology and Latin language. He is also a member of The Czech Aristotelian Society. He regularly publishes and attends professional conferences. Currently (for 5 years) he is a primary school teacher at an English-private school in Ostrava.

Théophile de Giraud, the author of the chapter *Antinatalism in Early Christianity* (pp. 69–88), is a French-speaking Belgian writer born in 1968. He is one of the main contemporary advocates of antinatalism in the French language. Among other works, he has written an essay entitled *L'art de guillotiner les procréateurs: Manifeste antinataliste* (*The Art of Guillotining the Procreators: Antinatalist Manifesto*). This book was published in French in 2006 and is currently being translated into English.

Mgr. Markéta Poledníková, the author of the chapter *Solovyov and His Godmanhood: Antinatalism in Russia* (pp. 111–124), is currently studying at the Department of Philosophy and the Department of Slavonic Studies (both on the Masaryk University in Brno). She is interested mainly in the philosophy of Vladimir Sergeyevich Solovyov and in recent times in the great novels by Fyodor Mikhailovich Dostoyevsky as well. Her other professional interests include the theory of literature, translatology, and ethics. The last of them brought her to effective altruism. For the first time she heard about antinatalism in 2016 and it immediately reminded her about selected passages from Solovyov's *The Justification of the Good*.

Dr. phil. Karim Akerma, the author of the chapter *Kurnig and His Neo-Nihilism: The First Modern Antinatalist* (pp. 125–145), was born in Hamburg in 1965 where he studied philosophy, history and literature. In addition to a number of articles, he is also the author of a series of books on antinatalism. In 1997 Karim Akerma defended his postgraduate thesis for professorship at Hamburg University which was entitled: *Verebben der Menschheit? Neganthropy und Anthropodizee* [*Ebbing away of Mankind? Neganthropy and Anthropodicy*, 2000]. His thesis was rejected in a narrow decision due to his antinatalism. In his book *Lebensende und Lebensbeginn* [*The Beginning and the End of a Life*, 2006] he defends a mental view on the beginning and the end of a life. According to this view, a new life begins when an entity gains consciousness whereas a life ends when an entity has irreversibly ceased to produce consciousness. Karim Akerma makes a living as a professional translator, lives a vegan lifestyle in order to diminish animal and human suffering and is a singer-songwriter to help spread the message.

Mgr. Jan Koumar, the author of the chapter *Antinatalism and Sexual Ethics* (pp. 149–165), is currently a postgraduate student of applied ethics at the Charles University in Prague. The main area of his expertise is ethics, in particular ethics of sexuality and quotidian activities. He has got degree in historical sociology, finished with a thesis *Ethical Context of Sexuality*. The title of his dissertation thesis is *Ethics of Sexual Behaviour*.

Julio Cabrera, Ph.D., the author of the chapter *Antinatalism and Negative Ethics* (pp. 167–288), is actually an associate researcher in the Bioethics Program at the University of Brasilia, an expert in ethics and philosophy of language and informal logic. He graduated from the University of Córdoba, Argentina, with postdoctoral studies in France, Spain and Mexico. He is an author of around 15 books in his areas and several articles published in Europe (Spain, France, Germany, Italy, Portugal) and America (US, Mexico, Colombia, Venezuela, Argentina, Brazil). He writes about morality of procreation since 1989, with the publication of his book *Project for a Negative Ethics*.

INDEX OF NAMES

Kateřina Lochmanová et al.
HISTORY OF ANTINATALISM:
How Philosophy Has Challenged the Question of Procreation

218 pages
ISBN 9798645624255

Made in the USA
Monee, IL
12 August 2021